A WORLD GOVERNMENT?

SABINO CASSESE

A WORLD GOVERNMENT?

GLOBAL LAW PRESS
EDITORIAL DERECHO GLOBAL

SEVILLA • 2018

RECOMMENDED CITATION:

Sabino Cassese, *A World Government?*
Global Law Press-Editorial Derecho Global
Sevilla, 2018

Serie Albero
(Administrative Law Beyond the State)

© 2018: Global Law Press-Editorial Derecho Global
www.globallawpress.org
Sevilla (España)

Diseño y maquetación: Los Papeles del Sitio

ISBN: 978-84-947415-2-4
DL: S-280-2018

(Hecho en España)

TABLE OF CONTENTS

CHAPTER III
GLOBAL REGULATION

CHAPTER IV

JUDGING AND GLOBALIZATION

INTRODUCTION

T HE idea of uniting humanity, or – at least – of developing a concert of civilized nations is an old one: Dante's one government under one ruler and a shared end; Hobbes's league of commonwealths; Kant's *civitas gentium* embracing all the peoples of the Earth; Einstein's world government; Mann's new order of the world, a society of free peoples with equal rights and duties. Are these only aspirations, or should it be recognized that there has been progress since the time of States as the only rulers, such that the division of the world into a hundred and ninety-three different and divided national governments is no longer entirely true?

There are now many features of a new world order: the circulation of concepts, techniques, rules; the development of global epistemic communities; an increasing mix of national and supranational institutions; the formation of more horizontal links among States, which do not disappear, but rather become accountable to one other; the generalization of common usages and rules. Overall, this is conventionally called globalization[1].

Globalization is the major development in the field of public law in the second half of the twentieth century. It has evolved according to an incremental pattern. First, it was applied to peace and human rights (the United Nations); then, to areas such as the sea, nuclear waste, health, labor, the environment. Subsequently, it was applied to trade, and, finally, to global terrorism and global crises. The process of globalization has been piecemeal, and globalization has developed through crises and unbalances, by accretion and accumulation.

---

[1] For an overview of this progress and the difficulties it has encountered, see A. Cassese (ed.), *Realizing Utopia. The Future of International Law*, Oxford, Oxford University Press, 2012.

In the global space, there is no global government, but rather several global regulatory regimes (from health to labor, to trade, to sea, to banking) without one single hierarchically superior regulatory system. The global polity is the empire of "ad-hoc-cracy:" global regulatory regimes that do not follow a common pattern. This highly a-systematic structure has been nicely encapsulated in the formulation "governance without government" (a formulation which already dates back a quarter of a century[2]). What unifies this mosaic of legal orders is reciprocal interest.

Vertically, there is continuity and no clear dividing line between global and national levels. "Global" does not mean that the State is excluded. National civil societies, national bureaucracies, and national executives are all important actors in the global arena, where they accept losing some of their autonomy (sovereignty) in exchange for obtaining influence in a much larger area than that of the national State. The bazaar replaces the cathedral[3].

Global does not mean intergovernmental. In the global space, there are transnational networks and links among civil societies that are as important as International Governmental Organizations (IGOs). While global regulatory regimes are approximately two thousand, Non-Governmental Organizations (NGOs) number more than sixty thousand[4].

There is no representative democracy and there are no periodic elections at the global level; but deliberative democracy can work as a surrogate, granting participation in the decision-making processes.

Global regulatory regimes impose democratic principles on national governments. In particular, some democratic principles (free elections, freedom of association, free speech) are imposed by global actors (such as the European Union and the Council of Europe) on national governments. An example is the conditionality of accession

---

[2] J. N. Rosenau and E. O. Czempiel (eds.), *Governance without Government: Order and Change in World Politics*, Cambridge, Cambridge University Press, 1992.

[3] The metaphor is taken from E. S. Raymond, *The Cathedral and the Bazaar: Musings on Linux and Open Source by an Accidental Revolutionary*, Sebastopol, Calif., O'Reilly and Associates, 2001. See also M. Xifaras, *The Global Turn in Legal Theory*, in *Canadian Journal of Law and Jurisprudence*, 2016, vol. 29, February, pp. 215-243.

[4] Union of International Associations, *Yearbook of International Organizations*, München, Saur, 2005.

to the European Union (EU). Another example of this phenomenon is provided by the European Convention on Human Rights, which provides for individual complaints to be brought before the European Court of Human Rights, which in turn has compulsory jurisdiction over its Member States[5].

Finally, the global polity is porous and open: national governments, other global regulatory regimes, and civil societies can interfere with and influence the global institutions.

I wish to thank Giorgio Mocavini for his assistance with the editing of this book.

The chapters of this book have been published or will be published in the following periodicals or books (the previous publishers have all agreed on this re-publication):

1) *From the Nation-State to the Global Polity*, in D. King – P. Le Galès (eds.), *Reconfiguring European States in Crisis*, Oxford, Oxford University Press, 2017, pp. 78-96 (with permission of Oxford University Press)

2) *The Globalization of Law*, in *New York University Journal of International Law and Politics*, 2005, vol. 37, n. 4, pp. 973-993

3) *Governing the World*, in S. Cassese (ed.), *Research Handbook on Global Administrative Law*, Cheltenham-Northampton, Edward Elgar, 2016, pp. 502-511

4) *Does a "Global Constitution" exist?*, keynote speech delivered at the *colloque* on "*Le constitutionalisme globale – Peut-on penser la Constitution sans État?*", Institut Villey, Université de Paris 1, Paris, 29-30 May 2017, to be published in the proceedings of the conference

5) *The Global Dimensions of Democracy*, lecture for the Carl Friedrich von Siemens Stiftung series on democracy, Munich, 22 June 2017, to be published in a book on *Die Zukunft der Demokratie*

6) *Administrative Law without the State? The Challenge of Global Regulation*, in *New York University Journal of International Law and Politics*, 2005, vol. 37, n. 4, pp. 663-694

---

[5] Council of Europe, *Convention for the Protection of Human Rights and Fundamental Freedoms*, as amended by Protocol No. 11, art. 34.

7) *Is There a Global Administrative Law?*, in *The Exercise of Public Authority by International Institutions*, Heidelberg, Springer, 2010, pp. 761-777

8) *Global Standards for National Administrative Procedure*, in *Law and Contemporary Problems*, 2005, vol. 68, pp. 109-126

9) *Ruling Indirectly: The Judicial Subsidiarity in the ECTHR*, in *Subsidiarity: a two-sided coin?*, in *Dialogue between judges 2015*, European Court of Human Rights – Council of Europe, pp. 11-18

10) *The Development of Global Administrative Law*, in S. Cassese (ed.), *Research Handbook on Global Administrative Law*, Cheltenham-Northampton, Edward Elgar, 2016, pp. 1-11

11) *Global Administrative Law: The State of the Art*, in *International Journal of Constitutional Law*, 2015, vol. 13, n. 2, pp. 465-468

12) *Legal Comparison by the Courts*, in *Revista Jurídica Piélagus*, 2010, n. 9, pp. 21-25

13) *The Constitutional Function of Supranational Courts: From Global Legal Space to Global Legal Order*, in *International Administrative Tribunals in a Changing World*, London, Esperia Publications Ltd., 2008, pp. 238-247

14) *The Constellation of Global and National Courts: Jurisdictional Redundancy and Interchange*, in A. Seibert-Fohr – M. Villiger (eds.), *Judgments of the European Court of Human Rights - Effects and Implementation*, Baden-Baden, Nomos, 2014, pp. 151-163

15) *Interactions between National and Supranational Jurisdictions: The Hedgehog Dilemma*, in *International Journal of Procedural Law*, 2015, vol. 5, n. 2, pp. 190-200

CHAPTER I

NATIONAL GOVERNMENTS AND GLOBALIZATION

I. FROM THE NATION-STATE TO THE GLOBAL POLITY

1. THE AMBIGUITIES OF THE STATE

THIS chapter is divided into three parts: the first concerns the rise of the State, the second discusses the decline of the State and the third is on the resurgence of the State.

In 1931, an American scholar wrote that "a cursory examination of the term 'State' brought to light no fewer than one hundred forty-five different definitions;" and he concluded that "from now on State will need to be accompanied with subscript brackets indicating the particular definition that is being used."[1] Therefore, it is important to handle the concept of "State" with caution.

As Max Weber first noticed, the State is but one of the many forms of polity that emerged in the sixteenth century and developed through the nineteenth century.[2] Later, Otto Brunner[3] and Otto Hintze[4] took up the concept of the historical nature of the State, recently developed

---

[1] C. H. Titus, "A Nomenclature in Political Science", in *American Political Science Review*, 1931, vol. 25, n. 3, pp. 615 ff. See also S. Cassese, "Fortuna e decadenza della nozione di Stato", in *Scritti in onore di Massimo Severo Giannini*, Milano, Giuffrè, 1988, vol. I, pp. 91 ff.

[2] M. Weber, *Staatssoziologie*, J. Winckelmann ed., Berlin, Duncker und Humblot, 1966.

[3] O. Brunner, *Land und Herrschaft. Grundfragen der territorialen Verfassungsgeschichte Österreichs im Mittelalter*, Baden bei Wien, 1965 (Engl. translation: *Land and Lordship. Structures of Governance in Medieval Austria*, University of Pennsylvania Press, 1995).

[4] O. Hintze, *Wesen und Wandlung des modernen Staats*, in *Sitzungsberichte der Preussischen Akademie der Wissenschaften*, 1931, Berlin, de Gruyter, p. 790; see also *The Historical Essays of Otto Hintze*, with an introduction by Felix Gilbert, New York, Oxford University Press, 1975.

by Bertrand Badie and Pierre Birnbaum. According to the latter two authors, *"[o]ften seen as the unescapable result of political development, the construction of the state should by contrast be understood as an original innovation located in time and space."*[5]

As for the concept of the State, this formed slowly in the seventeenth century and was explored by a wide range of thinkers, from Hobbes to Hegel, to whom we owe the idea that "civil society" and the State are both connected and opposed at the same time. The contribution of jurists was essential to the construction of the State. The German jurist Ernst Forsthoff observed: *"Der moderne Flächenstaat ist eine Hervorbringung des Juristen. Die Juristen haben ihn im 16 Jahrhundert geschaffen, die Juristen haben ihn auf seinem Wege begleitet."*[6] The Austrian jurist Hans Kelsen noted that the concept of the State is essential for two different purposes: to unify diverse entities and to direct them towards a unitary objective, the general interest; and to ensure the neutrality of the officials called to work for the State, distinguishing the holder of the office from the office itself.

In other words, the conceptual construction of the State has been instrumental in uniting countries (civil societies) around their ruling class and in giving a common purpose to separate parties.[7]

2. THE FIRST CYCLE: RISE AND GROWTH

If we consider the cycle experienced by Europe's political bodies over the last few centuries, we may see that in the fourteenth century, there were one thousand political bodies in this part of the world. In the sixteenth century, there were only five hundred; in the age of the French Revolution there were three hundred and fifty, and at the beginning of the twentieth century there were only twenty-five political bodies that could be called nation-States. As the British historian Mark Greengrass

---

[5] B. Badie and P. Birnbaum, *Sociologie de l'État*, Paris, Grasset, 1979, p. 243 (English translation by A. Goldhammer, *The Sociology of the State*, Chicago, Chicago University Press, 1983).

[6] F. Forsthoff, *Rechtsstaat im Wandel*, Stuttgart, Kohlhammer, 1964, p. 77.

[7] H. Kelsen, *General Theory of Law and State*, Cambridge, MA, Harvard University Press, 1949, p. 191.

writes: "[s]wallowing and being swallowed up, were fundamental features of Europe's political past."[8]

Notwithstanding this process of mergers, the States that resulted were not fully united. For example, even after the merger of German States (what is called the unification of Germany), there were several political bodies within the larger unit: after 1871, in the *Kaiserreich*, under Prussian rule and *Kanzler* Bismarck, there were twenty-six political bodies; some of these even had power in military affairs.

Why has there been such a thorough change since the fourteenth century? Why did nations become nation-States? What are the explanatory factors for this development? What were the catalysts of State-building?

There are three explanations.[9] The first was developed by the American historian and political scientist, Charles Tilly, in a book entitled "Capital and Coercion"[10] and can be summarized with the following sentence: "States make war, war makes States." In other words, the military-fiscal State emerges from dynamics of conquest and domination.

The second explanation characterizes nation-building as a process of self-perpetuation and self-aggrandizement that is governed by the insiders. Those who occupied State offices were able to act with a certain degree of autonomy from the ruling classes and were able to bring about the ends they desired. The State is a development of monocratic power: central institutions were built to serve the Prince and were organized in

[8] M. Greengrass, "Introduction: Conquest and Coalescence", in M. Greengrass (ed.), *Conquest and Coalescence: The Shaping of the State in Early Modern Europe*, London, Edwards Arnold, 1991, p. 2.

[9] For a taxonomy of the theories of State formation, see T. Ertman, "State Formation and State Building in Europe", in T. Janoski, R. Alford, A. Hicks, M. A. Schwartz, *Handbook of Political Sociology*, Cambridge, Cambridge University Press, 2003, p. 367; H. Spruyt, "The Origins, Development, and Possible Decline of the Modern State", in *Annual Review of Political Science*, 2002, vol. 5, pp. 127 ff.; L. Tedoldi, "Dove eravamo rimasti? Lo Stato in età moderna tra problemi storiografici e questioni aperte", in *Le carte e la storia*, 2009, vol. 15, n. 2, pp. 19 ff.; P. Carroll, "Articulating Theories of States and State Formation", in *Journal of Historical Sociology*, 2009, vol. 22, n. 4, p. 553; T. Vu, "Studying the State through State Formation", in *World politics*, 2010, vol. 62, n. 1, pp. 148 ff.; and H.P. Glenn, *The Cosmopolitan State*, Oxford, Oxford University Press, 2013 (challenging the concept of the nation-State, claiming that all States are cosmopolitan).

[10] C. Tilly, *Coercion, Capital, and European States AD 990-1992*, Oxford, Blackwell, 1992.

concentric circles around the ruler,[11] as *"le roi a un pouvoir préexistant aux lois"* (the king's powers preexist the legal system).[12]

The third explanation has to do with culture, identity, language, ideas, national traditions and beliefs. On 11 March 1882, a great French historian, Ernest Renan, gave a lecture in Paris on *"Qu'est-ce qu'une Nation?"*. His conclusion was that *"une nation est une âme, un principe spirituel,"* *"une grande solidarité,"* *"un héritage;"* *"l'existence d'une nation est un plébiscite de tous les jours"* ("a nation is a soul, a spiritual principle, a great solidarity, a heritage; the existence of a nation is a plebiscite held every day")[13]

The classical German eighteenth- and nineteenth-century school of philology also established a direct link between culture and the State. For Friedrich August Wolf, school and State were one;[14] for Ulrich Wilamowitz-Moellendorf, there was a direct relationship between *"Volk, Staat, Sprache:"* a people has no right to exist if it does not have a common culture and a shared language.[15]

In conclusion, war is not the only path to bureaucratic centralization and to State-building; there are other explanations too, which are complementary to that of war. This does not mean that war becomes less important. States continue to prepare for wars, to be able to defend their territories or their citizens even beyond their territories, or to maintain peace in other parts of the world.

What is the nation-State? What are the peculiarities of this polity compared to previous forms (city-states, confederations, federations, empires)? First, the State is a polity that develops in a nation. This does not mean that it is established as a representative body, but that the *"fab-*

---

[11] P. Molas Ribalta, "L'impact des institutions centrales", in W. Reinhard (ed.), *Les élites du pouvoir et la construction de l'État en Europe*, Paris, PUF, 1996, pp. 25 ff.

[12] F.-R. Chateaubriand, *Mémoires d'outre-tombe*, Ed. Livrée par J.-Cl. Berchet, Bordas, «Classique Garnier», 1989-1998, vol. II, p. 2204.

[13] Available at http://www.lexilogos.com/document/renan/nation.htm. For an Italian translation, see E. Renan, *Che cos'è una nazione? E altri saggi*, Rome, Donzelli, 2004. See E.-W. Böckenförde, *La nascita dello Stato come processo di secolarizzazione*, in E.-W. Böckenförde, *Diritto e secolarizzazione. Dallo Stato moderno all'Europa unita*, Rome-Bari, Laterza, 2007, pp. 33 ff. for another explanation for the birth of the State.

[14] D. Lanza, *Interrogare il passato. Lo studio dell'antico tra Otto e Novecento*, Rome, Carocci, 2013, p. 33.

[15] U. von Wilamowitz-Moellendorf, *Volk, Staat, Sprache*, Berlin, Büxenstein, 1898; see also D. Lanza, *Interrogare il passato*, cit., p. 67.

rication collective des identités nationales"[16] is largely the product of the State-building process, because the construction of the State runs parallel to a nation's self-recognition.

Second, it has a minimum size, which must be sufficient for a certain degree of economic development in a world where trade is under State control, and for resisting pressures from other States.[17] Therefore, State-building occurs against and in contrast to other entities.

Third, unlike the political bodies of the Middle Ages, that were fluid and polycentric and did not have a vocation for absolutism, the State is stable, hierarchical, unitary, and centralized.[18]

Fourth, within the State, a division of labor exists such that decision-making, implementation and conflict resolution are assigned to different bodies.

Finally, the State is also a culture, an important component of which is legal positivism. This was developed by lawyers, who played a significant role in the rise and development of the State.[19] Positivism is an expression of faith in the State.[20] Thus, the State has become a quasi-divine entity, belonging to a superior, sacred world.[21]

As seen above, the cultural aspect of the State – that is, the State as an idea, not as an entity – has played an important role throughout the State's entire history. For almost two centuries now, however, this role and its meaning has been challenged by authors as diverse as Karl Marx, Léon Duguit and Philip Abrams, to cite only a few. For Marx, the State is a "superstructure" of civil society. Duguit wrote that "in public law we no longer believe that behind those who hold office there is a collective personal and sovereign substance of which they are only the agents and

---

[16] A.-M. Thiesse, *La création des identités nationales. Europe XVIII – XX siècle*, Paris, Seuil, 1999, p. 13.

[17] A. Alesina and E. Spolaore, *The Size of Nations*, Cambridge, MA, MIT Press, 2005.

[18] M. Ascheri, *Istituzioni medievali. Una introduzione*, Bologna, Il Mulino, 1994; P. Grossi, *L'ordine giuridico medievale*, Rome-Bari, Laterza, 1995.

[19] R. Schnur (ed.), *Die Rolle der Juristen bei der Entstehung des modernen States*, Berlin, Duncker und Humblot, 1986.

[20] As noted by E. Forsthoff, *Lo Stato nella società industriale* (1971), Italian translation, Milan, Giuffrè, 2011, p. 12.

[21] F. Werfel, *Twilight of a Word* (1936), Italian translation *Nel crepuscolo di un mondo*, Milan, Mondadori, 1954, p. 151 (short story with the title: "Class reunion").

organs."[22] Abrams concluded that the State "is a spurious object of sociological concern and... we should now move beyond Hegel, Marx, Stein, Gumplowicz and Weber on from the analysis of the State to a concern with the actualities of social subordination."[23]

Once established, nation-States began to grow. There were three factors of growth. First, the suffrage: with the advent of elections, governments became more representative, becoming the "citizens' States."[24] With the extension of suffrage came a growth in popular demand for schools, healthcare, social services and public enterprises. Then there were wars: suffice it to consider the rise in public employment in England, Italy or France after World Wars I and II.

The law-and-order State became the "avuncular State", which undertakes to protect the people from illness and accident, to provide education, to remove distinctions based on gender and ethnicity, and to ensure welfare and well-being.[25] As Tocqueville had foreseen, the State is now *"un pouvoir immense et tutélaire... Il est absolu, détaillé, régulier, prévoyant et doux."*[26]

These developments affected the State's constitutional aspects (Parliament and Government) much less than its administrative one: as noted by Carl Schmitt, "the total State (the State that occupies every space of society...) is by nature an administrative State."[27] Consequently, the State has engaged in a new endeavor: that of distributing and allocating resources among its citizens.

Throughout its history, the State has turned out to be a highly adaptive polity, capable of adjusting to various internal and external pres-

[22] L. Duguit, *Law in the Modern State*, New York, Fertig, 1970, p. 243 (English translation of *Les transformations du droit public*, Paris, Colin, 1913).

[23] P. Abrams, "Notes on the Difficulty of Studying the State" *(1977)*, in *Journal of Historical Sociology*, vol. 1, n. 1, 1988, p. 58.

[24] O. Beaud, *La puissance de l'État*, Paris, PUF, 1994.

[25] T. Caplow, "Evaluating State performance", paper presented at the Conference on Social Change in Western Europe, Poitiers, 8-9 October 1997. See also M. L. Dauber, *The Sympathetic State*, Chicago, University of Chicago Press, 2012.

[26] A. Tocqueville, *La démocratie en Amérique II* (1840), Paris, Laffont, 1986, p. 648.

[27] C. Schmitt, "Legalità e legittimità", in Id., *Le categorie del "politico"*, Bologna, Il Mulino, 1972, p. 215.

sures. States have adapted to democratic and authoritarian rule; to large territories and small; to liberal and to communist policies.

In this process of adaptation, the State has developed a great ability to negotiate and mediate,[28] contrasting strongly with the traditional *"Hoheitlichkeit,"* following different patterns of bureaucratic rationalization.[29] Therefore, in many countries, the State is now no different from a modern factory and the managerial techniques applied therein.

Another indicator of the State's adaptive nature is its ability to assimilate elements that were originally foreign to its traditional foundations. For example, the merit system was unknown in Europe until the eighteenth century, when it was imported from China and became a permanent feature of the major European States (later, China imported electoral systems from Europe, which were previously unknown to it).[30]

In the course of this long history, beyond the apparent uniformity, there are several substantial differences and different styles of statism.[31] One major difference is that between strong States (for example, French *"étatisme,"* the Prussian tradition and the powerful, Hegelian theory of the State) and weak States (such as in Italy, where a hundred and twenty-seven different executives were established in the one hundred and fifty years of its life).

A second difference is between European and non-European States: the first share the common tradition of the *ius publicum europaeum*, based on the German reinterpretation of Roman law.[32]

---

[28] B. Jobert and P. Muller, *L'État en action. Politiques publiques et corporatismes*, Paris, PUF, 1987, pp. 69 ff. and 74 ff.

[29] B. S. Silberman, *Cages of Reason: The Rise of the Rational State in France, Japan, the United States and Great Britain*, Chicago, Chicago University Press, 1993.

[30] G. Bertuccioli, "Riflessioni su un anniversario", in *Mondo cinese*, 1994, n. 87, pp. 3 ff., but especially p. 6.

[31] P. Baldwin, "Beyond Weak and Strong: Rethinking the State in Comparative Policy History", in *Journal of Policy History*, 2005, vol. 17, n. 1, pp. 12 ff. and especially p. 18; S. Steinmo, *The Evolution of Modern States. Sweden, Japan and the United States*, Cambridge, Cambridge University Press, 2010, pp. 29 and 206.

[32] C. Schmitt, *Ex captivitate salus*, Italian translation, Milan, Adelphi, 1987, pp. 64-80. L. Garofalo, "Carl Schmitt e la "Wissenschaft des römischen Rechts". Saggio su un cantore della scienza giuridica europea", in *Diritto e società*, 2007, n. 2, pp. 171 ff..

The third, most important, difference is that between States with a significant martial component and States where, instead, this has become less important.[33]

Recent literature prefers to abandon the strong States/weak States dichotomy in favour of the idea that it is necessary to broaden the notion of stateness,[34] and that there are differing degrees of stateness and statehood: "[t]he State's importance cannot be captured on a one-dimensional strong-weak continuum or through a model that builds on a Weberian conception of coercive capacity located in centralized bureaucracies."[35] This conclusion, however, prompts a question: "how does the State evolve and succeed without the traditional elements of State building, or the customary apparatus of power and authority?"[36]

Another important point is the interaction between the process of State-building and the way in which the concept of State is approached; in other words, how the State is perceived and studied. Voltaire believed that there were two models, embodied by France and England, respectively. In France, the State was at the centre, while England was based on self-government (however, it must be noted that while we now conceive of self-government as synonymous with local government, in the nineteenth and twentieth century, scholars such as von Gneist believed that *Selbstverwaltung*, as opposed to *Staatsverwaltung*, had a much greater meaning, i.e. that society itself could run the State[37]).

---

[33] T. Caplow, *Evaluating State performance*, cit.

[34] The first author to stress the importance of "different levels of stateness" is J. P. Nettl, "The State as a Conceptual Variable", in *World Politics*, 1968, vol. 20, n. 4, 1968, pp. 559 ff. This idea was then expanded by C. Tilly, "Reflections on the History of European State-Making", in C. Tilly (ed.), *The Formation of National States in Western Europe*, Princeton, Princeton University Press, 1975 (Italian translation: "La formazione dello Stato in Europa. Riflessioni introduttive", in C. Tilly (a cura di), *La formazione degli Stati nazionali nell'Europa occidentale*, Bologna, Il Mulino, 1984, pp. 7 ff.). See also O. Nay, "Fragile and Failed States: Critical Perspectives on Conceptual Hybrids", in *International Political Science Review*, 2013, vol. 34, p. 326.

[35] D. King and R. Lieberman, "Ironies of State Building: A Comparative Perspective on the American State", in *World Politics*, 2009, vol. 61, n. 3, p. 581.

[36] D. King and R. Lieberman, *Ironies of State Building*, cit., p. 548.

[37] R. von Gneist, *Das heutige englische Verfassungs- und Verwaltungsrecht*, 2 vols., Berlin, Springer, 1857-1863, vol. II, p. 818 and 1863. R. von Gneist, *Geschichte und heutige Gestalt des englischen Communalverfassungs oder das Selfgovernment*, 2 vols., Berlin, Springer, 1863. On Gneist, see F. Ferraresi, "Il modello costituzionale inglese e la Germania fra Otto e Novecento",

England is a paradox: a very powerful State, with strong military might and the centre of a colonial empire, but one without any notion of State.[38] In his book "Introduction to the Study of the Law and Constitution,"[39] the British master of nineteenth-century constitutionalism, Professor Albert Venn Dicey, ignored both the word and the notion of State, while scholars such as Georg Jellinek in Germany or Vittorio Emanuele Orlando in Italy placed the theory of the State at the very centre of their reflections. Authors such as Bertrand Badie and Pierre Birnbaum go so far as to write that in countries like the United Kingdom and the United States, the organization of society makes the construction of the State unnecessary. The centre does not erect itself into a State, nor does it delegate its agents to do so. The "self-organization of society" is sufficient.[40]

The same is true for the United States, where the concept of State "slipped in importance during the 'behavioral revolution' of the 1950s and 1960s"[41] and had a revival in the 1980s. In 1985, a book entitled "Bringing the State Back In"[42] was published and noted "a sudden upsurge of interest in 'the State.'" It is now clear that "the apparent 'statelessness' of the United States is an illusion."[43]

These paradoxes draw attention to a further one. There is not necessarily a convergence between States and theories of the State: strong States may have poor, or no, theories of the State at all (such as the United Kingdom), while weak States may have developed strong theories of the State (such as Italy). It has been noted – with reference to the latter case – that "in their initial self-construction as fully-inclusionary centers of

---

in E. Capozzi (ed.), *Le costituzioni anglosassoni e l'Europa: riflessi e dibattiti tra '800 e '900*, Soveria Mannelli, Rubbettino, 2002, pp. 79 ff. and especially pp. 83 ff.

[38] A different opinion in J. McLean, *Searching for the State in British Legal Thought. Competing Conceptions of the Public Sphere*, New York, N.Y., Cambridge University Press, 2012.

[39] A. V. Dicey, *Introduction to the Study of the Law of the Constitution* (1885), Indianapolis, Liberty Fund, 1982.

[40] B. Badie-P. Birnbaum, *Sociologie de l'État*, cit.

[41] T. Vu, *Studying the State through State Formation*, cit., p. 148.

[42] P. Evans, D. Rueschemeyer, and T. Skocpol (eds.), *Bringing the State Back In*, Cambridge, Cambridge University Press, 1985.

[43] D. King and R. Lieberman, *Ironies of State Building*, cit., p. 547.

political power, States produced an inflated and over-centric semantic form for themselves, which they were not able to realize."[44]

Today, there are a hundred and ninety-three States that belong to the United Nations, a hundred and eighty-five States that are members of the International Labour Organization, and a hundred and fifty-six States that are part of the World Trade Organization. To become a member of one of these organizations, it is necessary to be a State. This is another paradox. Through treaties, States establish international organizations; but then international organizations induce, promote, support, and control States; they establish standards of democracy and of rule of law for States. Therefore, State-building is now both a bottom-up and a top-down process.

3. THE SECOND CYCLE: THE DECLINE OF THE STATE

The second cycle began in the early twentieth century, with the first crisis of the State. It continued into the 1970s, with the second crisis and the "retreat of the State," and into our days with the State's third crisis and the process of globalization.

Why did politicians and scholars begin talking of the crisis of the State in early twentieth-century Europe? This was because State authority was then challenged from within for the first time, by a variety of forces: associations, especially trade unions, which replaced the atomistic civil society, collectivism and corporatism of previous times. At that point, unable to represent these interests, political representation revealed its deficiencies. This societal "malaise" relating to the State, an indicator of the difficult relations between State authority and civil society, led many authors to write that the State was decaying, or being eclipsed.

This weakening of the State had three interpreters, one in France, just before World War I, one in Italy during World War I, and the third

---

[44] C. Thornhill, *The Future of the State*, in P. F. Kjaer, G. Teubner and A. Febbrajo, *The Financial Crisis in Constitutional Perspective. The Dark Side of Functional Differentiation*, Oxford, Hart, 2011, p. 372. On the theories of the State, see also M. Fioravanti, "Per una storia dello Stato moderno in Europa", in *Quaderni fiorentini per la storia del pensiero giuridico moderno*, 2010, n. 39, p. 69 ff.

in Germany, during the Weimar Republic. The first was Léon Duguit, who declared that "*l'État est mort.*"[45] The second, Santi Romano, proposed to replace the State with the "legal order" (*ordinamento giuridico*) as the central concept of public law.[46] The third was Johannes Popitz, followed by Carl Schmitt, who introduced the concept of "policracy" as a substitute for democracy.[47]

The first crisis met different reactions. One was the Italian reaction: the restoration of State authority. Mussolini and Fascism were a reaction to the first crisis of the State.

On a theoretical level, there was another reaction. Duguit wrote that "[l]'*État n'est pas une personne juridique; l'État n'est pas une personne souveraine. L'État est le produit historique d'une différentiation sociale entre les forts et les faibles dans une société donnée ;*" "*[f]aux le postulat de l'État-personne; faux celui de la puissance droit subjectif [...]*" and proposed to abandon the concept of the State in favour of more realistic concepts, such as the "*service public*" and "rulers" (*gouvernants*).[48] In several countries, but especially in Italy and Germany, the authoritarian reactions to the crisis of the State produced another result: a *Staatsmüdigkeit* (State-weariness) and *Entzauberung* (deconsecration or de-mythisation) of the State.[49]

The second crisis occurred in the 1970s and 1980s. At the political level, the indicators of this new crisis were the reforms introduced by Margaret Thatcher and President Reagan. At the scholarly level,

---

[45] L. Duguit, *Law in the Modern State*, cit., p. 243.

[46] S. Romano, *L'ordinamento giuridico (1917-18)*, Firenze, Sansoni, 1946.

[47] E. Forsthoff, *Lo Stato nella società industriale*, cit., p. 14.

[48] L. Duguit, *L'État, les gouvernants et les agents*, Paris, Fontemoing, 1903, p. 1 and p. 53. This book was a development of another book on the State, by the same author: *L'État, le droit objectif et la loi positive*, Paris, Fontemoing, 1901. The purpose of the latter text was to "*montrer que l'État n'est point cette personne collective, investie d'un pouvoir souverain, imaginée par l'esprit inventif des publicistes*" (p. 1) and to critique the work published by George Jellinek in 1892 and previous works of P. Laband and C. F. Gerber. See also Id., *Les transformations du droit public*, Paris, Colin, 1913, p. XIX: "*Ainsi la notion de service public vient remplacer celle de souveraineté. L'État n'est plus une puissance souveraine qui commande; il est un groupe d'individus détenant une force qu'ils doivent employer à créer et à gérer les services publics. La notion de service public devient la notion fondamentale du droit public moderne. Les faits vont le démontrer*".

[49] G. Dahm, *Die Stellung des Menschen im Völkerrecht unserer Zeit*, Tübingen, J. C. B. Mohr, 1961, p. 11.

the book authored by Guy Peters and Richard Rose, "Can Government Go Bankrupt?" set the tone.[50] This crisis was due to the modern State's failure to perform its duties, to governments' inability to meet popular demands, to the difficulties suffered by the welfare State, to ungovernability, to the financial crisis,[51] and to failures in policy implementation.[52] Could Hegel only suppose that the State could go bankrupt?

The State responded to the internal signs of this crisis in several ways: the rollback of State regulation of the economy, liberalizations, privatizations, sale of State ownerships, cuts in public expenditure, decentralizations.

These developments have reduced not only the size of governments, but also the differences between the public sphere and the private arena.[53] As a consequence, new problems have arisen. These include establishing the essence of the State and of sovereign authority, the location of the "hard core" of government powers and the dividing line between public and private, how to map the State, where to establish State boundaries and how to classify State agencies.

These problems have many practical implications. For example, since the German *Grundgesetz* establishes that the exercise of sovereign authority is, as a rule, entrusted to members of the public service (Art. 33, par. 4), can forensic treatment facilities be privatized in Germany?[54] Or, since the Israeli Constitution protects human dignity and liberty, can

---

[50] G. Peters and R. Rose, *Can Government Go Bankrupt?*, New York, Basic Books, 1978.

[51] R. Mayntz, "Governing Failures and the Problem of Governability: Some Comments on a Theoretical Paradigm" in J. Kooiman (ed.), *Modern Governance: New Government-Society Interactions*, London, Sage, 1993, pp. 11 ff.

[52] J. L. Pressman and A. Wildavsky, *Implementation: How Great Expectations in Washington are Dashed in Oakland, Or Why It's Amazing that Federal Programs Work at All*, Berkeley, University of California Press, 3rd edition, 1984.

[53] M. P. Maduro, "The Chameleon State. EU Law and the Blurring of the Private/Public Distinction in the Market" in R. Nickel (ed.), *Conflict of Laws and Laws of Conflict in Europe and Beyond: Patterns of Supranational and Transnational Juridification*, Antwerp-Oxford-Portland, Intersentia, 2010, pp. 279 ff. See also J. C. Alexander, *The Civil Sphere*, Oxford, Oxford University Press, 2006.

[54] See *Bundesverfassungsgericht*, 2 BvR 133/10 (2012). This decision established that the law did not give rise to objections concerning insufficient protection against unjustified interference with fundamental rights.

a law authorize a private, for-profit corporation to operate a prison in Israel?[55]

At a higher level, beyond the State, the blurring of the line between public and private has given rise to another problem: that of redefining an area that all members of a union can consider public. For this purpose, the European Union has identified a new institution, the "body governed by public law," which also includes private entities that are under public control, either through participation or through financing. Thus, the State becomes an entity "*à géométrie variable.*"

But there are also external signs of crisis. These include transnational corporations exercising "parallel authority" alongside national governments;[56] big businesses, insurers, accountants and international bureaucrats all encroach on the sovereignty of the State. There is, therefore, a "declining authority of the States" and a growth of "authority beyond the State."[57]

The third crisis is now under way. In Europe, national governments have lost control over their currencies. In 1998, there were thirty-seven currencies in Europe; from 2014, only twenty. At the global level, the phenomenon of globalization is unfolding: there are two thousand global regulatory regimes and sixty-thousand nongovernmental organizations; there are international organizations such as the WTO, networks of national regulators such as the Basel Committee; hybrid public-private regulators such as the International Standardization Organization, and private global regulators such as ICANN, the Internet Corporation for Assigned Names and Numbers. These

---

[55] The answer of the Supreme Court of Israel (Case No. HJC 2605/05 of 2009) was that the constitutional provision according to which the government is the executive branch of the State (Section 1) implies that there is a "hard core" of sovereign powers that the government must exercise itself, in order to ensure personal liberty and human dignity. Similar cases have arisen in Costa Rica and India in relation to the privatization of prisons and police. See D. A. Slansky, "Private Policing and Human Rights" in *Law & Ethics of Human Rights*, 2011, vol. 5, pp. 112 ff.

[56] S. Strange, *The Retreat of the State: The Diffusion of Power in the World Economy*, Cambridge, Cambridge University Press, 1996, especially pp. 91 ff.

[57] S. Strange, *The Retreat of the State*, cit., pp. 3 ff. and pp. 91 ff. See also S. Cassese and V. Wright, *La restructuration des États en Europe occidentale*, in V. Wright and S. Cassese (eds), *La recomposition de l'État en Europe*, Paris, Éditions de la découverte, 1996, pp. 7 ff. and D. King and P. Le Galès, "Sociologie de l'État en recomposition" in *Revue française de sociologie*, 2011, vol. 52, n. 3, pp. 453 ff.

regulators have the power to impose standards. See, for example, the *Codex Alimentarius* Commission, that establishes food standards that reach our very tables. These international organizations are not part of a unitary legal order, but rather of a fragmented legal space.[58]

Globalization is, at the same time, denationalization of State institutions and a cumulative process of expansion of trade, communication, media, migration, crime, terrorism and even fashion.[59] This development has two levels: one is global or universal, the other is supranational.

The main features of the global level are the following: development through mutual connections; a fluid organization; joint decision-making techniques; absence of any separation between the global and the domestic levels; three powers, legislative, executive and dispute-settling (but more continuity between them, rather than a true separation, a legislative branch acting mainly as standard-setter, and an executive branch less developed than in domestic legal orders, as the global polity is reliant to a great degree upon national implementation through indirect rule); an administration and administrative law with weak constitutional foundations; the growth of a global rule of law (i.e. principles that are common to all regulatory regimes: the right to a hearing, participation, the right to be informed, access to a judge) and legalization of global administrative networks towards a universal rule of law; and finally, control of the State by the economy, which replaces State control over the economy (indeed, through rating agencies, it is markets that control States, rather than States that control markets).[60]

As for Europeanization – which is but one example of supranationalism – we may see multiple citizenships (European, national and sub-national); multiple *demoi* (akin to the *Vielvölkerstaat* of the Middle

---

[58] See S. Cassese (ed.), *Global Administrative Law*, Cheltenham, Elgar, 2016.

[59] See J. Habermas, *The Divided West*, Cambridge, Ciaran Cronin, 2006, p. 175; S. Sassen, *Territory, Authority, Rights: from Medieval to Global Assemblages*, Princeton, Princeton University Press, 2006, p. 1; C. Zürcher, *When Governance Meets Troubled States*, in M. Beisheim and G. F. Schuppert (eds), *Staatszerfall und Governance*, Baden-Baden, Nomos, 2007, p. 11.

[60] S. Cassese, "Administrative Law without the State? The Challenge of Global Regulation" in *Journal of International Law and Politics*, 2005, vol. 37, n. 4, pp. 663 ff. (now in this book, p. 109 ff.) and S. Cassese, *The Global Polity*, Seville, Global Law Press, 2012.

Ages)[61] in which national identities become less important; several languages, as in the *Mehrsprachenstaat* of the past; a concentration of power that is replaced by networks (for example, the structure of the European Central Bank and the role of national governors); and a plurality of polities, such as the *imperium* which included several *regna*.

However, it is necessary to highlight that States are organized in "layers," and that not all developments occur simultaneously. Therefore, the three crises mentioned above did not all occur at the same time and did not all span the same number of years, as noted by several authors.[62]

The decline of the State poses a major problem: if the State is the place where democracy has developed, what will happen to democracy if the State disappears or becomes less important? Will it evaporate? Or will it be replaced by a cosmopolitan democracy? The democratic deficit of the global polity is compensated by many surrogates. One is legitimacy through procedure, by participation in decision-making processes (deliberative democracy), that is widespread in the global space (from the World Trade Organization – WTO – to the Internet Corporation for Assigned Names and Numbers – ICANN). Another is horizontal accountability, that is global actors, national and international governments, being accountable to each other (Hungary versus the European Union; the European Union versus the United Nations Organization). Another is judicial review acting as a "fire alarm" system (the approximately one hundred and twenty global courts and an equivalent number of quasi judicial bodies open the way to civil societies to keep under control both national and international bodies). Another is capacity-based authority, power based on reputation and expertise (as in the case of the International Electrotechnical Commission – IEC[63]).

[61] K. F. Werner, *Naissance de la noblesse. L'essor des élites politiques en Europe*, Paris, Fayard, 1998 (Italian translation, *Nascita della nobiltà*, Turin, Einaudi, 2000, p. 58).

[62] L. Jacobs and D. King, "America's Political Crisis: The Unsustainable State in a Time of Unraveling" in *Political Science and Politics*, 2009, April, pp. 277 ff.

[63] D. D. Avant, M. Finnemore, and S. K. Sell (eds), *Who Governs the Globe?*, New York, Cambridge University Press, 2010.

4. THE THIRD CYCLE: RESURGENCE OF THE STATE

At the end of the second cycle, one could reasonably wonder whether the State could survive so many crises without defeat. Fortunately, many of the second cycle's developments were replete with ambiguities. To implement the Big Government reforms, Margaret Thatcher required a very strong central government: to make the State smaller, one needs greater powers. A lesser State ownership went hand-in-hand with greater regulation on part of independent regulatory agencies. State activism shifted from a market-steering orientation to a market-supporting one[64]. Also, greater emphasis on consumer protection implies more State regulation.

These ambiguities show that the State has not disappeared with liberalizations and globalization, but, on the contrary, is alive and is only self-restructuring, to adjust its structure and functions to the new spaces, so that it can overcome its internal weaknesses. The developments analyzed above are simply part of the dynamics of the State.

States cope with internal fragmentation (next-steps agencies, *enti pubblici, établissements publics*) by governing without State-centric government models[65]; by learning the lessons of government without governance; by "societal replacement for the incapacity of government to steer and row"; by its "management of networks and [....] self-organizing systems of interaction" as an alternative to conventional governance; by a "decentralized rowing"[66]; and finally, by using an instrument of the British colonial tradition – indirect rule. Indeed, it can be said that the world is rediscovering indirect rule: the European Union is ruling indirectly, and the same is true for the WTO.

As for the external pressures, States are surrendering sovereignty to regional and global institutions, but at the same time they promote

---

[64] J. Levy (ed.), *The State After Statism. New State Activities in the Age of Liberalization*, Cambridge, MA, Harvard University Press, 2006.

[65] J. Pierre and B. G. Peters, *Governing Complex Societies: Trajectories and Scenarios*, Basingstoke, Palgrave Macmillan, 2013.

[66] B. G. Peters, "Shouldn't Row, Can't Steer: What's A Government to Do?", in *Public Policy and Administration*, 1997, vol. 12, n. 2, pp. 51 ff.

competition among nations[67]. Thus, from being "guardians of national security", they become "guardians against economic insecurity"[68].

Next to the thousands of international organizations, there are the regional supranational organizations like those established in Europe, Southeast Asia, North America, and South America. The most developed is the European Union, which presents many distinctive features.

First, while domestic administrations depend on a single centre of power, the European administration does not have only one centre. Unlike the situation in domestic governments, in the European Union there is no one single branch of government entrusted with the implementation of rules. Implementing power can be exercised by the Commission, by the Council, or by Member States.

Second, while domestic administrations have exclusive powers of implementation, the European administration is not the Union's only implementing authority. In the Union, the Member States take all measures necessary for implementing legally binding Union acts, and the Commission or the Council have implementing power where uniform conditions are required. Consequently, the Union's implementing power is residual and not monopolistic.[69]

Third, while domestic administration is binomial,[70] European administration is trinomial. For example, in the area of competition

---

[67] V. Cable, "The Diminished Nation-State. A Study in the Loss of Economic Power", in *Daedalus*, 1995, vol. 124, n. 2, pp. 23 ff. (issue topic: "What future for the State").

[68] S. Strange, "The Defective State", in *Daedalus*, 1955, vol. 124, n. 2, pp. 55 ff.

[69] Court of Justice, C-8/88 Germany v. Commission. See A. J. Gil Ibanez, *El control y la ejecución del derecho comunitario. El papel de las Administraciones nacionales y europea*, Madrid, Instituto nacional de administración pública, 1998; K.-H. Ladeur (ed.), *The Europeanisation of Administrative Law. Transforming National Decision-Making Procedures*, Dartmouth, Ashgate, 2002; J. H. Jans, R. de Lange, S. Prechal and R. J. G. M. Widdershoven, *Europeanisation of Public Law*, Groningen, Europa Law Publishing, 2007. On the relationship between European law and national administrative laws, G. Vesperini, *Il vincolo europeo sui diritti amministrativi nazionali*, Milan, Giuffrè, 2011.

[70] A.V. Dicey, *Introduction to the Study of the Law of the Constitution*, London, Macmillan, 1935, pp. 332-333: "*Droit administratif*", or "administrative law", has been defined by French authorities in general terms as "the body of rules which regulate the relations of the administration or of the administrative authority towards private citizens;" and Aucoc, in his work on *droit administratif*, describes his topic in very general language: "Administrative law determines the constitution and the relations of those organs of society which are charged with the care of those interests (*intérêts collectifs*) which are the object of public administration, by which term is meant

and State aid, the administration and the private party are not the only two players. On the contrary, there are several players: the European Commission, acting as the guardian of competition; one national government, the grantor of the aid; a private party that has benefited from the aid as grantee; other interested States; and other interested parties. This multiplicity of players generates "polycentric adjudication" processes.[71]

Fourth, unlike national law, the European Union features a double legality.[72] Indeed, the European treaties state that the Union is a "community based on the rule of law" and has a "complete system of legal remedies and procedures," in accordance with the "basic constitutional charter, the treaty." These treaties state that there are two ways of implementing the "general measures" of the Union's institutions: community implementation (where private parties can bring an action before the Court of Justice) and national implementation (where private parties can bring an action before national courts). These treaties state that all measures that are intended to have legal effects can be subject to judicial review.[73]

Fifth, while national governments have a single component, the European Union government is composite. In the EU, there are indeed four essential components, of differing natures: purely European (the Commission and the Court of Justice), multinational (the Parliament), inter-governmental (the Council), and inter-bureaucratic (the Committees).

---

the different representatives of society among which the State is the most important, and the relation of the administrative authorities towards the citizens of the State."

[71] L. L. Fuller, "The Forms and Limits of Adjudication", in *Harvard Law Review*, 1978, vol. 92, pp. 394-395. Polycentric adjudication processes require inter-institutional agreements: M. Cini, "EU Decision-Making on Inter-Institutional Agreements: Defining (Common) Rules of Conduct for European Lobbyists and Public Servants", in *West European Politics*, 2013, vol. 36, n. 6, pp. 1143 ff.

[72] On the features of the legality principle in European law, K. Lenaerts, "The Rule of Law and the Coherence of the Judicial System of the European Union", in *Common Market Law Review*, 2007, pp. 1625 ff.; L. Azoulai, "Le principe de légalité", in J.-B. Auby and J. Dutheil de la Rochére (eds), *Droit administratif européen*, Bruxelles, Bruylant, 2007, pp. 393 ff.; A. von Bogdandy, *Constitutional Principles*, in A. von Bogdandy and J. Bast (eds), *Principles of European Constitutional Law*, Oxford, Hart, 2006, pp. 15 ff.

[73] Court of Justice C-294/1983 Les Verts. See also Court of Justice C-46/87 and 227/88 Höchst and C-103/88 Fratelli Costanzo.

Sixth, while national law is imposed on national societies, European law leaves space for a choice of law.

Seventh, administrative development in the national context depends on national government policies, but administrative development at the European level depends on the interaction between national and European administrations. *Wechselseitige Eigennutz* ("reciprocal expediency") is the first and most important reason for which the State opened up and established standard-setting supranational and global bodies. One of the first to observe this was Immanuel Kant.[74]

States share their sovereignty (from a traditional point of view, this is an oxymoron: true sovereignty cannot be shared – if it is shared, it is not sovereignty). They join forces with other States and accept global standard-setting bodies, but they also try to reduce the asymmetry between the globalized economy and national governments.

Each State is confined by its own borders and, therefore, has no power to fight global terrorism and global warming, or to organize Olympic Games. To engage in these endeavors, the U.N. Sanctions Committee, the Kyoto Protocol, and the International Olympic Committee respectively are necessary.

Because they must share tasks and power, States become part of global networks and replace hierarchies with horizontal links, and command and control with negotiation. Clear departmental boundaries, clear lines of authority, detailed reporting mechanisms, and formal decision-making procedures are replaced with complementarity and reciprocity, vertical and horizontal interdependence, and mutually supportive actions.[75]

The result is often negative, because these confused new arrangements frequently lead to traps for joint decision-making. At this point, States have less power, because they must share decision-making with other States; but, at the same time, they are able to enter areas previously closed to them. Here is another paradox: States have less power and more power at the same time.

In conclusion, "contrary to the brave new world many expected in the wake of globalization and global economy integration [...] the State is

---

[74] I. Kant, *Zum ewigen Frieden*, Italian translation, *Per la pace perpetua*, Milan, Feltrinelli, 2010, p. 78 (observations on the *Handelsgeist* (the spirit of trade)).

[75] G. Thompson, J. Frances, R. Levacic, and J. Mitchell (eds), *Markets, Hierarchies and Networks: The Coordination of Social Life*, London, Sage, 1991.

doggedly present"[76] and "the notion of growing statelessness in the international system and the global economy has quickly evaporated."[77] There is no decline, no retreat, no crisis of the State. There is only a process of reconfiguration, adaptation, and restructuring which is part of the State's dynamics. This process may overlap with severe short-term crises and policy challenges but that is distinct from implosion of the State as the key organizing entity for political communities.

Contrary to a widespread view that opposes globalization and national governments, States are a constitutive element of globalization, as in Kant's dove flight.[78]

In the process of globalization, there are several paradoxes that strengthen the links between the State and globalization. First, globalization is a process through which States establish global regulators by agreement.[79] But the reverse is also true, as global regulators sustain, promote, and provide incentives for States and the rule of law, as is the result of the United Nations' global efforts to promote democracy through the United Nations Democracy Fund or the European Union Democracy Initiative.

Second, global institutions promote and develop global indicators with the expectation of self-harmonization and reciprocal pressure. Examples are the "State Capacity Survey" developed by Columbia University; the "State Fragility Index" published by the Center for Systemic Peace and the Center for Global Policy at George Mason

---

[76] D. King and R. Lieberman, *Ironies of State Building*, cit., p. 550. Similar conclusions are drawn in G. Corso, "Persistenza dello Stato e trasformazioni del diritto", and in L. Condorelli, "Crisi dello Stato e diritto internazionale: simul stabunt simul cadent?", both in *Ars interpretandi*, 2011, vol. 16, special issue on *Lo Stato contemporaneo e la sua crisi*, pp. 107 ff. and 173 ff., and in P. Du Gay and A. Scott, *Transformation de l'État ou changement de régime? De quelques confusions en théorie et sociologie de l' État*, in *Revue française de sociologie*, 2011, vol. 52, n. 3, pp. 537 ff.

[77] D. King and R. Lieberman, *Ironies of State Building*, cit., p. 547. On the challenge posed by globalization to the State, see also T. J. Lowi, "La globalizzazione, la guerra e il declino dello Stato", in *Rivista italiana di scienza politica*, 2009, vol. 39, n. 1, pp. 3 ff. and K.-H. Ladeur, *The State in International Law*, Osgoode Hall Law School Research Paper n. 27/2010.

[78] I. Kant, *Kritik der reinen Vernunft*, Riga, Hartknoch, 1781, 1787, Einleitung, III.

[79] This point has been recently stressed by R. Kwiecién, "On Some Contemporary Challenges to Statehood in the International Legal Order: International Law Between Lotus and Global Administrative Law", in *Archiv des Völkerrechts*, 2013, vol. 51, pp. 279 ff.

University;[80] the "Sovereignty Index" elaborated by the joint venture between the Brookings Institution, the Institute for State Effectiveness, and the Australian National University;[81] the "Index of State Weakness in the Developing World," published by the Brookings Institution;[82] the "Failed States Index" produced by the Fund for Peace and published by Foreign Policy;[83] and the Worldwide Governance Indicators (WGI).

5. THE STATE IN FLUX

As a result of these developments, retreats and advances, the State has become more malleable, better able to adjust, adapt, and change according to the new challenges and contexts.

These adjustments have produced several outcomes. The first is the de-differentiation of society and State. Over the past few centuries, the State established itself through a process of differentiation from the various social interests and the public interest. The separation of the political and the social led the State to become an entity separate from society. Today, the dividing line is blurring, and the State is a marketplace, or arena, of competing economic and social forces.

The second outcome is internal fragmentation. Originally, the State was more or less united around a centre which was able to keep the periphery under strict control, thereby ensuring the unity of the legal system. Today, the growth in the dimensions and powers of territorial and functional bodies has resulted in the development of multiple legal systems within the State. Therefore, the centre is obliged to replace rule with negotiation.

---

[80] J. A. Goldstone, R. H. Bates, D. L. Epstein, T. R. Gurr, M. B. Lustik, M. G. Marshall, J. Ufelder and M. Woodward, "A Global Model for Forecasting Political Instability", in *American Journal of Political Science*, 2010, vol. 54, n. 1, pp. 190-208.

[81] A. Ghani, C. Lockhart, and M. Carnahan, *Closing the Sovereignty Gap*, London, Overseas Development Institute (ODI), 2005.

[82] S. E. Rice and S. Patrick, *Index of State Weakness in the Developing World*, Washington, DC, The Brookings Institution, 2008.

[83] N. Haken, J. J. Messner, K. Hendry, P. Taft, K. Lawrence, T. Anderson et al., *Failed States Index 2012*, Washington, DC, The Fund for Peace Publication, pp. 1–48.

Third, as Parliaments became more representative through universal suffrage, the power of civil society grew. As a result, the State and its body of servants have been compelled to replace command and control with leadership, hegemony and negotiation.

Fourth is joint decision-making. When both a national and a supranational, or global, administration intervene in the decision-making procedures, there are arrangements that allow for both levels of government, the national and the supranational, to make their voices heard. From the first perspective, the most interesting institutions are the European Union committees.[84] First established to keep the European Commission under the control of the Council and domestic administrations, they subsequently became a means for the Commission to broaden the scope of its jurisdiction, obtain information from domestic administrations, consult and receive support from national constituencies, and hold national administrations' actions under review. Moreover, the committees unite national bureaucracies and provide a "forum" for discussion and exchanging ideas. They are a means for the formation of a common understanding among domestic administrations. Consequently, committees play three important roles: bottom-up, to represent the views of domestic administrations in the Union; top-down, to transmit European policies to national administrations; and horizontal, to open and facilitate dialogue among national administrations. Committees, however, are not the only kind of mixed – national and European – organizations. There are many more such entities, which exist at a metaphorical halfway point between Brussels and national capital cities to ensure a balance among national and supranational governments.

The fifth outcome is interdependence of State and non-State actors. Non-governmental Organizations ("NGO") are established in order to interact with global regulatory regimes. National governments become

---

[84] T. Christiansen and E. Kirchner (eds), *Committee Governance in the European Union*, Manchester, Manchester University Press, 2010, M. Savino, *I comitati dell'Unione. La collegialità amministrativa negli ordinamenti compositi*, Milan, Giuffrè, 2005; F. Gencarelli, "Il Trattato di Lisbona e la nuova comitologia", in *Diritto comunitario e degli scambi internazionali*, 2012, n. 1, pp. 1 ff.; T. Christiansen and M. Dobbels, "Delegated Power and Inter-Institutional Relations in the EU after Lisbon: A Normative Assessment", in *West European Politics*, 2013, vol. 36, n. 6, pp. 1159 ff.

more transparent and must hear national, supranational and global pressure groups. The global disputes are multi-polar and involve both private parties and States.

Finally, like Ulysses, the State has committed itself through international treaties, thus renouncing full sovereignty and agreeing to share power with other States and global institutions. Globalization and the ensuing State-global space interactions produced two paradoxes.

The first paradox is clear in the role played by globalization in the constitution and development of States. The United Nations Organization supports States as members of the international community. The traditional relationship between States and the international community is reversed: previously, States created the international community. Now, the international community supports States. States establish global organizations, which, in turn, legitimizes States.

This reversal is amplified when global or supranational institutions impose on national governments, or promote among them, certain basic models of democracy, or rule of law. For example, the United Nations Democracy Fund (UNDEF) finances civil society organisations for the promotion of democracy, and the Office for Democratic Institutions and Human Rights (ODIHR) of the Organization for Security and Cooperation in Europe (OSCE), is active in the fields, *inter alia*, of democratic development, election observation, and non-discrimination.

The second paradox is that, while global institutions are entirely new organizations, they mimic national governments. For example, they allocate rule-making, executive and dispute-settlement functions to separate bodies. This does not mean that the separation of powers principle is replicated in the global space, as the different environment leads to changes that, in turn, result in different organizational arrangements in the two areas. Here, once again, the "myth of the State" and the conceptual reduction of all public powers to the State affects the development of globalization.

6. METHODOLOGICAL IMPLICATIONS

This analysis has two methodological implications. First, one must take an evolutionary approach to social institutions.[85] Lawyers and political scientists are good at analyzing and dissecting dead bodies. But States are subject to "a continuous adaptive process," and are "moving in different directions."[86] One has to learn to analyze and study these living institutions and move towards understanding the rules governing their change, the way the American sculptor Alexander Calder moved from "stabiles" to "mobiles."

Second, while seeking to ameliorate the poor state of empirical measures on the quality of States,[87] one must also try to conceptualize the complex web of integrated global and national polities. States are a constituent part of globalization. They expand in the global space and, at the same time, are limited by global institutions.

National governments split, as noticed by the French international law scholar Georges Scelle, in his theory of the *"dédoublement fonctionnel:"* they establish global institutions and become their servants or implementers. Between States and global institutions, and among States, new kinds of relations are established, which one could call of horizontal accountability;[88] national governments monitor their counterparts, since their actions are interrelated.

---

[85] O. Lewis and S. Steinmo, *How Institutions Evolve: Evolutionary Theory and Institutional Change*, paper presented at the APSA in Seattle, 2011.

[86] S. Steinmo, *The Evolution of Modern States*, cit., p. 210 and p. 206.

[87] F. Fukuyama, "What is Governance?", in *Governance*, 2013, vol. 26, n. 3, pp. 347 ff. and the World Bank, *The State in a Changing World: Selected World Development Indicators*, Washington, DC, The World Bank, 1997.

[88] For this concept as applied within national governments, see G. O'Donnell, "Horizontal Accountability in New Democracies", in A. Schedler, L. Diamond, and M. F. Plattner (eds), *The Self-Restraining State: Power and Accountability in New Democracies*, London, Lynne Rienner, 1999, especially pp. 38 ff.

CHAPTER II

THE GLOBALIZATION OF LAW

I. THE GLOBALIZATION OF LAW

1. SOME MOTIVATING QUESTIONS: THE CIRCULATION AND SPREAD OF LEGAL INSTITUTIONS

C AN democracy be exported to Iraq by means of military occupation? Can the President of the United States ask Russia to respect democracy, that is, "a rule of law and protection of minorities, a free press and a viable political opposition?"[1] Can the World Trade Organization (hereinafter WTO) require that the public administration of Malaysia – like the governments of all other States – meet the obligation to openly participate in the tendering procedures for the awarding of government contracts? Can all nations be asked to respect a single, universal catalogue of human rights? Can the United States require that domestic consultation procedures be adopted by international organizations? Can free trade liberalization be used to induce China to introduce the rule of law into its domestic legal system?

These are all controversial issues, not to mention complex, ambiguous, and multifaceted questions. In this Section, I endeavor to examine and disentangle each of them and to formulate some additional questions. I begin by explaining each of the questions in turn.

---

[1] Press Release, Office of the Press Secretary, President and President Putin Discussion Strong U.S. - Russian Partnership (Feb. 24, 2005) http://whitehouse.gov/news/releases/2005/02/20050224-9.

A. Can democracy be exported to Iraq by military force?

The achievements of occupation forces in Germany and Japan after World War II, as well as the more recent achievements of the UN-authorized, multinational stabilization force in Bosnia and Herzegovina could be repeated. Foreign military forces imported democracy into those three countries. Nonetheless, our common understanding of democracy is that of a complex set of institutions which have developed over time in the Western world, first in the United States, and then elsewhere. Is it right to consider these institutions as superior to others, and to transplant them into countries with different traditions? Or, would it be more desirable to allow the indigenous development of political institutions, making it more likely that they would be accepted by their respective societies? Insofar as there exist different forms of democracy, which of them should be exported? On the contrary, does the diversity of democratic forms actually facilitate their successful transplant in different social and political contexts? How long can a democratic government last if such conditions as economic development (almost always correlated with democracy) are not achieved?[2] For example, would the United States, which often demands that other States introduce democratic regimes, ever agree to the abolition of the death penalty – a condition for Turkey's accession to the European Union?[3]

---

[2] See generally E. Bellin, "The Iraqi Intervention and Democracy in Comparative Historical Perspective", in *Political Science Quarterly*, 2004-2005, vol. 119, p. 595, and A. Sen, *La democrazia degli altri*, Italian translation by A. Piccato, Milan, Mondadori, 2004.

[3] The United States actually behaves in the opposite way. On March 7, 2005, it decided to withdraw from the optional protocol to the 1963 Vienna Convention on Consular Relations granting compulsory jurisdiction to the International Court of Justice in disputes arising out of the Convention. The decision was adopted in response to death penalty opponents, who began to invoke the Vienna Convention in order to challenge capital sentences imposed on foreign citizens in the United States. See Charles Lane, "U.S. Quits Pact Used in Capital Cases", Wash. Post, Mar. 10, 2005 at A01, available at http://www.washingtonpost.com/wp-dyn/articles/A21981-2005Mar9.html.

B. Can the WTO standardize government procurement?

A similar range of questions has been raised by the "Government Procurement Agreement" signed in 1994 in the WTO framework.[4] Originally conceived as a means for promoting the free circulation of goods and services, this agreement requires that government suppliers be chosen on the basis of open tendering procedures applied in a non-discriminatory manner.[5] It requires transparency, competition, equal treatment and a reasoned decision on the award of the contract.[6] These principles also apply in countries where the awarding of government contracts is aimed at pursuing specific goals, such as the development of disadvantaged areas or assistance to socio-economically disadvantaged populations.[7] In Malaysia, for example, domestic legislation accords the indigenous Bumiputera population a preferential treatment in terms of access to bids, prices and other contractual provisions.[8] How, then, can we reconcile the requirements of global free trade with helping the disadvantaged? Can the law governing public procurement be conceived so as to harmonize domestic goal of protection with global demands for free trade? In this case, how should Malaysia behave? Should it not adhere to the agreement altogether or ask for *ad hoc* derogations in favor of the Bumiputera?[9]

---

[4] See generally Agreement Establishing the World Trade Organization annex 4 (b), April 15, 1994 (1996) (Agreement on Government Procurement), available at http://www.wto.org/english/docs_e/legal_e/gpr-94_e.pdf [hereinafter Agreement on Government Procurement].

[5] Id. arts. 3, 7, 13.

[6] Id. arts. 3, 10.1, 17, 18.3.

[7] Id. art. 4.

[8] Office of the United States Trade Representative, *National Trade Estimate Report on Foreign Trade Barriers*, 2004, p. 321, available at http://www.ustr.gov/Document_Library/Reports_Publications/2004/2004_National_Trade_Estimate/2004_NTE_Report/Section_Index.html.

[9] See generally C. McCrudden and S.G. Gross, *WTO Rules on Government Procurement and National Administrative Law*, in *European Journal of International Law*, 2006, n. 17, p. 151 ff.

C. Can all nations be asked to respect a single catalogue of human rights?

The question whether all nations may be asked to respect a single, universal catalogue of human rights refers to the 1948 International (later "Universal") Declaration of Human Rights, as codified by the 1966 Covenants on Civil and Political Rights and Economic, Social and Cultural Rights.[10] It has been pointed out that the Declaration both attenuates the monopoly of States, by allowing individuals to become active subjects of global law, and weakens their sovereignty by enabling judicial authorities to condemn breaches of the supranational legal order.[11] Born as a "common ideal to be pursued," the Declaration has become a "parameter for evaluating behavior,"[12] thereby also becoming increasingly exposed to criticism. In Islamic and sub-Saharan African cultures, some argue for the rejection of modern Western political values.[13] A Chinese legal scholar pointed out that, in his traditional language, no term fully corresponds to the notion of "individual right" as established in the Western legal tradition.[14] Universality, it has been emphasized, is a myth. The legal protection of human rights varies according to cultural traditions and political structures.[15]

---

[10] See International Covenant on Economic, Social and Cultural Rights, opened for signature December 16, 1966, 993, U.N.T.S. 3, 6 I.L.M. 368 (1976); International Covenant on Civil and Political Rights, opened for signature December 16, 1966, 999 U.N.T.S. 171, 6 I.L.M 368 (1976).

[11] M. Delmas-Marty, *Le Relatif et l'Universel*, Paris, Seuil, 2004, p. 72.

[12] L. Condorelli, "L'azione delle Nazioni Unite per l'attuazione della dichiarazione universale", in *Società Italiana per l'Organizzazione Internazionale*, "Il sistema universale dei diritti umani all'alba del XXI secolo", Rome, 1999, Acts of the National Conference for the Celebration of the 50th Anniversary of the Universal Declaration of Human Rights, Rome, SIOI, 1999, p. 32.

[13] See, e.g., Y. Ghai, "Universal Rights and Cultural pluralism: Universalism and Relativism: Human Rights as a Framework for Negotiating Interethnic Claims", in *Cardozo Law Review*, 2000, vol. 21, p. 1095; G. Binder, "Cultural Relativism and Cultural Imperialism", in *Human Rights Law*, in *Buffalo Human Rights Law Review*, 1999, vol. 5, p. 211-213.

[14] D. Zolo, "Fondamento della universalità dei diritti dell'uomo", in E. Diciotti and V. Velluzzi (eds), *Ordinamento giuridico, sovranità, diritti*, Turin, Giappichelli, 2003, p. 202; J. Yacoub, *Les droits de l'homme sont-ils exportables?*, Paris, Ellipses, 2005.

[15] See A. Cassese, *I diritti umani nel mondo contemporaneo*, Rome-Bari, Laterza, 8th ed., 2003, p. 51 (1988).

D. Can the United States require that consultation procedures be adopted by international organizations?

Not surprisingly, the United States has been accused of "legal imperialism" due to its demands that international organizations adopt consultation procedures modeled on American ones.[16] Indeed, between the 1970s and the 1990s, the United States introduced powerful instruments to promote participation in administrative decision-making procedures. For example, in order to adopt an environmental protection regulation, an administrative authority has to notify the affected industries and environmental associations by sending them a draft of the proposed regulation.[17] Those that will be affected by the regulation and other interested parties may then put forward comments and proposals before the authority issues its decision.[18] On the contrary, when decisions are not made by domestic authorities but by an international organization, private actors see their right of participation under domestic law evaporate. The United States, therefore, argues that international organizations also ought to guarantee an analogous right of participation by consulting interested parties.[19] In this regard, is it fair to require that international organizations, whose frameworks are defined by informality and negotiation, adopt American-style adversarial procedures? Additionally, how can such criteria be transplanted into a wider context where, considering the interests involved in global decisions, consultation may slow or even paralyze proceedings? Finally, does the duty to consult interested parties not change when transferred to the global level?

•

[16] U. Mattei and J. Lena, "U.S, Jurisdiction Over Conflict Arising Outside of the United States: Some Hegemonic Implications", in *Hastings International and Comparative Law Review*, 2001, vol. 24, p. 381-388.

[17] *Akron, Canton & Youngstown R.R. Co. v. United States*, 370 F. Supp. 1231, 1240 (D. Md. 1974).

[18] *Ogden Chrysler Plymouth, Inc. v. Bower*, 809 N.E.2d 792, 803 (Ill. App. 2d 2004) ("in adopting rules, Administrative agencies must comply with the public notice and comment requirement set forth in the Procedure Act.")

[19] See D. A. Wirth, "Reexamining Decision-Making Process in International Environmental Law", in *Iowa Law Review*, 1984, vol. 79, p. 769-778.

E. Can free trade induce the rule of law in China?[20]

The following issue has been debated in view of China's participation in the WTO. During the negotiations, China's membership in the Organization was advocated on the condition that it promote the rule of law within the country.[21] Yet, is it legitimate to transplant fundamental legal principles developed in some Western countries to the East? Can principles that work in London or Washington work just as well in Beijing? And how may the rule of law take root in legal systems where the authority of the judiciary is constrained and may not extend to ideas such as political freedom?[22]

2. PHASES AND MODES OF LEGAL GLOBALIZATION

In addition to all being controversial issues at the forefront of international debate, these questions have one thing in common: they address the circulation of legal institutions among national systems and their spread from the national to the global level, and *vice versa*. Transfers like these are no novelty but their speed has increased as we have left behind the rigid world of 18th- and 19th-century nationalism.

This unitary problem takes five different forms. The first is the direct transfer of institutions from one national system to another – for example, American democracy in Iraq. The second is the imposition of a global legal principle upon national public administrations – for example, the tendering rule that the WTO requires of member States' administrations, including Malaysia). The third is the imposition by a global judicial body of a common legal principle, not only upon States, but also within national legal systems – for example, universal human rights, respected by everyone at the national level. The fourth form captures legal principles which are transplanted from national legal systems to the

---

[20] See generally B. Kingsbury, N. Krisch, and R. Stewart, "The Emergence of Global Administrative Law", in *Law and Contemporary Problems*, 2005, vol. 68, p. 15.

[21] See e.g. M. G. Hu, WTO's "Impact on the Rule of Law in China", in *The Rule of Law: Perspectives from the Pacific Rim*, Mansfield foundation pub., 2000, p. 101.

[22] On these problems, G. Silverstein, "Globalization and the Rule of Law: 'A machine that runs of itself?'", in *International Journal of Constitutional Law*, vol. 1, n. 3, 2003, p. 427.

global level – for example, the duty to consult, from the American legal system to the global one. Finally, one or more institutions may spill over into other contexts at the global level – for example, free trade used to introduce the supremacy of law.

The questions raised above have helped us to focus on the progressive globalization of law. I now investigate the main phases and modes of legal globalization before turning to the laws governing this process.

Legal thought is the first area affected by the circulation and spread of law. Here, globalization does not concern positive institutions but rather research approaches, techniques and methodologies. This is the domain of the universality of legal thought. It is limited to legal culture and does not extend to positive law.

As natural law retreated in the eighteenth century – and remained behind the scenes into the 19th century –[23] legal thought began to distinguish "local jurisprudence" from "universal jurisprudence" (as per Jeremy Bentham's idea),[24] or "particular jurisprudence" from "general jurisprudence" (according to John Austin).[25] Universal or general legal thought drew on principles common to several systems of positive law. Its scope is however quite limited. It includes the writings of Roman jurists, the decisions of English judges, and the provisions of the French and Prussian codes. It is universal, but this universe is narrow and atemporal.[26] Gian Domenico Romagnosi's "Universal Public Law", written in 1833, illustrates this well.[27]

In the twentieth century, the universality of legal thought was not under-discussed; rather, its scope widened because people no longer distinguished between particular (or local) jurisprudence and universal (or

[23] G. Fassò, *La filosofia del diritto dell'Ottocento e del Novecento*, Bologna, Il Mulino, 1988, p. 306.

[24] J. Bentham, *An Introduction to the Principles of Morals and Legislation* (1789), p. 294 (J.H. Burns & H.L.A. Hart eds., Oxford, Oxford University Press, 1970).

[25] J. Austin, *The Province of Jurisprudence Determined* (1832), p. 10, 15-16. W. E. Rumble, ed., Cambridge, Cambridge University Press, 1995.

[26] See generally M. Barberis, "John Austin, la teoria del diritto e l'universalità dei concetti giuridici", in *Materiali per una storia della cultura giuridica* , 2003, n. 2, pp. 407-427.

[27] G. D. Romagnosi, *Introduzione allo studio del diritto pubblico universale*, Florence, Piatti, 3rd ed., 1833.

general) jurisprudence. According to Saleilles (1904), "all legal thought is necessarily international and universal."[28]

Twentieth-century legal thinkers are, however, positivists and assumed that universal law requires a single sovereign and a single, worldwide legal community.[29] Universality, thus, extends as far as legal thought and did not affect the relativism of positive legal systems.

Nonetheless, in the second half of the twentieth-century, the idea that law reaches beyond a particular positive legal system began to take root, especially in the area of private law. While the doctrines and institutions of public law are intimately tied to the State and to the design thereof enshrined in State norms, private law institutions like property, family, contract and tort law may have had common rules. In the mid-1900's, the Italian jurist Filippo Vassalli affirmed that private law that never been "a servant of the State." With the codifications, States have taken control over the rules governing private law relationships; nonetheless there was a trend towards overcoming the statist dogma and towards dismantling the barriers between nations.[30]

Legal theorists later recognized that public law too resorts to imitation, whereby the institutions of one legal system are copied by others. Nineteenth century English "bicameralism,"[31] the Napoleonic "*Conseil*

---

[28] R. Saleilles, "Le Code civil et la Méthode historique", in « Le Code Civil 1804-1904 » Livre du Centenaire publié par la Société d'Etudes Législatives, I, Paris, Librairie Edouard Duchemin, 1904, reprinted 1969, p. 127. The French jurist Raymond Saleilles (1855-1912) played a pivotal role in criticism of legal positivism and the isolation of legal thought.

[29] On the limits of legal positivism, P. Grossi, "Un diritto senza Stato (la nozione di autonomia come fondamento della Costituzione giuridica medievale", in *Quaderni fiorentini per la storia del pensiero giuridico moderno*, 1996, n. 25, pp. 267-284; P. Grossi, "Il disagio di un "legislatore" (Filippo Vassalli e le aporie dell'assolutismo giuridico)", in *Quaderni fiorentini per la storia del pensiero giuridico moderno*, 1997, n. 26, pp. 377-405; P. Grossi, "Il ruolo del giurista nell'attuale società italiana", in *Rassegna forense*, 2002, n. 3, pp. 501-515; P. Grossi, "Le molte vite del giacobinismo giuridico (ovvero: la "Carta di Nizza", il progetto di "Costituzione europea", e le insoddisfazioni di uno storico del diritto)", in *Jus*, 2003, n. 3, pp. 405-422; P. Grossi, "Dalla società di società alla insularità dello Stato fra medioevo ed età moderna", Lezioni Magistrali, Series directed by F. De Sanctis, Istituto Suor Orsola Benincasa, Naples, 2003. For a critique of the myth of the law and the legislature, see the pivotal work of C. Schmitt (*La condizione della scienza giuridica europea*, Rome, Antonio Pellicani Editore, 1996).

[30] F. Vassalli, "Estrastatualità del diritto civile", in *Studi Giuridici*, vol. III, book II "Studi vari (1942-1955)", Milan, Giuffrè, 1960, p. 753 and p. 755.

[31] See D. Shell, "The History of Bicameralism", in *The Journal of Legislative Studies*, 2001, vol. 7, n. 5, p. 7-9.

d'État"[32], the Swedish "Ombudsman" (1809),[33] the Austrian "fair proceeding" (1925) were all applied and adapted in many other national systems.[34] Very diverse legal systems then presented many similarities. Once the obstacles to adapting public law institutions to foreign legal contexts (in which they would become different from their archetype) had been removed, it was possible to recognize that institutions considered to be specific to a particular legal tradition actually originated elsewhere. For example, the model of the "*grandes écoles*" and the "*grands corps*," believed to be typical of the French administrative *élite*, was in fact formed under the influence of the Chinese Mandarinate, which had fascinated Enlightenment philosophers.

The last phase of law development continues to this day. It is characterized by transfers from one domestic legal context to another domestic legal context, as well as to the universal level, and it includes the repercussions of such transfers in domestic legal systems.

Mutual recognition agreements illustrate well the transfer of legal institutions from one country to another. On the basis of such agreements, a product that can be sold in one country can also be sold in another country, under the same conditions. Similarly, an accountant from one State may offer his services in other States subject to the law of his country of origin; once authorized to operate in one country, a bank may rely on that same authorization to carry out its activity in another.

Insofar as the product, the accountant, and the bank all "carry their national law" with them when they change countries, the recognition of the validity of foreign administrative norms and procedures results in a reciprocal exportation of national laws, as well as in ongoing and evolving cooperation among States.

Mutual recognition agreements do not consist in the mere acceptance by one State of the law that applies to goods, services and businesses in another State in a given moment. They may also provide that the other State's rules change. They require that the potentially affected

---

[32] See e.g. E. T. Beller, "The Headscarf Affair: The Conseil d'État on the Role of Religion and Culture in French Society", in *Texas International Law Journal*, 2001, vol. 39, p. 581.

[33] See W. Gellhorn, "The Swedish Justitieombudsman", in *Yale Law Journal*, 1965, vol. 75, p. 1.

[34] See, e.g., id.

States be notified of possible rule changes and have an opportunity to comment upon them.

Moreover, if a State enters into a mutual recognition agreement with another State, and the latter enters into one with a third State, the agreements will have a transitive force, favoring the circulation of institutions between national legal systems. Finally, the recognition not only of products but also of productive processes implies a broader horizontal cooperation between States in areas that intersect with trade, such as the environment, working conditions and safety protection.[35]

With mutual recognition, national laws mix together, increasing the need for common standards implemented by multilateral organizations. At the same time, this enables one to choose from among multiple national law regimes.

Three examples of typical State activities – labor protection, criminal justice and government-citizen relations – illustrate the transfer from the national to the universal context: a transfer that takes place along a vertical axis rather than a horizontal one.

A. Labor protection

Some countries export goods that have not been produced in conformity with the internationally recognized standards for labor protection set by the International Labour Organization (ILO).[36] These States not only allow for unfair competition *vis-à-vis* producers from other countries, but they also threaten the labor protection standards in the importing countries, and can trigger a race to the bottom. This form of "social dumping" may be countered by invoking a provision of international trade law that requires that imported goods be regulated according to a regime that is no less favorable than that governing other "simi-

---

[35] On mutual recognition, K. Nicolaidis and G. Shaffer, "Managed Mutual Recognition Regimes: Governance without Government", in *Law and Contemporary Problems*, vol. 68, pp. 263 ff.

[36] Convention for the Conservation of Southern Bluefin Tuna, Austl.-Japan-N.Z., art. 16, 1-2, May 10, 1933, 1819 U.N.T.S. 360 (entered into force on May 20, 1944).

lar" imports.[37] To apply this norm however, the term "similar" must be interpreted to mean goods produced according to procedures, methods and techniques that comply with the "Core Labor Standards," a lowest common denominator for working conditions.

Once the relevant norm has been identified by following the convoluted path outlined above, the next question is: which authority ought to enforce it? Should it be an individual country, like the United States, which banned trade with Burma on account of serious labor and human rights abuses? Or should it be the international community, under the *aegis* of the WTO?[38]

B. Criminal Justice

Criminal law traditionally was precisely the kind of "particular law"[39] left up to individual States. Can extremely unjust State laws (*"extremes Unrecht"*[40]) be accepted at all? If they are not acceptable, crimes carried out in compliance with unjust laws must be defined at the supranational level and enforced by a supranational judge. International enforcement is all the more necessary when considering that national tribunals tend not to punish genocide, war crimes, and crimes against humanity because these crimes are usually committed by domestic organs, like the military, that State authorities either protect, or, in any case, do not wish to judge. Therefore, it is necessary that international authorities replace domestic judges in the promotion, defense and pursuit of universal values. To these ends, universal criminal law protects peace and security, and defines war crimes, crimes against humanity and genocide as international crimes. The international community considers it legitimate

---

[37] *S. Bluefin Tuna Case (Austl. & N.Z. v. Japan)*, 13 I.L.M. 1359, 1391 (Arb. Trib. Constituted under annex VII of the UNCLOS 2000).

[38] On this question, M.J. Trebilcock and R. Howse, "Trade Policy and Labour Standards", in *Minnesota Journal of Global Trade*, 2005, vol. 14, p. 261.

[39] G. Carmignani, *Elementi del diritto criminale*, Naples, Printing Press of P. Androsio, 1854, p. 8.

[40] On this expression used by Gustav Radbruch, see G. Vassalli, *Formula di Radbruch e diritto penale*, Milan, Giuffrè, 2001, especially p. 281; by the same author, see also *La giustizia internazionale penale*, Milan, Giuffrè, 1995.

to investigate and punish such crimes independently of where they are committed, and independently of who the victims and the perpetrators are.[41] Special courts have been established, from the Nuremberg and Tokyo tribunals to those for the former Yugoslavia and Rwanda, to the International Criminal Court.

Two important changes characterize this new environment: the first has to do with norms, and the second regards judicial bodies. As for norms, "[i]n claiming that these actions are wrong, we put aside the purely parochial interests of particular nations."[42] With respect to judges, "global" crimes could be judged by national courts. The choice of establishing non-State tribunals overcomes national legal systems by providing the global one with the panoply of instruments that national judges usually have at their disposal. A "universal" criminal law thus integrates or sometimes counters "parochial" criminal law.[43]

C. GOVERNMENT-CITIZEN RELATIONS

The third and final example regards the law governing the relationship between citizens and the government and, in particular, due process of law. This principle traces back to a 1354 Statute of Edward III,[44] and was also included in the American Constitution.[45] It refers to both the right to be ruled by law and the right to a fair trial. In national legal systems, it has been applied widely to the relationship between citizens and the government. Understood as the right to "procedural fairness"[46] in

---

[41] G. Werle and F. Jessberger, "Concetto, legittimazione e prospettive del diritto internazionale penale, oggi", in *Rivista italiana di diritto e procedura penale*, 2004, n. 3, p. 743.

[42] G.P. Fletcher, "Parochial versus Universal Criminal Law", in *Journal of International Criminal Justice*, 2005, n. 3, p. 4.

[43] Id. at p. 23 See also O. Höffe, *Globalizzazione e diritto penale*, Italian translation by S. Dellavalle., Turin, Edizioni di Comunità, 2001 (elaborating on the effects of globalization on the birth of international and intercultural criminal law).

[44] See 28 Edw. III, c.3.

[45] U.S. Const. amend. XIV, 1.

[46] The Bill of Rights: Original Meaning and Current Understanding 217-19 (Eugene W. Hickok, Jr. ed., 1991).

Italy, the application of this principle requires the public administration to give notice and hearing to the citizen.[47]

The principle is now applied globally. Three cases decided by three different international courts provide evidence of this. In the first case, the Appellate Body of the WTO held that a State, when limiting imports from other countries, has to give exporting countries the chance to be heard, must provide a reasoned decision and recognize the right to defense.[48] In the second case, the International Tribunal for the Law of the Sea (ITLOS) decided that a government that sequesters a ship and takes away the crew's passports must respect the due process of law and the principle of fairness, informing the ship's owner and the crew and giving them the chance to be heard.[49] Finally, in a more specific area, the European Court of Human Rights (ECHR) held that administrative decisions affecting individual rights can be taken only after the interested parties have been heard.[50]

As to the application of the due process of law in the global legal order, three features are worth emphasizing. First, the principle of "procedural fairness" is not always declared by international treaties, but is often developed by judicial bodies. These bodies derive it from provisions of sectoral regulation which prohibit arbitrary decisions and require reasonableness (as in the areas of trade and the law of the sea),[51] or from clauses requiring due process and the right of defense (as in the European Convention of Human Rights).[52] The generation of "constitutional" principles by judicial bodies leads to a process of

[47] The Constitution of the Italian Republic, art. 13.

[48] Appellate Body Report, United States – Import prohibition of certain shrimp products, WT/Ds58/AB/R 12 October 1998, For commentary see, for example, S. Cassese, "Gamberetti, tartarughe e procedure. Standards globali per i diritti amministrativi nazionali", in *Rivista trimestrale di diritto pubblico*, 2004, n. 3, pp. 657-678.

[49] ITLOS, "*Juno Trader Case*", 18 December 2004, n. 13.

[50] ECHR, "*Credit and Industrial Bank v. the Czech Republic*" – Case n. 29010/95 of 21 October 2003.

[51] United Nations Convention on the law of the see Annex VII, art. 8, Dec. 10, 1982, 3 U.S.T.R. 1833 (entered into force on Nov. 16, 1944), available at http://www.un.org/Depts/los/convention_agreements/texts/unclos/.

[52] See European Convention for the protection of Human Rights and Fundamental Freedoms, art. 6, Nov. 4, 1950, 213 U.N.T.S. 221.

constitutionalization.[53] Second, the growth of global law through lateral connections, especially with regard to trade, is open to expansion because of its many ties to related issues as the environment, working conditions, human rights, health protection, security, and other sectors in which "constitutional" principles developed by global judges may be easily transported. Finally, under global law, both the State and private actors enjoy the right of participation in their relationship with public administrations.

Bodies of relatively uniform rules of universal application are increasing in a number of areas. The growth of world trade requires common standards for product conformity, consumer protection and product liability;[54] States' inability to control such phenomena as financial crises, global warming, the use of the seas and maritime resources and migratory fish species mandates that these universal public goods be protected at the global level.[55]

---

[53] D. Z. Cass, "The 'Constitutionalization' of International Trade Law: Judicial Norm-Generation as the Engine of Constitutional Development in International Trade", in *European Journal of International Law*, 2001, vol. 12, n. 1, pp. 39-75. On proceduralization and its functions in the global legal order, A. von Bogdandy, "Legitimacy of International Economic Governance: Interpretative Approaches to WTO law and the Prospects of its Proceduralization", in S. Griller (ed.), *International Economic Governance and Non-Economic Concerns – New Challenges for the International Legal Order*, Wien-New York, Springer, 2003, p. 128 and 129. On "procedural fairness" as a principle of global law, G. della Cananea, *The EU and the WTO: A "Relational" Analysis*, paper presented at the Vienna Conference on "New Foundations for European and Global Governance", 29-30 November 2004, p. 9. On the development of domestic jurisdictions, N. Picardi, "La vocazione del nostro tempo per la giurisdizione", in *Rivista trimestrale di diritto e procedura civile*, 2004, n. 1, pp. 41-71.

[54] M. Shapiro, "The Globalization of Law", in *Global Legal Studies Journal*, 1993, vol, 1, n. 37, p. 59 and following section.

[55] On legal globalization see M.R. Ferrarese, *Le istituzioni della globalizzazione. Diritto e diritti nella società transnazionale*, Bologna, Il Mulino, 2000; A. von Bogdandy, "Democrazia, globalizzazione e futuro del diritto internazionale", in *Rivista di diritto internazionale*, 2004, n. 2, p. 317-344; E. Denninger, "L'impatto della globalizzazione sulle democrazie contemporanee", in *Rassegna parlamentare*, 2004, n. 1, pp. 25-41; J. V. González García, *Globalización económica, Administraciones públicas y Derecho administrativo: presupuestos de una relación*, in *Revista de Administración Pública*, 2004, p. 7-39; S. Kadelbach, "Ethik des Völkerrechts unter Bedingungen der Globalisierung", in *Zeitschrift für ausländisches öffentliches Recht und Völkerrecht*, 2004, n. 64, pp. 1-20.

3. LAWS GOVERNING LEGAL GLOBALIZATION

We have thus far examined the evolution of principles, norms and institutions that we can regard as "common," because they have either developed simultaneously, been transplanted from one national context to another, been exported from domestic to global law, or emerged directly in the global legal system to address specific needs. I now consider the laws governing this process of legal globalization.

I first address the following question: is there a mechanism driving this process of mutual penetration and harmonization, or does this process depend on the uncertain and contradictory policies of domestic governments?

The most striking feature of the relationship between legal unity and differentiation is the contrast between a universal legal patrimony which reinforces the legal unity of the world, and the extreme variety of local legal system. On the one hand, there are some common principles and institutions that no domestic legal system can do without. On the other hand, there are marked differentiations across domestic (or local) systems. And this gap tends to widen over time. The number of international organizations dealing with issues of uniformity or, at least, harmonization grows in proportion with the number of States.[56] Insofar as the States are the main causes of differentiation, the gap is a permanent feature of the new legal order.

This tension between increasing unity and an increasing differentiation lends itself to rival interpretations. Those who believe in the central role of the States see this as a confirmation of their theory. Those who argue, by contrast, that the global legal order has taken root, emphasize unity over differentiation. The real challenge is to interpret these apparently contradictory elements in a holistic way.

Relativists, who believe that every society has its own State-created law, underestimate the ability of legal systems to adapt, to live together, and thus to change. At the other end of the theoretical spectrum, a smaller group of universalists, who believe that legal globalization is

---

[56] A. Alesina and E. Spolaore, *The Size of Nations*, Cambridge-London, The MIT Press, 2003, and A. Caffarena, *Le organizzazioni internazionali*, Bologna, Il Mulino, 2001.

now dominant, overestimate the unity and uniformity of the global legal order, as well as its ability to compel domestic legal systems.[57]

It is hard to analyze the vertical and horizontal concatenation of national, supranational and global law because we still do not know the (incomplete, despite being quite developed) global legal "grammar," while we know our native domestic legal terminology all too well. We can draw, however, one safe conclusion: legal globalization allows for diversity of national laws, and leaves them the right to be different,[58] either by leaving entire fields uncovered – to be regulated by State law – by providing special derogatory measures, or else by applying techniques that leave spaces, margins, and interstices, weave networks, establish balances and create compensations.

The emerging legal order appears as a binary order, in which differences coexist with a set of common principles: on the one hand, an extreme and even growing variety of national or sub-national regimes; on the other hand, an ever-stronger fabric of universal principles and procedures. The resulting system is not fundamentally different from other historical examples: pre-State law, like Roman law, with a universal vocation and a tolerance for diverse internal rules;[59] Common Law, which in the Middle Ages lived together with local laws and put them into communication with each other; imperial systems, which include indigenous nationalities and public powers governing by "indirect rule."[60]

This binary system is particularly evident in the two-level area of criminal law. At the first level, universal courts exercise absolute jurisdiction over specific subject in defense of universal values. At the second level, national criminal courts exercise conditional universal jurisdic-

---

[57] One area in which these two perspectives particularly clash is the regulation of Internet, according to D. W. Drezner, "The Global Governance of the Internet: Bringing the State Back In", in *Political Science Quarterly*, 2004, vol. 119, n. 3, pp. 477-498.

[58] M. Delmas-Marty, *Le Relatif et l'Universel*, cit., p. 11, p. 65-66 (referring to the European Convention on Human Rights as an example).

[59] See generally, S. Riccobono, "Outlines of the Evolution of Roman Law", in *University of Pennsylvania Law Review*, 1925, vol. 74, p. 1; L. R. Yankwich, "Aspects of Roman Civil Law", in *Southern California Law Review*, 1953, vol. 26, p. 292.

[60] For a historical reference, see generally F. Calasso, *Medio Evo del diritto, I, Le fonti*, Milan, Giuffrè, 1954; P. Grossi, *L'ordine giuridico medievale*, Rome-Bari, Laterza, 1995.

tion: they are assigned to be guardians of global law, but only within the limits set by the higher level.[61]

The cohabitation between world legal unity and local differentiation requires a vast and complicated system of enabling rules. These rules often appeal to science in order to prevent accusations that they originate from international negotiations or global regulators in which representatives of the Western world dominate, which in turn, enact rules favoring industrialized countries.[62] This is indeed a subject that deserves further investigation.

My second point concerns the dynamic growth of the global legal patrimony of institutions, rules and principles. I already mentioned that legal globalization is a consequence of the emergence of problems that no national legal order can solve on its own – for example, the expansion of trade and the need for a "corpus" of rules to accompany it; the need to exercise control over some of the sources of environmental pollution; the need to regulate phenomena that escape the control of individual States, from air traffic to the use of the seas, postal transport, and financial crises; and the need to establish international criminal tribunals to compensate for the inertia of local judges in pursuing crimes that the whole international community regards as deserving punishment.

Another factor explains the last quarter of the twentieth century and the recent acceleration of legal globalization. There exists a cycle: the more communication, the more we apprehend the world, the more differences are manifest, the more global instruments are applied to resolve these differences, the more we care about the democracy and accountability of these instruments, the more we seek to strengthen the ties

---

[61] For this distinction, A. Cassese, "Y a-t-il un conflit insurmontable entre souveraineté des Etats et justice pénale internationale?", in A. Cassese and M. Delmas-Marty (eds.), *Crimes Internationaux et Juridictions Internationales*, Paris, Puf, 2002, pp. 1-29; on the role of national judges as guardians of global law, see also M. Delmas-Marty, *Le Relatif et l'Universel*, cit., p. 204, and R. Stewart, "U.S. Administrative Law: A Resource for Global Administrative Law?", in *New York University Journal of International Law and Politics*, 2005, vol. 37, p. 695.

[62] There is thus less deference to governments and more faith in the impartiality of science. On this, see J. Peel, *Risk Regulation Under the WTO SPS Agreement: Science as an International Normative Yardstick?*, Jean Monnet Working Paper n. 02/04, New York University School of Law, 2004, available at http://www.jeanmonnetprogram.org/papers/04/040201.pdf (referring to rule-making bodies such as the WTO).

between global institutions and civil society, and the greater the frustration with a world that has "governance" without having a government.

This is ultimately a cumulative process, marked by both the ongoing development of a global legal order and the growing dissatisfaction with it; this dissatisfaction in turn drives further developments. Even the no-global movements have been important vehicles of globalization, because they have attracted the world's attention to local inequality and to the uneven effects of globalization itself. Additionally, they have triggered correction mechanisms. As a result, we live in a more unified world, while also being more aware of its fractures, and driven by this awareness to reconcile national differences.

The third and final point concerns the emerging balance among domestic legal systems within the global legal order. The global legal order features several sectoral imbalances; it is more developed in some areas, while embryonic or inexistent in others. The variability of "international regimes"[63] thus produces a different form of relativism, one that is sectoral, rather than national. These asymmetries also provoke reactions. They are contagious: an institution or principle introduced in one sector quickly spreads into others, under the pressure of interests that do not accept sector-dependent treatment.

The greatest asymmetry comes from the different status of select States in the global legal order. In 1947, the Italian lawyer Vittorio Emanuele Orlando wondered whether what he called "world revolution" would lead to a single dominant State or to a network or association of States.[64] Today, Orlando's question would receive a twofold answer: at present, the processes of *both* globalization and Americanization are under way.[65]

---

[63] See, e.g., D. J. Puchala and R. F. Hopkins, "International Regimes: Lesson for Inductive Analysis", in S. D. Krasner (ed.), *International Regimes*, Ithaca, Cornell University Press, 1983, pp. 62 ff. (3rd ed. 1995).

[64] V. E. Orlando, *La rivoluzione mondiale e il diritto*, in *Studi di diritto costituzionale in memoria di Luigi Rossi*, Milan, Giuffrè, 1952, pp. 777–778.

[65] M. Shapiro, *The Globalization of Law*, cit., p. 48. On American legal imperialism, U. Mattei, *The Rise and Fall of Law and Economics. An Essay for Judge Guido Calabresi*, paper for the Symposium in honor of Judge Guido Calabresi, 4 October 2003, available at http://jus.unitn. it/dsg/ricerche/dottorati/materiali/mattei04.pdf and "A Theory of Imperial Law: A Study on U.S. Hegemony and the Latin Resistance", in *Indiana Journal of Global Legal Studies*, 2003, vol. 10, pp. 383-447. On the balance between globalization and Americanization see also M.

4. STUDYING THE GLOBAL LEGAL ORDER

Finally, I consider how to study the new universe created by legal globalization. Although in different ways, a number of legal scholars at the end of World Wars I and II – Santi Romano, Gustav Radbruch, Filippo Vassalli and Vittorio Emanuele Orlando – signaled that globalization was advancing. After the world wars, however, scholarly treatment of this phenomenon languished, and it has been resumed only in the last decade, particularly in the United States. Some grand themes do emerge from this scholarship, yet the focus of these studies is somewhat dispersed by excessively detailed analyses.

One major theme concerns the legal concepts that operate at the global level, but remain rooted in positive law.[66] How are we to study them? What is their relationship with national law? For example, the right to be heard by the administration before it makes a decision is by now widely recognized, both in national legal systems and in the global legal system.[67] This requires us to study due process in a new way, by comparing national legal systems with each other and with the global one, whose innovative components – for example, the fact that under global law, the right to be heard extends to both States and private actors – require further analysis.

A second theme is the role of the rule of law in the global legal order: can we say that the rule of law is "a machine that runs of itself"[68] in the global legal context? Domestic systems feature the recognition of rights, formalized conflicts between the State and the bearers of individual rights, the right of defense and the presence of a judge. Together these ensure the conditions for a mechanical process, so that the rule of law is

---

Bussani, "Funzioni e limiti del diritto globale", in P. Annunziata, A. Calabrò and L. Caracciolo (eds), *Lo sguardo dell'altro. Per una governance della globalizzazione*, Bologna, Il Mulino, 2001, p. 117-137; U. Mattei, "Il diritto giurisprudenziale globalizzato ed il progetto imperiale. Qualche spunto", in *Politica del diritto*, 2005, n. 36, p. 85.

[66] See generally M. Delmas-Marty, *Le Relatif et l'Universel*, cit., who drew my attention to this issue.

[67] See Appellate Body report; credit and Indus. Bank v. Czech Rep., 2003-XI Eur. Ct H.R. 44.

[68] G. Silverstein, *Globalization and the rule of law*, cit., p. 427, n. 2 (citing James Russell Lowell).

to law what the market is to the economy. But do the conditions exist for a similar development outside and above the States?

A third theme is the role of judges in the global legal system. Almost every sector of this legal order has witnessed a judicial "explosion."[69] Many parties are admitted to proceedings before global judges, making them choral in character. These judges impose sanctions that contain a mix of top-down interventions and countermeasures by the offended party. Thus, we may ask whether, in the global arena, legal proceedings and trials are becoming a surrogate for democracy.

A fourth theme asks to what extent globalization can tolerate governance without government. There is now a network of sectoral governments above the State. This network has developed incrementally and has been facilitated by the lack of a center (or by the presence of a center – the UN – operating as a "forum"). How long can this precarious, structurally incomplete balance last?

The rupture of the equation between law and State ultimately requires a new approach to research and new forms of communication. For the former, I will limit myself to pointing out the need for international scholarly societies, numerous in many areas other than law.[70] For the latter, I note the need to use the most widespread linguistic vehicle – English. In this respect, at least in Italy, legal scholarship is more backwards than in all other fields[71].

---

[69] M.R. Ferrarese, *Inclusion, no "Exit-Option" and Some "Voice": "Democratic" Signals in International Law*, paper presented at the Vienna conference on "New Foundations for European and Global Governance", 29-30 November 2004, p. 11, and A. Garapon and C. Guarnieri, "La globalizzazione giudiziaria", in *Il Mulino*, 2005, n. 417, n. 1, p. 165.

[70] The establishment of European-wide organizations is a recent phenomenon, an example of which is the newly-formed "European Society of International Law". European Society of International Law, *Welcome to ESIL*, available at http://www.esil-sedi.org/english; see also D. Prosser, "Scholarly Communication: The View from Europe, Creating International Change", in *College and Research Libraries News*, 2004, vol. 65, n. 5, p. 265 ff. (highlighting the need for new forms of scholarly communication).

[71] This statement draws on data collected by the Italian Committee for Research Evaluation (CIVR) and based on information provided by all Italian research centers and universities. See generally Center of research Evaluation, http://www.civr.it/ecivr/meet_civr.asp (last visited January 25, 2006).

5. CONCLUSION

I conclude with the title of this section: The globalization of law.

This is an ambiguous formulation. It assumes a reality that does not and may never exist. A unitary cosmopolitan legal system is not on the horizon, nor is it perhaps among current ambitions. Instead a process is under way that affects certain positive principles and branches of law. Recognizing the existence of shared principles in some sectors is useful not for "drafting cosmopolitan legal codes, but only for demonstrating the fundamental ability of all cultures to communicate."[72] It helps to show the extraordinary ability of legal instruments to coexist, overlap, order themselves and, even, integrate. Moreover, when shaping the tools of harmonization, it highlights the importance of appreciating the differences among legal systems. To acknowledge that common research approaches, methodologies and criteria are being developed is not aimed at emphasizing the successes of an already established academic *"koinè"*, but only at valuing the stable ties that already exist among different national legal cultures.

II. GOVERNING THE WORLD

1. THE PARADOXES OF GLOBALIZATION

"The contemporary, now global Westphalian system—what colloquially is called the world community — has striven to curtail the anarchical nature of the world with an extensive network of international legal and organizational structures designed to foster open trade and a stable international financial system, establish accepted principles of resolving international disputes, and set limits on the conduct of wars when they do occur. This system of States now encompasses every culture and region. Its institutions have provided the neutral framework for

---

[72] F. D'Agostino, *Pluralità delle culture e universalità dei diritti*, Turin, Giappichelli, 1996, p. 45.

the interactions of diverse societies — to a large extent independent of their respective values."[73]

"The international economic system has become global, while the political structure of the world has remained based on the nation-State."[74]

"[....] the nature of the State itself — the basic formal unit of international life — has been subjected to a multitude of pressures: attacked and dismantled by design, in some regions corroded from neglect, often submerged by the sheer rush of events"[75].

These three quotes from the latest book of the political scientist and diplomat Henry Kissinger highlight the basic dilemma of the contemporary world: a process of globalization is developing, a process that is binding on national governments, but that is mainly economic; in the meantime, the old sovereigns, the States, are no longer in command. Thence arises the question: who runs the world – strong multinationals, States, or global regulators?[76] Is there a world government, or there is governance without government?[77]

This examination will commence with some empirical evidence. In 1453, it took forty days for the Pope to learn that Constantinople had fallen to the Turks. In 2001, by contrast, the Twin Towers of the World Trade Center in New York fell during a live television broadcast[78]. A Nokia telephone is made of nine hundred parts produced in forty different countries, and is sold in eighty different national markets. Poliomy-

[73] H. Kissinger, *World Order*, New York, Penguin Press, 2014, p. 7.

[74] Ibid p. 368.

[75] Ibid p. 367 - 368.

[76] This question was asked first by José Ortega y Gasset in 1930, in his famous book *La rebelión de las masas*, in the second part of which he raised the question "¿Quién manda en el mundo?" (J. Ortega y Gasset, *La rebelión de las masas*, Madrid, Espasa Calpe, 1930, Italian translation: *La ribellione delle masse*, Bologna, Il Mulino, 1962). Recent analyses in J. L. Dunoff and J. P. Trachtman (eds), *Ruling the World? Constitutionalism, International Law, and Global Governance*, Cambridge, Cambridge University Press, 2009; D. B. Avant, M. Finnemore and S. S. Sell (eds), *Who Governs the Globe?*, Cambridge, Cambridge University Press, 2010 and T. Büthe and W. Mattli, *The New Global Rulers. The Privatization of Regulation in the World Economy*, Princeton, Princeton University Press, 2011.

[77] As suggested in a well-known book edited by J. N. Rosenau and E.-O. Czempiel (eds), *Governance without Government. Order and Change in World Politics*, Cambridge, Cambridge University Press, 1992.

[78] N. Chanda, *Bound Together. How Traders, Preachers, Adventurers, and Warriors Shaped Globalisation*, New Haven, Yale University Press, 2007.

elitis, that caused millions of deaths in the last century, was eradicated thanks to the campaign launched by the World Health Organization in 1988; in 2011 and 2012 not a single case of polio was reported in India. It can be concluded that national barriers to the economy are being destroyed and that world policies are successful.

However, on the other hand, globalization is not equally distributed. As for the population, only two percent of people live outside their country of birth. Only two percent of students attend universities outside their home countries. Only seven percent of the directors of Standard & Poor 500 companies are foreigners. As for trade and investment, exports are equivalent to only twenty percent of global GDP. Foreign direct investment accounts for only nine percent of all fixed investment. Less than twenty percent of venture capital is deployed outside the fund's home country. Only twenty percent of shares traded on stock markets are owned by foreign investors. Only seven percent of rice is traded across borders. The level of concentration in vital industries has fallen since 1950, and has remained constant since 1980.[79] It can be concluded that globalization should not be overestimated, because we live in an era of semi-globalization, and that the world is not being taken over by a handful of giant companies.

The internal fabric of globalization is complex. Consider that, in a world with seven billion inhabitants, seven thousand languages and a hundred and ninety-three States, there are sixty thousand global Non-Governmental Organizations and around two thousand global regulatory regimes. Moreover, there is "an array of partially overlapping and non-hierarchical institutions governing a particular issue area."[80] "[R] egime complexes, including different mixes of states, sub-state units, international organizations, civil society organizations and private actors, have in various issue areas replaced more tightly integrated international regimes. Regime complexes have been identified in the areas of climate

[79] P. Ghemawat and S. A. Altman, *DHL Global Connectedness Index 2014: Analyzing global flaws and their power to increase prosperity*, 2014, NYU Stern School of Business and IESE Business School, available at http://www.dhl.com/content/dam/Campaigns/gci2014/downloads/dhl_gci_2014_study_low.pdf; see also "The Case Against Globaloney", *The Economist*, 23 April 2011, available at http://www.economist.com/node/18584204.

[80] K. Raustiala and D. G. Victor, "The Regime Complex for Plant Genetic Resources", in *International Organization*, 2004, vol. 58, pp. 277 – 310.

change, food security, refugee policy, energy, intellectual property and anti-corruption."[81] It can be concluded that what we call "globalization" is in fact a plurality of phenomena.

Another paradox of globalization is that it opens the way to new exploitations: between fifteen and twenty million hectares of African land are owned or used by foreign firms, which produce fruit and vegetables for their own markets, for consumption or for bio-fuel (e.g. Korea, Saudi Arabia). This brings financial resources to Africa, but also strips it of natural resources (mainly water), relocates people, has an impact on their customs, and obliges the FAO to provide more food to local populations through the World Food Program.[82] It can be concluded that globalization is a process that is full of ambiguities.

If the extent of globalization is limited and its internal fabric is composite, can one say that national governments are still in command? This aspect too is contradictory. Europe is attempting to transcend the Member States by means of the Union (and the same may happen soon in Africa, North America, South America and Southeast Asia). Parts of the Middle and Far East and of Africa have dissolved into ethnic components conflicting with one another, producing the well-known phenomenon of "failed States," with ungoverned territories (think of Libya). Most States are self-established, but some are not: they are the product of international action, and were established not from below, but from above. It can be concluded that it is not the State as such, but only a few States (today mainly the United States, Russia, and China) that play a dominant role in the world; and that many States are experiencing a period of crisis.

2. GLOBALIZATION AS SHARED GOVERNANCE

In such a context, it can no longer be said that the world is run by national governments according to the Westphalian model, nor that the rulers of the world are to be found beyond the States, in the global

---

[81] G. de Búrca, R. O. Keohane and C. Sabel, "Global Experimentalist Governance", in *British Journal of Political Science*, 2014, vol. 44, p. 481.

[82] International Food Policy Research Institute, *"Land Grabbing" by Foreign Investors in Developing Countries: Risks and Opportunities* (Joachim von Braun and Ruth Meinzen-Dick), IFPRI Policy Brief 13 April 2009.

space. It can only be concluded that power is shared between national and supranational rulers.[83]

A few examples from the fields of environmental protection, oil and gas exploitation in the Arctic, and global health security, can demonstrate this conclusion.

To control global warming, the 1997 Kyoto Protocol (which entered into force in 2005), conferred upon the United Nations Framework Convention on Climate Change the power to set caps for each nation, which are basically limits on the amount of pollutants that can be emitted. Countries that emit less than their quota of greenhouse gases can sell emission credits to polluting countries. This system requires the collaboration of global regulators, national governments (acting as co-regulators and implementers) and civil societies (i.e. polluters that buy or sell emission credits). Soon after this program started, managing emissions became one of the fastest-growing specializations in financial services.

The Arctic, the region around the Earth's North Pole, is surrounded by five States: Russia, the United States, Canada, Norway and Denmark. When a country ratifies the United Nations Convention on the Law of the Sea, it enjoys special rights over the exploitation and use of marine resources in the Exclusive Economic Zone (EEZ), which extends to a distance of two hundred nautical miles (three hundred and seventy kilometers) adjacent to their coasts. The five countries launched projects to establish claims over parts of the Arctic, but in 2008 met and pledged to strive for "the orderly settlement of any possible overlapping claims". From then on, the five countries try to find a solution to their problems through regional cooperation and multilateral coordination.

The "World Health Report 2007 – A Safer Future: Global Public Health Security in the twenty-first Century" noted that "new diseases

---

[83] On the interactions between the global and the national level, see these seminal works by Stefano Battini: "Taking outsiders' interests into account: il diritto amministrativo come Costituzione materiale dell'interdipendenza globale", in *Rivista trimestrale di diritto pubblico*, 2014, n. 4, pp. 927-935; "Extraterritoriality: an Unexceptional Exception", in T. Zwart, G. Anthony, J. B. Auby and J. Morison (eds), *Values in Global Administrative Law*, Oxford, Hart Publishing, 2011, pp. 61-80; "The Procedural Side of Legal Globalization: The Case of the World Heritage Convention", in *International Journal of Constitutional Law*, 2011, vol. 9, pp. 340-368; "Il diritto amministrativo internazionale, oggi", in *Rivista italiana di diritto pubblico comunitario*, 2010, n. 6, pp. 1405-1427; *Amministrazioni nazionali e controversie globali*, Milan, Giuffré, 2007.

are emerging at the historically unprecedented rate of one per year. Air-lines now carry more than 2 billion passengers annually, vastly increas-ing opportunities for the rapid international spread of infectious agents and their vectors." "Vulnerability is universal." "A more secure world [...] requires global partnerships that bring together all countries and stakeholders in all relevant sectors."[84] This requires global cooperation in surveillance, sharing of knowledge, and cross-sector collaboration.

These examples share some features. In all three cases, they pre-sent global problems that cannot be solved nationally. They require the establishment of global rules and regulatory bodies.

As observed by Robert Howse: "some of today's most pressing problems [...] are problems that cannot be solved by the uncoordinated exercise of sovereignty by strong individual nation-states. The most obviously serious is climate change; another example is biodiversity. A national interest model of sovereign regulation, where the state is free to regulate to satisfy the balance of diverse constituencies within its borders without regard to external effects, does not take into account these kinds of global "commons" problems"[85].

However, global rules and global regulators are not sufficient: national cooperation is also necessary, both among States and with global regulators, because global regulations cannot be implemented or enforced without local/national cooperation. New regulatory machiner-ies are established, but without a constitutional basis.

3. THE 'MARBLED' STRUCTURE OF GLOBAL GOVERNANCE

In this new context, States cooperate by signing treaties and estab-lishing global regulators, but are also obliged to cooperate as implement-ers and enforcers of global regulations. This occurs not only in the area

---

[84] WHO, *The world health report 2007 - A safer future: global public health security in the 21st century*, World Health Organization, 2007 (available at http://www.who.int/whr/2007/en/), pp. 2, 6, 8 and 19.

[85] R. Howse, "The End of the Globalization Debate: a Review Essay", in *Harvard Law Review*, 2008, vol. 121, n. 6, p. 1531. He also observes that "the recognition of the inherent inseparability today of national and global security illustrates the end of the globalization debate: national security cannot protect people against global insecurity" (p. 1542).

of global warming, Arctic exploitation, or health security, but in many other areas too, such as the fight against global terrorism, the control of the fishing of highly migratory sea species, and the regulation of nuclear waste transportation.

The interaction between States and global regulators is very complex. National governments negotiate, establish global regulators, confer upon them public tasks, control them, but at the same time are controlled by them, and act as their agents, implementers or enforcers. Therefore, States have a triple role *vis-à-vis* global regulatory regimes. They are fragmented: they are both masters and servants.

Another factor contributing to the fragmentation of national governments is the result of their contradictory behaviours: upon pressure from their multinational corporations, countries such as the United States fostered the establishment of the World Trade Organization, to impose upon other States obligations to lower trade barriers; however, they thus become obliged to submit themselves to the World Trade Organization Dispute Settlement Body.

Principles of global law percolate into national legal orders and are, as a rule, limited to a specific area (health, trade, labour). However, they can, and are, easily transplanted to adjacent areas (pursuant to the impact of the equal treatment standard) and influence the entire national legal order. States are masters of their own competences, but they cannot avoid shaping them according to global standards.

The new world order brings together components that originated as different and separate. Now, they are combined and interpenetrated. Therefore, shared power is the rule. The overall picture is not hierarchical, because there are no multiple layers, in which fields are exclusive and interference between two arenas does not exist. Rather, it resembles a marble cake, in which global and national powers mix.

The global legal space is not an additional layer with respect to the national level. The two "levels" are not distinct, but are, rather, intertwined. States are not the only subjects, but combine with other subjects and thus lose their unity.

States are at the same time both stronger and weaker: stronger, because they operate in the global space, beyond their own territory; weaker because, within international organizations, they must share power with other States and with non-State institutions, and because global rules directly impact national legal systems, without any need for State intermediation.

"State sovereignty has neither disappeared nor been surrendered to global actors or forces; rather, sovereignty has been re-shaped by globalization, and its exercise occurs in tandem and interconnection with global actors and forces"; "the real issue is how the state has been remade and reordered and the resulting degree of tractability of the new or emerging state and its institutions to the underlying normative agenda of the anti-globalizers."[86]

How can the combination of national and supranational be explained? Along which lines are national and global governments divided? One is the high politics/low politics split. The first remains under the control of the States, while the second is delegated to global regulatory regimes. As an example, refer to the situation in Ukraine. The European Union and the Organization for Security and Cooperation in Europe have been active, imposing standards and economic and financial sanctions upon Russia. However, when the military aspect emerged, it was not the Union, but rather the French and German national governments to take the lead. At this point, States return to the stage. Therefore, the conferral of national competences to supranational bodies is area-sensitive.

Another is the economics/politics line. There is a division between the former and the latter, with economics in the domain of global regulators, and politics in the hands of the States.

As observed by Joseph E. Stiglitz, "in effect, economic globalization has outpaced political globalization. We have a chaotic, uncoordinated system of global governance without global government, an array of institutions and agreements dealing with a series of problems, from global warming to international trade and capital flows. Finance ministers discuss global finance matters at the IMF, paying little heed to how their decisions affect the environment or global health. Environment ministers may call for something to be done about global warming, but they lack the resources to back up those calls."[87] Therefore, State control of the economy is very difficult.

---

[86] S. Sassen, *Territory, Authority, Rights: From Medieval to Global Assemblages*, Princeton, Princeton University Press, 2006, as summarized by R. Howse, *The End of the Globalization Debate*, cit., p. 1546.

[87] J. E. Stiglitz, *Making Globalization Work*, New York, Norton, 2006, p. 21.

This produces responses: "The international order thus faces a paradox: its prosperity is dependent on the success of globalization, but the process produces a political reaction that often works counter to its aspirations. The economic managers of globalization have few occasions to engage with its political processes."[88]

4. THE GLOBAL SPACE

At the centre of national public powers is the government, also known as the executive power. In the global legal space, there is no one supreme authority, nor the hierarchy peculiar to States, nor a body of general rules that can endow uniformity upon its structure and operation. So how can the global administrative machine operate?

The first condition of its very existence and operation is transnationalism. The global legal space has not only developed along vertical lines – from the national to the global level – but also along horizontal lines, connecting national authorities and global agencies, and global agencies to each other. The system is based largely on cooperation at both inter-state and global levels. Cooperation between national authorities is an essential element of the global system. Two examples are the consultative and deliberative committees of international organizations, and mutual recognition agreements.

As occurs in the European Union, in which the strictly European component is accompanied by a multinational one (the intergovernmental bodies and the comitology committees), the global legal space presents several committees of international organizations, with representatives of national administrations. These representatives perform a three-fold role: they are an instrument for informing global bodies, a conduit for transmitting the decisions of the latter to the national level, and a means to ensure dialogue and negotiation between national administrations.

The transnational component of the global legal space originates from the very limitations of legal globalization. The more national markets open to one another, the more conspicuous the asymmetries and contrasts become. To reduce them and level the playing field, global

[88] H. Kissinger, *World Order*, cit., p. 369.

rules establish general principles, but cannot govern every detail: this leaves room for mixed transnational committees and mutual recognition agreements to develop.

This component of the global legal space reduces its verticality, as the *superioritas* of global authorities is based on a dense network of horizontal relations of a contractual nature. The network facilitates the transfer or transplant of institutions from one national legal system to another, and stimulates the quest for the functional analogies concealed by the formal differences between national systems. Finally, the transnationalism of the global legal order suggests the need for caution before proclaiming the crisis of the State and a flight towards the global level: the dynamics of the global administrative system are largely dependent on the State or its fragments.

The multi-national component of the global space is connected to two of its characteristics, the first related to its mode of operation, and the second to its decision-making processes. The first characteristic is that of transactionalism, meaning that the global system's operation is based on transactions. For example, several international treaties prescribe that conflicts between national administrations must be solved through negotiations, inquiries, mediation, conciliation, arbitration, judicial decisions or other peaceful means of dispute resolution. In other words, treaties establish other contractual or semi-contractual means to solve conflicts.

A strict application of the transnational principle would require global decisions to be taken unanimously. However, although expressly required in certain treaties, unanimity is tempered in various ways. International norms establish that collegial organs must make every effort to reach an agreement through "consensus." Should this not be possible, the decision can be taken through a two-thirds or simple majority vote of the parties present.

The horizontal relations that compose the global system are accompanied by vertical ones. However, these too are not hierarchical and are not based on a strict separation, but rather, on the logic of collective action.

First, vertical relations are established in the case of concurrent competences, which require mixed procedures. For example, the Patent Cooperation Treaty of 1970 provides for the possibility to request a preliminary international examination, which is undertaken jointly with the requester. The request results in an investigation that is transferred to the national authority; this authority then takes the final decision. The proceedings are, therefore, half-global and half-national. The two "levels of government" share powers.

Second, the heterogeneity of the various sector-based regimes and the inherent complexity of relations within the global space require the establishment of functionally different relations depending on the sphere of activity (defence, the environment, or food safety) and, often, on the nature of the national parties involved (for example, the States' degree of development), also in relation to the existing structures at the global level.

This latter variable is extremely interesting. Contrary to the traditional description, there are several different types of global administration. In addition to the bodies formally constituted as international organizations which employ their own staff, there are those which consist of networks of national authorities, and which operate collectively through national officers; distributed administrations led by national regulating bodies and based on cooperation and mutual recognition agreements; hybrid, semi-public administrations founded on private-type structures; and private administrations performing regulatory functions that are recognized as public.

In conclusion, while national governments are unitary and have an executive body at their centre, in the global space there are several different regulatory regimes, and there is no single executive.

In national legal orders, a central executive is accompanied by a body of general rules, which is then divided into sector-specific norms. The former confers coherence and uniformity to the latter. At the global level, the situation is different. Almost all human activities are regulated by global norms. The latter are highly diverse. Some establish only framework legislation, for States to flesh out through regulatory activity; some provide guidelines for national authorities; others directly impose certain obligations upon private parties; others may rely on global authorities for implementation or to control their implementation; some rely on national authorities for these activities; some provide instruments for judicial conflict resolution, while others yet do not have such mechanisms and resort only to negotiation or national judges. However, they do present a common trait, outlined above: these normative entities are all sector-based; there is no general set of rules (or meta-rules) that operates as a unifying element.

The global legal space compensates for the disadvantages of this sectoralism in several ways. The first and most common course is a process of accretion and accumulation of legal principles, as highlighted by the first decision issued by the Arbitral Tribunal established by the Convention on the Law of the Sea.

The second is the establishment of horizontal connections between different normative bodies. For example, prior to 1995, the standards established by the *Codex Alimentarius* Commission were voluntary, but have since acquired legal force because the WTO required the parties that did not wish to observe them to prove their capacity to guarantee an adequate level of protection. These connections are usually established starting from, and surrounding, the most important global normative bodies, such as that on trade; these, due to their scope, exert a strong gravitational pull on other sector-based regulations.

Thus, the various regulatory bodies are distinct but not separate. As established by the first decision issued by the Appellate Body of the WTO, the global laws on trade are not to be interpreted in isolation, separate from general international law. This gave rise to the ever-closer interconnections between rules on trade, on one hand, and those on environmental protection, worker protection standards etc. on the other.

The rules produced by global institutions address national administrations or national civil societies directly. In the former case, global institutions take on the task of keeping national administrations in check. For example, the WTO imposes various obligations upon national administrations, such as that of transparency and equivalence, and of introducing consultation procedures.

When global norms address private subjects, compliance with global standards is ensured in various ways. The national administration can be used as a tool for implementation through coercion or sanctions. Otherwise, spontaneous implementation can occur, prompted by market-based incentives.

Although the global legal space does not possess a set of general and common rules, is it nevertheless subject to general principles, such that the global governance system cannot be considered a system of absolute government? In other words, is there a global rule of law?

5. LOOKING TO THE FUTURE

In the final pages of Mark Mazower's *Governing the World*, one may read a skeptical and critical evaluation of the present situation of the globalized world: "That international institutions may not be internally democratic in their workings has been known for some time and does not appear particularly surprising. They are, after all, chiefly executive bureaucracies, [....] What does seem novel, in historical terms, is the collapsing importance of the public bodies that give national sovereignty meaning and the way that organs of international government and regulation have come to assail the internal legitimacy, capacity, and cohesion of individual states. [...] international institutions and norms have developed into means of curtailing sovereignty rather than enhancing it, trends that could not but affect the standing of international bodies themselves and undercut their ability to command continued support."[89] Also "[o]ur representatives continue to hand over power to experts and self-interested self-regulators in the name of efficient global governance while a skeptical and alienated public looks on. The idea of governing the world is becoming yesterday's dream."[90]

This point of view cannot free itself from the Westphalian approach to international law as a rule for a community of sovereign States. The reality has changed. National governments are part of the global space, play an important role in it, while being constrained by global rules that oblige them to negotiate and to comply with global judicial and quasi-judicial bodies. National governments can reach new areas and control new phenomena, while their sovereignty is increasingly limited. Henry Kissinger is correct in noting that "[a] reconstruction of the international system is the ultimate challenge to statesmanship in our time"[91] and that a new culture is necessary "to translate divergent cultures into a common system."[92]

---

[89] M. Mazower, *Governing the World. The History of an Idea, 1815 to the Present*, New York, Penguin, 2012, pp. 421-422.

[90] Ibid. p. 427.

[91] H. Kissinger, *World Order*, cit., p. 371.

[92] Ibid. p. 373.

III. DOES A "GLOBAL CONSTITUTION" EXIST?*

1. IS THE STATE THE DOMICILE OF CONSTITUTIONALISM?

"The modern State was for long the undisputed domicile of constitutionalism", as observed by Neil Walker.[93] However, today, this is no longer true. Constitutionalism is "a template [...] within and beyond the State", as remarked in the program of the periodical "Global constitutionalism. Human Rights, Democracy and the Rule of Law," which is now in its fifth year of publication. Half of the book on the "Sociology of Constitutions", edited by Alberto Febbrajo and Giancarlo Corsi and published in 2016,[94] examines the transformation of classical constitutionalism and the relationship (the existence of which is disputed) between constitutionalism and globalization. In February 2017, two professors, one British and the other German, edited the "Research Handbook on Global Constitutionalism," the basic premise of which is that "the international order cannot be understood without an understanding of constitutional theory."[95]

* Thanks to Pasquale Pasquino for his comments on a previous version.

[93] N. Walker, "Beyond the Holistic Constitution", in P. Dobner, M. Loughlin (eds), *The Twilight of Constitutionalism*, Oxford, Oxford University Press, 2010, p. 291.

[94] A. Febbrajo, G. Corsi (eds), *Sociology of Constitutions*, Abingdon, Routledge, 2016.

[95] A. F. Lang, A. Wiener (eds), *Handbook on Global Constitutionalism*, Cheltenham, Northampton, Elgar, 2017. See also A. Von Bogdandy, "Constitutionalism in International law: Comment on a proposal from Germany", in *Harvard International Law Journal*, 2006, vol. 47, n. 1, pp. 223 ff.; J. Dunhoff, J. Trachtman (eds), *Ruling the World: Constitutionalism, International Law and Global Governance*, Cambridge, Cambridge University Press, 2009; T. Kleinlein, "On Holism, Pluralism and Democracy: Approaches to Constitutionalism Beyond the State", in *European Journal of International Law*, 2010, vol. 21, p. 4; M. Koskenniemi, P. Leino, "Fragmentation of international law? Postmodern anxieties", in *Leiden Journal of International Law*, 2002, vol. 15, p. 3; G. Amato, "Il costituzionalismo oltre i confini dello Stato", in *Rivista trimestrale di diritto pubblico*, 2013, n. 1, p. 1-8; G. Silvestri, "Costituzionalismo e crisi dello Stato-nazione. Le garanzie possibili nello spazio globalizzato", in *Rivista trimestrale di diritto pubblico*, 2013, n. 4, p. 905-919; L. J. Kotzé, *Global Environmental Constitutionalism in the Anthropocene*, Oxford and Portland, Hart Publishing, 2016; C. Schwöbel, *Global Constitutionalism in International Legal Perspective*, Leiden, Nijhoff, 2011; C. Tomuschat, "International law: Ensuring the survival of mankind on the eve of a new century", in *Recueil des Cours*, 1999, vol. 281, p. 10; E. De Wet, "The International Constitutional Order", in *International and Comparative Law Quarterly*, 2006, vol. 55, p. 1; N. Gibbs, "Human Rights, Symbolic Form, and the Idea of the Global Constitution", in *German Law*

Further evidence of the development of constitutionalism beyond the State consists in the references made by constitutional courts to supranational courts, such as that made by the Italian Constitutional Court to the European Court of Justice by means of Order (*ordinanza*) n. 207/2013. The order states that "the question referred to the Court of Justice for a preliminary ruling is relevant in the proceedings before the Constitutional Court, since the interpretation requested from that Court appears to be necessary in order to establish the precise meaning of the Community legislation for the purposes of the subsequent constitutionality proceedings which this Court will conduct with reference to the principle of constitutional law supplemented by the aforementioned Community legislation."

2. THE DEVELOPMENT OF GLOBAL CONSTITUTIONALISM: NOT AN UNDISPUTED PHENOMENON

At the global level, a process of constitutionalization is currently underway, with the strengthening of an international civil society, the creation of a global public sphere, a growing number of transnational networks and the proliferation of international courts.[96]

Journal, 2017, vol. 18, n. 3, p. 511 – 532. Seminal contribution to the study of global constitutionalism have been given by Anne Peters, Mattias Kumm and Alexander Somek. See the following articles or parts of books by Anne Peters: "The Merits of Global Constitutionalism", in *Indiana Journal of Global Legal Studies*, 2009, vol. 16, n. 2, p. 397 – 411; "Are we Moving towards Constitutionalization of the World Community?", in A. Cassese (ed.), *Realizing Utopia*, Oxford, Oxford University Press, 2012, p. 118 – 135; "Fragmentation and Constitutionalization", in A. Orford – H. Florian, *The Oxford Handbook of the Theory of International Law*, Oxford, Oxford University Press, 2016, p. 1011 – 1031; "Global Constitutionalism", in *Encyclopedia of Political Thought*, Wiley and Sons, 2015. By Mattias Kumm see "The Cosmopolitan Turn in Constitutionalism: on the Relationship Between Constitutionalism in and Beyond the State", in J.L.Dunoff, J.P.Trachtmann (eds.), *Ruling the World? Constitutionalism, International Law, and Global Governance*, Cambridge, Cambridge University Press, 2009, p. 258 – 324. See also M. Kumm, J. Havercroft, J. Dunoff and A. Wiener, "The end of 'the West' and the future of global constitutionalism", in *Global Constitutionalism*, 2017, vol. 6, n. 1, p. 1 – 11. A. Somek, *The Cosmopolitan Constitution*, Oxford, Oxford University Press, 2014.

[96] S. Cassese, *The Global Polity – Global Dimensions of Democracy and the Rule of Law*, Sevilla, Global Law Press, Editorial Derecho Global, 2012, p. 63.

However, such a conclusion is disputed by those who are willing to admit that a global legal order does exist, but that this higher law is purely administrative in nature, or that the constitutional foundations of such a global polity are only at an early stage of development. According to one scholar, "[t]he rule of law, division of power and democratic legitimacy are central to constitutionalism"; however, they are not present in the global form of constitutionalization.[97] "Constitutionalism provides a worthwhile goal for global governance. Making claims for its existence before it can be substantiated, however, creates more cynics than advocates of global constitutionalism"[98].

Another skeptical and more problematic point of view is that advanced by Dieter Grimm, who observes that "[t]he constitution emerged as the constitution of a State" and admits that there is now a "relativization of the boundary between the interior and the exterior", because external law is superimposed as if at a constitutional level; therefore, many countries are compelled to comply with global law even where no external law is superimposed. Grimm adds that "the real question is whether the achievement of constitutionalism can be raised to the supranational level". According to Grimm, "[t]he decline of statehood places [...] constitutionalism as such in question." "The two borders that are presupposed by and constitutive of the constitution, that between inside and outside, and that between private and public" become blurred. However, he concludes that "[...] for the time being, the State appears to remain the only place where the compliance with system boundaries and autonomy protected by fundamental rights can be asserted with consequences, and for the State, these derive from the national constitutions and international legal documents." "The submission of internationally exercised public power to law will always lag behind the achievement of constitutionalism at the national level. The conditions that would allow a reconstruction of the achievement beyond the nation State are not given."[99]

---

[97] A. O'Donoghue, *Constitutionalism in Global Constitutionalisation*, Cambridge, Cambridge University Press, 2014, p. 198.

[98] *Ibidem*, p. 248.

[99] D. Grimm, *Constitutionalism. Past, Present, and Future*, Oxford, Oxford University Press, 2016, pp. 32-35, 322-323, 366, 344 and 376.

3. GLOBALIZATION CHALLENGES CONSTITUTIONALISM

Let us now consider the question in further detail, without defining what is a constitution but rather considering only formal constitutionalism and its strict hierarchy of norms.[100]

The features of constitutionalism are: (1) a unitary legal order and a centralized authority; (2) a political community and a dialogue between civil society and the rulers; (3) a *"pouvoir constituant;"* (4) a body endowed with the power to legislate; (5) a clear hierarchy of norms; and (6) mechanisms of enforcement. These features do not exist in the global arena. The global realm does not feature one single legal system, but rather two thousand regulatory self-contained regimes; therefore, there is no "centre". There is a global space, but neither a global community[101] nor a dialogue between those who are ruled upon and the rulers. There is no global author of a global constitution comparable to a body enjoying *pouvoir constituant*;[102] there are many "fora" or assemblies, but not a cosmopolitan parliament with legislative power. Finally, there is no power to enforce.

Let us consider the other side of the problem. Over three percent of the world's population lives in a country different from that of their birth. In 2016, there were almost one and a half billion international air travel passengers. The majority of the men and women in the world dress in the same manner. Global warming and global terrorism attract global attention, not only of governments, but also of peoples. Between national legal orders, many interferences and horizontal accountability

---

[100] As suggested by M. Scheinin, *United Nations law: substantive constitutionalism through human rights versus formal hierarchy through Article 103 of the Charter*, in F. Fabbrini, V. C. Jackson (eds), *Constitutionalism Across Borders in the Struggle Against Terrorism*, Cheltenham, Northampton, Elgar, 2016, pp. 15-16. See also D. Grimm, *Constitutionalism. Past, Present, and Future*, Oxford, Oxford University Press, 2016, p. 363 where he lists the characteristics of constitutionalism (the constitution as a set of legal norms that regulate the establishment and exercise of public power with a comprehensive regulation, the people as the only legitimate source of power, constitutional law as higher law).

[101] P. Pasquino, "Costituzione e potere costituente: i due corpi del popolo", in *Rivista di Politica*, 2016, n. 4, p. 16: every political community has a constitution.

[102] P. Pasquino, "Costituzione e potere costituente: i due corpi del popolo", in *Rivista di Politica*, 2016, n. 4, p. 22.

procedures exist. Is it possible to conclude that a global society and a global public opinion has started to develop?

Many global or supranational charters, covenants or treaties proclaim and protect a set of human rights, including the "right to have rights". These norms are organized in a limited hierarchy. Article 103 of the United Nations Charter provides that "[i]n the event of a conflict between the obligations of the members of the UN under the present Charter and their obligations under any other international agreement, their obligations under the present Charter shall prevail." Can these documents be interpreted as constitutional in nature?

Some of the oldest international organizations consider their own statutory instruments to be constitutions. For example, since its very creation, the International Labour Organization has been governed by a basic regulatory instrument called "Constitution." The International Olympic Committee, established in 1908, has recognized since 1921 that its Charter is approved on the basis of its own "constitutional rights."[103] Today, the Introduction to the Charter states that it is "a basic instrument of a constitutional nature". Should not the will of the founders of those organizations be taken into consideration, and these documents not be downgraded to mere "statutes?"

Almost all global regulatory regimes have a basic set of rules that govern their structure, procedures and day-to-day regulatory activity. Why, therefore, should it not be recognized that there are two bodies of law, one higher and one lower, with the first playing the same role as that played in national contexts by constitutions?

Many regulatory bodies produce ample legislation on all areas, issuing rules that must be complied with by States and by individuals within nation-States. These regulators have well-developed legislative branches, developing dispute settlement procedures and bodies, and a less developed executive branch. Despite the regulators' fragmentation, is it possible to detect links being established between them, and a growing common administrative set of rules?

More than one-tenth of these regulatory regimes have compliance-checking procedures and bodies in place, and most of these bodies may

---

[103] The 1921 edition was in French, and therefore the term used there was "*prérogatives constitutionnelles*". Only in 1930 was the Charter drafted in English.

be considered courts. Indeed, they review global and national decisions to check their compliance with supranational rules and, in certain cases, act upon references from national courts.[104] National jurisdictions accept these higher courts as having the final word. Can this "judicial dialogue" be considered as the first step toward a global rule of law?

Finally, while a cosmopolitan parliament does not exist, civil society is indeed represented at the global level (think of the tripartite representation enjoyed by States, employees and employers within the International Labour Organization), or is at least heard by international bodies in procedures of deliberative democracy. Global organizations defend, protect and promote national democracy. Can one conclude that democracy is no stranger to global institutions?

4. NATIONAL CONSTITUTIONALISM AND GLOBAL CONSTITU-
TIONALISM ARE NOT SIMILAR

I shall now address the last question: is the emerging global constitutionalism similar to national constitutionalism?

First, the history of global constitutionalism is very different from that of national constitutionalism. The latter developed as an instrument to check strong executive powers, while in the global space, the executive branch is as yet embryonic. There is little need for a countervailing body, as there are powerful rule-making bodies but no executive branch.

Second, global constitutionalism is not international law that is slowly transforming into constitutional law. It is much richer than that, because it derives from the interactions between national constitutional traditions and from the interaction between the global and national legal orders. Cooperation, borrowing and transplanting are the rule in this highly complex net of mutual interactions. The best example is judicial dialogue, the interaction of global and national courts.

The national level is not excluded from the supranational level for two main reasons. One is the bottom-up openness proclaimed by national constitutions that the Germans have called *"Völkerrechtsfreundlichkeit"*,

---

[104] According to C. Thornhill, *The sociological origins of global constitutional law*, in A. Febbrajo, G. Corsi (eds), *Sociology of Constitutions*, p. 103, the judicial branch plays a more central role in the global space than it does within national legal orders.

because Articles 24 and 25 of the German Basic Law contains an opening clause that makes the borders of the State permeable to foreign public powers.[105] Similar clauses are included in many national constitutions, from that of South Africa to that of Italy. Another form of openness travels in the opposite direction, with global constitutional institutions influencing national legal orders: an example is the European Court of Human Rights adjudicating upon British constitutional provisions on voting rights. It is therefore appropriate to redefine global constitutionalism as "trans-constitutionalism."

My final conclusion is that if constitutionalism means establishing limits to restrict power and protect liberties, the global space is indeed progressing towards constitutionalism.

IV. THE GLOBAL DIMENSIONS OF DEMOCRACY*

1. HUNGARY AND THE EUROPEAN PARLIAMENT

Article 2 of the Treaty on European Union (TEU) establishes that "[t]he Union is founded on the values of respect for human dignity, freedom, democracy, equality, the rule of law and respect for human rights [...]". If a member State breaches these values, the Union can resort to a preventive procedure and to a sanction mechanism (Article 7 TEU).

On the basis of these provisions, the European Parliament passed two resolutions on 10 June and 16 December 2015[106], voicing serious con-

---

[105] D. Grimm, *Constitutionalism. Past, Present, and Future*, Oxford, Oxford University Press, 2016, p. 33. Article 25 of the German Basic Law provides that "[t]he general rules of international law shall be an integral part of federal law. They shall take precedence over the laws and directly create rights and duties for the inhabitants of the federal territory".

* Thanks to Valentina Volpe for comments to a previous version of this section.

[106] European Parliament, *Resolution of 10 June 2015 on the situation in Hungary* (2015/2700(RSP)); European Parliament, *Resolution of 16 December 2015 on the situation in Hungary* (2015/2935(RSP)). See also European Parliament, *Resolution of 3 July 2013 on the situation of fundamental rights: standards and practices in Hungary (pursuant to the European Parliament resolution of 16 February 2012)* (2012/2130(INI)) and European Parliament, *Resolution of 16 February 2012 on the recent political developments in Hungary* (2012/2511(RSP))

cerns on the situation of democracy in Hungary, and asking the Commission to activate the Article 7 procedures to ensure that the "national legislation is in conformity with democracy, the rule of law and fundamental rights". On 2 December of the same year, the Commission however "found that the conditions to start a rule of law framework procedure [were] not fulfilled."

This is not the only case in which supranational or global institutions have engaged with national democracy. The European Court of Human Rights has put British democracy under control, while the European Union (EU) has attempted to check Turkish democracy.[107]

These initiatives counter the widespread opinion that democracy is a matter only for the State. According to this opinion, national communities or civil societies are inextricably linked to a government. Both society and government are necessarily national and only the *demos* is entitled to choose its own rulers, while the rulers derive their legitimacy from the *demos* and are accountable only to it. Therefore, there is a "closed circuit," with which foreign authorities are not entitled to interfere.

Consider the difference between this approach to democracy and how we approach the rule of law or respect of human rights. One century ago, it was a well-established opinion that natural rights did not exist, as rights derive from the State, which is the only source of law – to use Vittorio Emanuele Orlando's terminology in his 1911 Preface to the Italian translation of Georg Jellinek's Theory of subjective public rights.[108] However, we now accept that observance of the rule of law and of human rights is a matter not only for the State, but also for the international community and for global and supranational institutions. We accept that the EU, the European Court of Human Rights and many more global institutions are capable of evaluating, controlling and judging whether and how national authorities respect the rule of law and human rights.

Today, if compliance with the rule of law, respect of human rights and observance of democratic principles are tasks not only for national legal

---

[107] V. Jourová, Commissioner, in a debate with MEPs, European Parliament, Press Release, "Hungary: no systemic threat to democracy, says Commission, but concerns remain", 2 December 2015. See J-W. MÜLLER, "Should the EU Protect Democracy and the Rule of Law inside Member States?" in *European Law Journal*, 2015, vol. 21, n. 2, pp. 141-160.

[108] V. E. Orlando, "Sulla teoria dei 'diritti pubblici subiettivi' di Jellinek", now in Id., *Diritto pubblico generale. Scritti varii (1881 – 1940) coordinati in sistema*, Milan, Giuffrè, 1954, p. 275.

orders, but also for supranational and global institutions, many questions readily arise. Is there a universal concept of democracy? Is democracy a universal and shared value? Is there a universal right to democratic governance, a right that is necessarily a *global* right? Is there, or can there be, democracy at the global level? Is global democracy similar to national democracy? Does globalization hollow out national democracy? Or, on the contrary, can global bodies enhance national democracies? If the State is the cradle of democracy, what will happen to democracy if the State becomes less important and decisions are increasingly taken by supranational or global actors? Will national democracy evaporate? Or will it be replaced with a cosmopolitan form of democracy?

I shall address some of these questions in the following order. I shall first examine the many legal documents that have entrusted global institutions with the task to introduce, promote, evaluate and defend democracy. I shall then consider the possibility of transplanting democracy at the global level. Next, I shall analyze how globalization affects national democracies and how global and national democracies interact. Finally, I will make an overall evaluation of national and supranational democracy.

First, however, I wish to make a caveat: it would be a mistake to consider the expansion of democracy as being a mere problem of multilevel governance, because there are actually many complex relations between the forms of democracy existing at the different levels. National democracy and global democracy are intermingled, and there is also room for the development of a universal concept of democracy, one that can influence local applications and reinterpretations of the concept. Be, therefore, ready to encounter a complex web of relations.

2. DEMOCRACY AS A UNIVERSAL PRINCIPLE

The United Nations Charter, signed on 26 June 1945 in San Francisco, mentioned peace, security, human rights and fundamental freedoms, not rule of law and democracy: this was because the Soviet bloc was against the inclusion of these principles.[109] However, only three years

---

[109] D. Archibugi, *Democracy at the United Nations*, in T. Inoguchi – E. Newman and J. Keane (eds.), *The changing nature of democracy*, Tokyo, New York, Paris, United Nations University Press, 1998, p. 244-254, p. 245.

later, the Universal Declaration of Human Rights, proclaimed by the General Assembly of the United Nations on 10 December 1948, provided, at Article 21(1), that "[e]veryone has the right to take part in the government of his country, directly or through freely chosen representatives." Direct or representative democracy were universally recognized as individual rights, but only within national contexts ("in the government of his country"). The "democratic society" referred to in the subsequent Article 29(2) was necessarily a national society. The same is true for the "democratic decision" mentioned in the 1944 Declaration of Philadelphia on the aims and purposes of the International Labor Organization, as Article 1 envisages the representatives of workers and employers joining "in a free discussion and democratic decision" with the representatives of (national) governments.

This recognition was expanded in the International Covenant on Civil and Political Rights (16 December 1966). Article 25, does not only grant to all citizen the right to directly or indirectly take part in the conduct of public affairs, but also the right to "vote and to be elected at genuine periodic elections, which shall be by universal and equal suffrage and shall be held by secret ballot, guaranteeing the free expression of the will of the electors."[110]

A step forward in the support and promotion of democracy, albeit in an optative form, was made with the Vienna Declaration and Program of Action adopted at the 1993 World Conference on Human Rights: Section 1(8) provides that "[t]he international community should support the strengthening and promotion of democracy [...]". The goals of promoting, strengthening and supporting the consolidation of democracy were further affirmed in Resolution 55/2, adopted by the UN General Assembly on 8 September 2000 (the Millennium Declaration), and in Resolution 70/1, adopted by the UN General Assembly on 25 September 2015 (the 2030 Agenda for Sustainable Development). The first resolved to "strengthen the capacity of all our countries to implement the principles and practices of democracy" (Para. 24), to "support the consolidation of democracy in Africa" (Para. 27), and to "strengthen the further

---

[110] Also, in this international document, a "democratic society" is a point of reference (Articles 14, 21 and 22). Freedom of association, equality and the right of assembly are also mentioned. The UN Resolutions 45/150 (1990) and 46/137 (1991) return to the subject of "periodic and genuine elections".

cooperation between the United Nations and national parliaments [...] in various fields, including [...] democracy" (Para. 30). The second resolution declared democracy to be "essential for sustainable development" (Para. 9). Therefore, these declarations took an even further step, by referring not only to the principle but also to the practices of democracy; and not only to democracy in the world generally, but also to democracy in a particular region (Africa) and as an instrument for development. Finally, by linking national parliaments with the United Nations, the Millennium Declaration touched upon global democracy, thus going beyond the principle of democracy in national settings.

These global declarations were followed by regional charters. Among these, that of the American and that of the European States are particularly noteworthy.

The Charter of the Organization of American States (30 April 1948) declares that representative democracy "is an indispensable condition for the stability, peace and development of the region" (Preamble); that the Organization has the purpose of "promot[ing] and consolidat[ing] representative democracy" (Article 2) and the "effective exercise of democracy" (Article 3) and provides for the suspension of non-democratic members' right to participate. These principles are developed in the Inter-American Democratic Charter (11 September 2001), in which democracy is considered to be "indispensable" and "essential" both for the stability, peace and development of the region and as the basis of the rule of law (Preamble and Articles 1-4). The Charter solemnly declares that "the peoples of the Americas have a right to democracy and their governments have an obligation to promote and defend it" (Article 1), and that any alterations and interruptions of democracy are unconstitutional. The Charter also envisages the organization of electoral observation missions (Articles 23-25) and the promotion of democratic culture.

As for Europe, the European Convention on Human Rights (4 November 1950) declares "an effective political democracy" to be the best way to maintain fundamental freedoms (Preamble) and refers to a "democratic society" (Articles 6, 8-11),[111] while the TEU (13 December 2007), "desiring to enhance further the democratic [...] functioning of the institutions [...]" (Preamble), declares that "the Union is founded

---

[111] See also Article 2, Protocol 4 and Preamble, Protocol 13.

on the value of respect for [...] democracy", that "the functioning of the Union shall be founded on representative democracy" (Article 10(1)) and that "every citizen shall have the right to participate in the democratic life of the Union. Decisions shall be taken as openly and as closely as possible to the citizens" (Article 10(3)). The TEU also declares that national governments should be "themselves democratically accountable either to their national Parliaments or to their citizens" (Article 10(2)). Accordingly, Article 12 regulates the relations between national Parliaments and the EU, and Article 11 establishes mechanisms for consultation and openness. Article 21(2) provides that the Union "shall define and pursue common policies and actions [...] in order to [...] consolidate and support democracy."

These European constitutional declarations were followed by the Charter of Fundamental Rights of the European Union (7 December 2000), which contains a proclamation of "respect for democratic principles" (Article 14)[112] and a commitment to "consolidate and support democracy (Article 21).

According to these provisions, democracy is also a matter for the EU, not only for national governments. In the EU, the principle of democracy is a supranational principle that is imposed not only on national governments, but also on the government of the EU itself.

As a conclusion to this part, it may be stated that the principle of democracy is codified in a range of supranational instruments and has therefore become a principle of international law; that – according to these supranational legal instruments – democracy must be promoted, supported and defended as a human right; that democracy is considered not only an asset *per se*, but also as instrumental to peace, development, actual respect of human rights and compliance with the rule of law; that democracy is considered a condition for becoming a member of some international organizations; that, where democracy is required of supranational bodies, it should not substitute, but rather supplement national democracy (as local democracy supplements national democracy within domestic legal systems); that democracy is therefore established on two levels, one peculiar to each national legal system, and one universal and

---

[112] The Preamble declares that the Union is "based on the principles of democracy and the rule of law".

shared; that "the international system is moving toward a clearly designated democratic entitlement, with national standards validated by international standards and systematic monitoring of compliance", as noted by Thomas Franck.[113]

Today, therefore, *"Demokratie ist nicht auf Staaten beschränkt."*[114] However, this conclusion is drawn after a seventy-year history, which may be divided into three main periods: a first period, during which democracy was not even mentioned at the global level; the second, when democracy was an established principle at the global level, but essentially as an obligation upon the participating States; the third, when democracy has emerged as a universal principle, to be respected not only by States but also by global or supranational institutions.

The turning point, when democracy was also addressed to the two levels of government, occurred with the establishment of the EU. Only then could the world escape the paradox of a global (and regional) polity establishing a sound principle that applied to other polities (national governments) but not to itself.

3. DO GLOBAL INSTITUTIONS HAVE DEMOCRATIC CREDENTIALS?

"Konstitutionalisierung des Völkerrechts bezeichnet nur die Verrechtlichung, nicht die Demokratisierung der internationalen Ordnung," observed Christoph Möllers.[115] Further, Robert Keohane has emphasized the "difficulties that stand in the way of genuine global democratic governance"[116]: "[t]he symbols of democracy are all around us as

---

[113] T. Franck, "The Emerging Right to Democratic Governance", in *The American Journal of International Law*, 1992, vol. 86, n. 1, p. 91. According to Franck, "the transformation of the democratic entitlement from moral prescription into international legal obligation has evolved gradually (p. 47). See also R. Rich, "Bringing Democracy into International Law", in *Journal of Democracy*, 2001, vol. 12, n. 3, pp. 20 ff.

[114] C. Möllers, *Demokratie – Zumutungen und Versprechen*, Berlin, Wagenbach, 2008, p. 82.

[115] *Ibidem*, p. 101.

[116] R.O. Keohane, "Nominal Democracy? Prospects for Democratic Global Governance", in *International Journal of Constitutional Law*, 2015, vol. 13, n. 2, p. 344. This article has attracted criticism from J. W. Kuyper and J. S. Dryzek, "Real, not Nominal, Global Democracy: A Reply to Robert Keohane", in *International Journal of Constitutional Law*, 2016, vol. 14, n. 4, p. 930

we contemplate the institutions of global governance, but the substance is elusive;"[117] global democracy is merely "nominal." While the global space is no longer a "bureaucratic bargaining system," global institutions appear to enjoy only indirect legitimacy through their member States,[118] as there is no cosmopolitan Parliament, no global public sphere and no universal elections.[119]

Let us pause on this conclusion and consider two elements that could lead the quest for global democracy down different paths. First, we should ask ourselves whether the global environment is similar to that of national governments, and, if it is different, where the peculiarities of the global context lie. Second, we should consider whether, given the different context, democracy could establish itself in the global space through different means.

The history of global institutions is rather different from that of national institutions. States grew out of divided societies, developed around a united and strong Executive and gained the power to enforce (the monopoly of the use of the force), the power to tax, and the power to wage wars and maintain armed and police forces. Later, States became welfare States and therefore developed spending power, which implies a great power to allocate resources.

During their relatively short lifespan, global and supranational institutions developed along very different lines. There is no authoritarianism

---

(who observe that "[a] deliberative view of democracy that puts inclusive and egalitarian reasoned communication at its core helps show how substantive democracy can be pursued in global governance") and from G. de Búrca, "Nominal democracy? A reply to Robert Keohane", in *Ibidem*, p. 425 (who notes that the values of democracy, such as participation, transparency, accountability, and the protection of minorities and of free media can indeed be promoted in the global setting). See also G. de Búrca, "Developing Democracy Beyond the State", in *Columbia Journal of Transnational Law*, 2008, vol. 46, p. 221.

[117] *Ibidem*, p. 351.

[118] R. Dahl, "Can International Organizations be Democratic? A Skeptic's View", in I. Shapiro, C. Hacker-Cordón, *Democracy's Edges*, Cambridge, Cambridge University Press, 1999, p. 33.

[119] A. Buchanan, R. O. Keohane, "The Legitimacy of Global Governance Institutions", in *Ethics and International Affairs*, 2006, vol. 20, n. 4, pp. 416-417. But see D. Archibugi, *The Global Commonwealth of Citizens: Toward Cosmopolitan Democracy*, Princeton, Princeton University Press, 2008; D. Held, *Democracy and the Global Order: From the Modern State to Cosmopolitan Governance*, Stanford, Stanford University Press, 1995; D. Archibugi – D. Held, *Cosmopolitan Democracy: Paths and Agents*, in S. Gupta – S. Padmanabhan (eds.), *Politics and Cosmopolitanism in a Global Age*, New Delhi, Routledge, 2015, pp. 17-36.

in their past. They are not united, but are, instead, fragmented. Each institution has a single task: to regulate the use of the sea, to control the use of nuclear waste, to oversee international trade, to deal with global health, etc. Therefore, power is divided. There is no centralized body and there are very limited powers of enforcement, as the enforcement of most global or supranational decisions requires State cooperation. There is no centralized police or army, no taxing power, and almost no spending power. Global institutions act as initiators or promoters. They do not impose burdens. If they can impose burdens, they cannot give orders. If they can issue guidelines, they must nevertheless rely on national authorities for implementation. They do not directly interfere with religious beliefs or with free speech. In limited cases, they may constrain, but they cannot impose obligations. Only in very limited cases, they may infringe upon individual rights[120]. It could therefore be said that global institutions are toothless.[121]

If the main task of democracy is to place and maintain power under control, if national parliaments, and subsequently universal suffrage, developed for the main purpose of imposing limitations upon the executive, democracy at the supranational and global level does not have any such duty to accomplish, for the simple reason that the nature of the global system is different. The concepts of democracy, as embedded in the State experience[122], cannot be transposed as such into the global polity.

As Bogdandy has noted, as global institutions became increasingly active, their need for democratic justification in their own right and the democratic question became more pressing.[123] For example, one of the most urgent challenges faced by the global arena is the need to find

---

[120] A. Reinisch, "Securing the Accountability of International Organizations", in *Global Governance*, 2001, vol. 7, n. 2, pp. 131-149.

[121] S. Cassese, *Il diritto globale. Giustizia e democrazia oltre lo Stato*, Turin, Einaudi, p. 161.

[122] E. Bécault, A. Braeckman, M. Lievens, J. Wouters, *Introduction: Global Governance and Democracy: Invitation to a Multidisciplinary Dialogue*, in E. Bécault, A. Braeckman, M. Lievens, J. Wouters (eds.), *Global Governance and Democracy. A Multidisciplinary Analysis*, Cheltenham, Northampton, Elgar, 2015, p. 3.

[123] A. von Bogdandy, "The European Lesson for International Democracy: The Significance of Articles 9–12 EU Treaty for International Organizations", in *European Journal of International Law*, 2012, vol. 23, n. 2, p. 317.

ways to implement democratic values and practices in the environmental policies.[124]

The first source of legitimacy for global institutions – the first way to democratize global policies – is State consent. National political leaders play a double role as they are both members of the national ruling classes and global policymakers. Therefore, they are twice accountable to the national electorate (although this does not apply to non-democratic States[125]).

This is a special type of indirect democracy, as global democracy through State consent and support does not only mean that every single member State supports the global institutions of which they are a part, but also that this support is provided by the collective action of national governments. These interact with each other, while influencing global choices.

A second source of legitimacy for global institutions consists in global parliamentary assemblies. Bogdandy has noted that "[s]ince the first decades of the 20th century, proposals were presented which aimed at some form of global representative assembly. Most important were proposals to establish a parliamentary assembly within the framework of the League of Nations"[126]. Parliamentary assemblies consisting of representatives of national parliaments are not unknown to supranational and global organizations: examples include the Parliamentary Assembly of the Council of Europe, the Mercosur Parliament, the Pan-African Parliament of the African Union, ASEAN's Inter-Parliamentary Assembly, NATO's Parliamentary Assembly and Parliamentary Assembly of the Organization for Security and Cooperation in Europe (OSCE)[127].

Progress towards a more comprehensive type of global democracy was made with the European Parliament, which is directly repre-

[124] E. Bécault, *Democratizing Global Environmental Governance? The case of Transnational Climate Governance*, in E. Bécault, A. Braeckman, M. Lievens, J. Wouters (eds.), *Global Governance and Democracy. A Multidisciplinary Analysis*, cit., p. 76 ff.

[125] As noticed by A. Buchanan, R. O. Keohane, "The Legitimacy of Global Governance Institutions", in *Ethics and International Affairs*, cit., p. 412 ff. The point on the "duality of global democracy" is made especially in a seminal contribution by Anne Peters, *Dual Democracy*, in J. Klabbers, A. Peters and G. Ulfstein, *The Constitutionalization of International Law*, Oxford, Oxford University Press, 2009, pp. 263-341.

[126] A. von Bogdandy, *The European Lesson for International Democracy*, cit., p. 320.

[127] A. Peters, *Dual Democracy, cit.*, pp. 322-326.

sentative of the peoples of the EU's member States and of its citizens. However, it does not possess all of the prerogatives enjoyed by national parliaments.

The 2014 European Parliament elections introduced a new procedure for choosing the President of the European Commission: the so-called *Spitzenkandidaten*. This experiment has been considered as a first step in overcoming the insufficient democratic control within the system, by strengthening the role of the European Parliament in the investiture procedure of the Commission's President at the expense of that of the European Council, which must now appoint the leader of the party that won the most seats in the European elections.

Some international organizations have social partners' representatives. The International Labour Organization (ILO) is a tripartite agency of the United Nations that brings together governments, employers and worker representatives. The ILO acts as a forum in which the governments and social partners of the economies of its member States can debate and elaborate labour standards and policies.

Indirect forms of legitimation and accountability of global policymakers have several drawbacks, the most important of which are the fragmentation of national electorates and their limited knowledge and control of foreign policy.

Allow me now to return to the question raised before. Does global democracy mirror national democracy? Or should one conclude that democracy acquires different characteristics in the global space?

An analysis of the structures and decision-making processes at the global level reveals that there are two prevailing forms of legitimacy and accountability-building mechanisms: one that is horizontal and another that is vertical.

As interdependence is a predominant feature of the global space, external restraints play an important role: as members of multilateral global bodies, national governments can control each other. This is different from State consent as a source of indirect democratic legitimacy, because the latter acts in a vertical bottom-up direction, while this mutual control mechanism acts horizontally[128].

---

[128] See G. O'Donnel, "Horizontal Accountability in New Democracies", in *Journal of Democracy*, 1998, vol. 9, n. 3, pp. 113 and 117 for the horizontal accountability inside national governments and A. Mulieri, *Can we democratize Global Governance? Two Guiding Scenarios*

Second, transparency, participation, review, contestation procedures, and the duty to provide reasons for decisions contribute to alleviate the perceived democratic deficit[129].

Principles such as the right to a hearing, the duty to provide a reasoned decision and the duty to disclose all relevant information developed and were enforced in the global arena in the course of only a few years, while their development in domestic legal orders required decades or even centuries, depending on the State in question.

Global rules grant participation rights to private parties *vis-à-vis* domestic authorities (thus strengthening the participatory rights already granted by several national legal orders); to national governments *vis-à-vis* global agencies or other national governments; to global institutions *vis-à-vis* other global institutions; and to private parties appearing before global institutions. Participation is therefore ensured both vertically (for private parties before national governments and global agencies, and for national governments before global organizations) and horizontally (as it is guaranteed to national governments before other national governments, and to global institutions before other global institutions). Thus, participatory rights created at the global level establish links between the different levels of government, and between the different governmental bodies involved and civil society.

Moreover, looking to the future, it may be observed that global institutions cannot promote human rights (including the right to participate to public affairs) without at some point accepting the idea that they themselves must recognize popular participation in their own structures and decision-making processes.

In conclusion, it cannot be said that global institutions are not democratic because citizens can never attain influence and control over global

---

based on a Narrative Approach, in E. Bécault, A. Braeckman, M. Lievens, J. Wouters (eds), *Global Governance and Democracy. A Multidisciplinary Analysis*, cit., p. 27 for the external forms of accountability.

[129] A. von Bogdandy, *The European Lesson for International Democracy*, cit., p. 21; A. Buchanan, R. O. Keohane, *The Legitimacy of Global Governance Institutions*, cit., p. 426. See also R. Dehousse, "Beyond Representative Democracy: Constitutionalism in a Polycentric Polity", in J. H. H. Weiler, M. Wind (eds.), *European Constitutionalism beyond the State*, Cambridge, Cambridge University Pres, 2003, pp. 135-156. On deliberative democracy in general, see A. Floridia, "Beyond Participatory Democracy, Towards Deliberative Democracy: Elements of a Possible Theoretical Genealogy", in *Rivista italiana di scienza politica*, 2014, n. 3, pp. 299-326.

decisions, because the views of the élites tend to prevail, or because there are no opportunities for political participation, information on political decisions of international organizations, public debate, political competition between the parties and individuals seeking office, or control over international bureaucracies[130]. On the contrary, it is possible to conceive of and practically achieve the democratization of governance beyond the State, as well as democratic politics beyond the borders of the nation-State and without one unified people[131].

I wish to make a final remark on this point. To understand the development of global democracy, it cannot be forgotten that national governments also developed very slowly toward democracy, first by establishing legislative bodies with very little countervailing power *vis-à-vis* the executive, and then legitimizing these legislative assemblies through elections and universal suffrage. It should be recalled that when Alexis de Tocqueville wrote *"La démocratie en Amérique,"* approximately three point five percent of the population participated in the ballots, the Northern States had only recently abolished slavery, and the Southern States did not grant political rights to slaves (who constituted eighteen percent of the population). Regardless, Tocqueville praised American democracy. Should we expect more from global institutions, given their current stage of development?

4. DO GLOBAL INSTITUTIONS REDUCE OR ENHANCE NATIONAL DEMOCRACY?

I will now leave aside the first problem (that of how democratic are global institutions themselves) and turn to the second issue identified, that of the impact of globalization upon national democracies. Is globalization a friend or a foe of national democracies? Does it have a positive or a negative impact on national democratic systems? Does it promote, defend and enhance national democracy, or, on the contrary, does it con-

---

[130] As observed by R. Dahl, *Can international organizations be democratic? A skeptic's view*, cit., p. 31.

[131] As noticed by A. von Bogdandy, *The European Lesson for International Democracy*, cit., pp. 316 and 323.

strain democracy at the national level? In other words, are democracy and globalization two opposed ideals?

If the State is the context in which democracy developed, what will happen if the State becomes less important, due to its conferral of a part of its powers upon global (unaccountable) institutions? Does this conferral of sovereign power from national governments reduce democracy and undermine the legitimacy of national governments, given that the national electorate cannot regain control over decisions that have been transferred to the competence of the global institutions[132]? This is a real concern for many Member States of the EU, as articulated for example by the German Federal Constitutional Court in the case on the European Stability Mechanism[133]. According to this judgment, if further EU integration is to be in line with the Basic Law, any additional transfer of power must be democratically legitimated by the *Bundestag*.

According to Dieter Grimm, "[a]s long as there is no convincing model of a global democracy, the source of democratic legitimacy and supervision must not run dry at the State level. Today sovereignty protects democracy". Further, "[s]overeignty's most important function today lies in protecting the democratic self-determination of politically united society with regard to the order that best suits it"[134].

Globalization undoubtedly has an impact on national democracies, because it produces an asymmetry between the input and the output. Many decisions are no longer under the control of national governments, because the power to make them has been transferred to global or supranational authorities. National executives can no longer act as guarantors for these decisions: they are only able to cooperate with their counterparts when taking them and are themselves subject to their binding power.

---

[132] Citations from S. Cassese, *Il diritto globale*, cit., p. 233. See also S. Cassese, *Universalità del diritto*, in ID, *Oltre lo Stato*, Rome – Bari, Laterza, p. 92 ff and ID., *Territori e potere. Un nuovo ruolo per gli Stati?*, Bologna, il Mulino, 2016, pp. 105 ff.

[133] BVerfG, Judgment of the Second Senate of 18 March 2014 - 2 BvR 1390/12.

[134] D. Grimm, *Sovereignty, The Origin and Future of a Political and Legal Concept*, New York, Columbia University Press, 2015, p. 128. Accordingly, for Grimm, the judgement of the German Constitutional Court "defended the sovereignty of the Federal Republic not in the interests of the nation-State, but in the interests of democracy" (p. 127).

At the same time, national governments are accountable to their respective peoples, which do not distinguish between the two levels of government and direct their criticism towards national executives, which are their representatives. As a consequence, national governments are held responsible for decisions that were taken in cooperation with other authorities and over which they did not have full control.

This asymmetry activates a process in which national political parties accentuate populism and demagogy while criticizing globalization, and national leaders must play the role of mediators between popular demand and global institutions.

However, on the contrary, globalization may also serve to democratize domestic governments[135]. Global actors can foster national democracy by establishing standards and evaluating best practices (as does, for example, OSCE); by funding, rewarding and promoting national grassroots initiatives (as the United Nations Democracy Fund – UNDEF – or the European Instrument for Democracy and Human Rights); by adjudicating cases involving national democratic institutions (as did the European Court of Human Rights in its decisions on British democracy);[136] by helping in drafting domestic legal

[135] A different problem is the export of democracy from one country to another. On this, see G. J. Ikenberry, "Why Export Democracy?", in *The Wilson Quarterly*, 1999, vol. 23, n. 2, pp. 56-65; P. C. Schmitter, I. Brouwer, *Conceptualizing, Researching & Evaluating*, in *EUI Working Paper SPS*, 1999, 9; L. Diamond, *The Spirit of Democracy. The Struggle to Build Free Societies Throughout the World*, New York Times Book, 2008, pp. 56-87; A. Magen, L. Morlino, "Hybrid regimes, the rule of law, and external influence on domestic change", in A. Magen, L. Morlino (eds), *International Actors, Democratization and the Rule of Law. Anchoring Democracy?*, New York, Routledge, 2009, pp. 1-25; N. S. Teixeira (ed.), *The International Politics of Democratization. Comparative perspectives*, New York, Routledge, 2008; G. Sørensen, *Democracy and democratization. Processes and prospects in a changing world*, Boulder, Westview Press, 2008, pp.79-98; P. T. Leeson, A. M. Dean, "The Democratic Domino Theory: An Empirical Investigation", in *American Journal of Political Science*, 2009, vol. 53, no. 3, pp. 533-551; T. Risse, "Conclusions: Towards Transatlantic Democracy Promotion?", in A. Magen, T. Risse, M. A. McFaul (eds), *Promoting Democracy and the Rule of Law. American and European Strategies*, Basingstoke, Palgrave Macmillan, 2009, pp. 244-271; M. McFaul, *Advancing Democracy Abroad. Why We Should and How We Can*, New York, Toronto, Hoover, 2010; P. Burnell, R. Youngs (eds), *New challenges to Democratization*, New York, Routledge, 2010; T. Carothers, *The continuing backlash against democracy promotion*, in P. Burnell, R. Youngs (eds), *New challenges to Democratization*, New York, Routledge, 2010, pp. 59-72.

[136] Consider the prisoners' voting rights saga that has been opposing British authorities and the European Court of Human Rights for more than ten years. See ECtHR, *Hirst v. the United*

frameworks (like in the case of the Venice Commission's constitutional assistance);[137] by putting national elections under observation by global institutions; by assisting and supporting national democratic processes; or by establishing that democracy is a condition to access global or supranational institutions.[138]

Let me make a few examples. UNDEF was established in July 2005 and equipped with an Executive Head, a Secretary-General, an Advisory Board and a Program Consultative Group. To date, forty-five member States have contributed to the Fund[139], which provides financing to civil society organizations every year for the ultimate aim of promoting democracy. Similarly, the European Instrument for Democracy and Human Rights (EIDHR) contributes to the development and consolidation of democracy through support for civil society organizations and has funded civil society initiatives directed at supporting action on democracy and transparency of democratic electoral processes, in particular through election observation.[140]

The Organization for Security and Cooperation in Europe (OSCE) is the world's largest regional security organization, with fifty-seven participating States. Its Office for Democratic Institutions and Human

---

Kingdom (No. 2), Strasbourg, 6 October 2005; *Greens and M.T. v. the United Kingdom*, Strasbourg, 23 November 2010; *Firth and Others v. the United Kingdom*, 12 August 2014; *McHugh and Others v. the United Kingdom*, Strasbourg, 10 February 2015; *Millbank and Others v. the United Kingdom*, Strasbourg, 30 June 2016.

[137] Taxonomies of these interventions are suggested in S. Cassese, *The Global Polity – Global Dimensions of Democracy and the Rule of Law*, Sevilla, Global Law Press, Editorial Derecho Global, 2012, pp. 61-62, 77-101, 103-104 and in V. Volpe, *Backing Democracy. Global Actors Raising Domestic Legal Standards*, forthcoming and V. Volpe, *Drafting Counter-majoritarian Democracy. The Venice Commission's Constitutional Assistance*, in *Heidelberg Journal of International Law*, 2016, vol. 76, n. 4, pp. 811 – 843.

[138] A. Peters, *Dual Democracy*, cit., pp. 283-286 on pro-democratic interventions.

[139] UNDEF, *Status of Contributions by Cumulative Amount as at 28 February 2017*, available at http://www.un.org/democracyfund/contribution-table.

[140] B. Carotti, "Who Promotes Democracy? The United Nations Democracy Fund and the European Instrument for Democracy and Human Rights: Causality or Convergence?", in *Global Administrative Law. The Casebook*, S. Cassese - B. Carotti - L. Casini - E. Cavalieri - E. MacDonald, with the collaboration of M. Macchia - M. Savino (eds.), Institute for Research on Public Administration (IRPA) - Institute for International Law and Justice (IILJ), Rome - New York, 2012, Chapter 7, § 7.A.3; see also the websites of the United Nations Democracy Fund (http://www.un.org/democracyfund/) and of the European Instrument for Democracy and Human Rights (EIDHR) (https://ec.europa.eu/europeaid/how/finance/eidhr_en.htm_en).

Rights (ODIHR) based in Warsaw, Poland, is active throughout the OSCE area in several fields, including democratic development and election observation. The ODIHR is organized in several different departments, one of which is the Democratization Department, which focuses on fostering equal participation in political and public life and on promoting democratic governance. Another particularly relevant unit is the Elections Department, which engages in election observation and in the creation and implementation of technical assistance projects, in areas including the review of elections, relevant legislation and the promotion of domestic observer groups throughout the OSCE region. "The OSCE is active in democracy assistance in seventeen countries, and spent over 162 million Euro in 2006 alone"[141]. In 2015, ODIHR conducted seventeen election-related activities and its overall budget was more than eighteen million Euros[142].

The EU enlargement strategy implies four important steps: the definition of benchmarks of democratic performance as conditions for accession; the securing of commitments from candidate countries; oversight of the implementation of these commitments on the basis of annual reports; and the provision of pre-accession assistance.

Article 3 of Protocol No. 1 of the European Convention on Human Rights provides that: "[t]he High Contracting Parties undertake to hold free elections at reasonable intervals by secret ballot, under conditions which will ensure the free expression of the opinion of the people in the choice of the legislature". In the case of *Yumak and Sadak v. Turkey* of 8 July 2008, App. No. 10226/02[143], the Grand Chamber of the Strasbourg Court maintained that "[d]emocracy constitutes a fundamental element of the 'European public order', and the rights guaranteed under Article 3 of Protocol No. 1 are crucial to establishing and maintaining the foundations of an effective and meaningful democracy governed by the rule of law". The Grand Chamber reached the conclusion that "in general a 10% electoral threshold appears excessive. In that connection, [the Court] concurs with the organs of the Council

---

[141] N. Bermeo, "Is Democracy Exportable?", in Z. Barany, R.G. Moser (eds), *Is Democracy Exportable?*, Cambridge, Cambridge University Press, 2009, p. 247.

[142] OSCE, *Annual Report 2015*, pp. 45 and 100, available at http://www.osce.org/annual-report/2015?download=true

[143] ECtHR, *Case of Yumak and Sadak v. Turkey*, Strasbourg, 8 July 2008.

of Europe, which have stressed the threshold's exceptionally high level and recommended that it be lowered [...]. It compels political parties to make use of stratagems which do not contribute to the transparency of the electoral process".

The mechanics of these means of global enhancement of national democracy presents many interesting features and paradoxes. First, global or supranational institutions often address their action to civil societies directly, to empower them. Therefore, national governments are under double pressure, from above and from below. This is the case with the EU conditioning accession upon the introduction, in the national context, of more democratic procedures and structures; and of the national civil society associations funded by the European Instrument for Democracy and Human Rights to fight for more democratic and inclusive national institutions.

Second, although democracy is traditionally generated by the people in a national context, it may also be encouraged, imported, transplanted, promoted, assisted and controlled from the outside. Democracy is not necessarily only the outcome of domestic political processes, without any influence by actors outside the nation-State. As has been observed, "international factors [...] influence domestic regime transition" and "democracy promotion has become a foreign policy goal [...] with international organizations as an important vehicle for achieving these ends"[144].

Third, in this context, we are witnessing the paradox of a set of new global and supranational institutions that are not entirely democratic, but that promote, assist, support and judge longstanding and well-established national democracies.

Fourth, by "upgrading" national democracies, global and supranational bodies "assist domestic publics to achieve goals that they would otherwise have difficulty realizing"[145]. However, by helping to control special interest groups and make democracy more inclusive, by protecting individual and minority rights, these bodies act like constitutional legislators and courts, and "may attenuate direct electoral control and

[144] J. C. Pevehouse, "Democracy from the Outside-In? International Organizations and Democratization", in *International Organization*, 2002, vol. 56, n. 3, pp. 515-516.

[145] R. O. Keohane, S. Macedo and A. Moravcsik, "Democracy-Enhancing Multilateralism", in *International Organization* 2009, vol. 63, p. 15.

may themselves be captured by special interests, or operate in a non-transparent and unaccountable fashion"[146].

Fifth, are democracy-enhancing global policies justified only in terms of democracy, or are there additional reasons they should be supported, such as their capacity to maintain peace, given that democracies are supposed to be more peaceful?

Sixth, one should ask how effective these external pressures are and what type of democracy they promote[147]. There is no doubt that the role of international and transnational actors in contemporary democratization processes is increasingly important, that "democratization and economic reform in east Europe have been materially affected by an external actor, the European Union"[148] and that "European Union influence has not disappeared, or even substantially weakened, after the end of pre-accession conditionality"[149].

In conclusion on this point, it may be said that global interventions, akin to foreign interventions, do not necessarily entail a loss for democracy; on the contrary, they can protect or even promote it, and can compensate for the powers that have been removed from national democracies[150].

However, democracy-enhancing policies raise a wealth of additional problems: which form of democracy should be promoted or defended? At which stage should global action be taken? "What actions constitute a violation sufficient to warrant international intervention"[151]? Which authority is endowed with decisive power, when conflicting values arise?

---

[146] *Ibidem*, pp. 22-23.

[147] A question raised by J. L. McCoy, *Transnational Response to Democratic Crisis in the Americas, 1990-2005*, in T. Legler, S. F. Lean and D. S. Boniface, *Promoting Democracy in the America's*, Baltimore, The Johns Hopkins University Press, 2007, p. 286.

[148] M. A. Vachudova, *The Leverage of International Institutions on Democratizing States: Eastern Europe and the European Union*, European University Institute Working Papers, RSC 33, 2001, p. 34.

[149] P. Levitz and G. Pop-Eleches, "Why No Backsliding? The European Union's Impact on Democracy and Governance Before and After Accession", in *Comparative Political Studies*, Sage Publications, 2010, vol. 43, p. 479.

[150] From a global constitutionalist perspective, see A. Peters, "Compensatory Constitutionalism. The Function and Potential of Fundamental International Norms and Structures", in *Leiden Journal of International Law*, 2006, vol. 19, pp. 579–610.

[151] J. L. McCoy, *Transnational Response to Democratic Crisis in the Americas, 1990-2005*, cit., p. 280.

5. AN OVERALL EVALUATION OF GLOBAL DEMOCRACY

I shall now proceed to an overall evaluation of the benefits and dis-advantages of the globalization of democracy, in both its forms. This evaluation shall be laid out in short points.

1. It is necessary to discard the purely national approach to democracy and to reject the concept of democracy as necessarily bound to a people and to a territory; it is necessary to cast aside the principle that a certain political actor need be accountable only to its own constituency.

2. Global democracy cannot be expected to be equivalent to national democracies, as the context (the global space) is significantly different from the national setting; in particular, there is no one *demos*, but rather many *demoi*.

3. There is a relocation of democracy: the people lose control over a certain amount of areas, but gain control upon larger areas, that are beyond the reach of the State.

4. Democracy and the rule of law progress very slowly but simultaneously, in the global space. However, in some cases, they may conflict. This occurred when in June 2017, the European Commission sent Poland an official warning that the changes made to its constitutional court endanger the rule of law, with a decision that could lead to sanctions imposed against the country (according to the European Commission, the recent alterations to the workings of Poland's highest court posed "a systemic risk to the rule of law"). The Polish Government reacted angrily in name of the sovereignty of the Polish people.

5. If the right to democracy has become an international right, world public opinion and the international community have an interest in ensuring that democratic rulers are in power everywhere in the world, also because a democratically ruled neighbour is more likely to be a peaceful neighbour.

6. The global expansion of democracy produces a wealth of external links – because there are more "fire alarms" in case of political crises not only within the national community, but also outside it – but this may endanger national democracies, because those accountable may escape from the national accountability process.

7. By ensuring democracy, global actors draw a constitutional moment out on the global space. Combining the respect for human rights and compliance with democratic principles at the global level enables the emergence of constitutionalism in the global arena.

8. Global democracy is very fragile, not only because many national governments are not democratic and because there are no cosmopolitan elections, but also because there are tensions between democracy at national and global levels: "[…] conflicts between domestic and international law increasingly cause national disrespect of international law which is justified or camouflaged with the argument that a conflicting international rule violates domestic democracy"[152].

9. Finally, many of these developments are still at the stage of "law in books". However, an evaluation of the progress made by democracy worldwide cannot avoid considering the process, and therefore a future in which we may hope that these proclamations will also become "law in action". New nationalistic revivals in the Anglo-Saxon world, in Eastern Europe and Turkey will not prevail, as forces supporting globalization and democracy are much too ingrained in the world's structures and processes.

---

[152] A. Peters, *Dual Democracy*, cit., pp. 333-337.

CHAPTER III

GLOBAL REGULATION

I. ADMINISTRATIVE LAW WITHOUT THE STATE? THE CHALLENGE OF GLOBAL REGULATION*

> *The giraffe is like a machine that, though made out of pieces from different machines, still functions perfectly... Mr. Palomar...wondered why he was so interested in giraffes. Perhaps because the world around him moved in disharmony and he always hoped to uncover a design, a constant.[1]*

1. TUNA FISHING: HOW GLOBAL ADMINISTRATIVE LAW WAS BORN

IN early 1960s, the fishing of Southern Bluefin Tuna rose to over seventy thousand tons per year, leading to a marked decrease in mature tuna[2]. As a result, the catch began to suffer.

---

* I wish to thank Lorenzo Casini for his assistance with research on the ICANN and Stefano Battini and Francesca Bignami for their comments on an earlier draft.

[1] I. Calvino, "La corsa delle giraffe", in C. Milanini (a cura di) *Romanzi e racconti*, Milano, Mondadori, 1992, p. 940-941.

[2] M. Hayashi, "The Southern Bluefin Tuna Cases: Prescription of Provisional Measures by the International Tribunal for the Law of the Sea", in *Tulane Environmental Law Journal*, 2000, vol. 13, p. 361-365, citing Statement of Claim and Grounds on Which it Is Based at t 3, Austl. v. Japan (lnt'l Trib. of the Law of the Sea) (July 15, 1999) [hereinafter Australian Southern Bluefin Tuna Claim]; New Zealand Ministry of Foreign Affairs and Trade, Backgrounder: Dispute between New Zealand and Japan concerning Southern Bluefin Tuna, http://www.mfat.govt.nz/support/legal/disputes/ disputeontuna.html [hereinafter New Zealand Backgrounder].

In 1973, the third United Nations Conference on the Law of the Sea met in New York.[3] It concluded its work in 1982 with a new treaty-the United Nations Convention on the Law of the Sea (UNCLOS).[4] This treaty went into force in 1994, with the signature of the seventieth state, Guyana. [5] Article 64 of the UNCLOS provides that "[t]he coastal State and other States whose nationals fish in the region for the highly migratory species listed in Annex I shall cooperate directly or through appropriate international organizations with a view to ensuring conservation and promoting the objective of optimum utilization of such species throughout the region, both within and beyond the exclusive economic zone."[6]

Articles 116 through 119 contain other provisions on the conservation of marine resources.[7] The Southern Bluefin Tuna is included in the list in Annex 1.[8]

In 1985, Australia, Japan, and New Zealand – which are the countries that do the most fishing of this type of tuna – stipulated voluntary agreements on tuna fishing.[9] These agreements proved to be inadequate because they were nonbinding, so in 1993, these three nations signed the Convention for the Conservation of Southern Bluefin Tuna (CCSBT), which went into force in 1994.[10] Other countries later acceded to this treaty.[11]

---

[3] See generally E. L. Miles, *Global Ocean Politics: The Decision Process at the Third United Nations Conference on the Law of the Sea 1973-1982*, The Hague, Martinus Nijhoff publishers, 1998.

[4] United Nations Convention on the Law of the Sea, opened for signature December 10, 1982, 21 I.L.M. 1261, 1833 U.N.T.S. 3 [hereinafter UNCLOS].

[5] The treaty entered into force on November 16, 1994.

[6] Id. art. 64(1).

[7] Id. art. 116-19.

[8] Id. annex I.

[9] M. Hayashi, *The Southern Bluefin Tuna Cases*, cit., p. 365.

[10] See generally Convention for the Conservation of Southern Bluefin Tuna, Austl.-Japan-N.Z., May 10, 1993, 1819 U.N.T.S. 360 (entered into force May 20, 1994) [hereinafter Bluefin Tuna Convention].

[11] Taiwan and the Republic of Korea have acceded to the convention, the Philippines was accepted as a formal cooperating non-member, and discussions with Indonesia and South Africa regarding non-member status are under way. Commission for the Conservation of Southern Bluefin Tuna [CCSBTJ, About the Commission, http://www.ccbst.org/docs/about.html (last visited Nov. 11, 2005) [hereinafter CCSBT].

The 1994 Convention establishes a Commission for the Conservation of Southern Bluefin Tuna.[12] The Commission has legal personality,[13] a budget and rules governing accounting and employment relations,[14] a Secretariat with its own staff,[15] and headquarters in Canberra.[16]

Within it, separate bodies carry out oversight and consultation tasks.[17] In 2001, the Commission established an Extended Commission, made up not only of the Commission's member states, but also of other "entities or fishing entities" whose flagships fish for tuna.[18]

With authority from the CCSBT treaty and the acts subsequently adopted, the Commission is in charge of gathering statistical and scientific information on tuna and similar species, adopting binding decisions establishing quotas of tuna that may be fished annually by each treaty adherent, monitoring respect for fixed trade limitations – for example, the Commission has established that the importation of tuna by party states must be accompanied by statistical information on its provenance[19] – adopting, "if necessary, additional measures,"[20] control-

---

[12] Bluefin Tuna Convention, cit., art. 6.

[13] Id. art. 6, 9 (granting legal personality to the Commission).

[14] Id. art. 11 (giving the Commission power to decide on a budget); Staff Regulations (Sept. 11 1995) (amended Sept. 24-28 1996), CCSBT, http:/ /www.ccsbt.org/docs/pdf/about_the_commission/staff_regulations.pdf (establishing employment policies for Commission employees).

[15] Id. art. 10, 11 (establishing the Secretariat).

[16] CCSBT, *Headquarters Agreement between the Commission for the Conservation of Southern Bluefin Tuna and the Government of Australia* art. 4, (March 10, 1999), http://www.ccsbt.org/docs/pdf/about_the_commission/ headquarters_agreement.pdf) (agreeing on Canberra as the Commission's headquarters).

[17] See, e.g., Bluefin Tuna Convention, cit., art. 10, 3 (establishing Commission oversight of the Secretariat), art. 9 (establishing Commission oversight of the Scientific Committee).

[18] CCSBT, *Resolution to Establish an Extended Commission and an Extended Scientific Committee and Rules of Procedure of the Extended Commission for the Conservation of Southern Bluefin Tuna* 1 (Apr. 18-21, 2001) (revised Oct. 7-10, 2003), https://www.ccsbt.org/userfiles/file/docs_english/basic_documents/the%20Extended%20Commission.pdf.

[19] Quotas are assigned to the party States but addressed to fishers. States in turn distribute the national quota among fishers.

[20] See Bluefin Tuna Convention, cit., art. 8, 1(a) (regarding the obligation of the Commission to gather statistical and scientific information), art. 8, 3(b)(obligating the Commission to determine the total allowable catch for each treaty adherent), art. 8, 1 3(b) (regarding additional measures which the Commission may adopt if necessary); CCSBT, *Southern Bluefin Tuna Statistical Document Program* 1, 1.1 (Oct. 2003), http://www. ccsbt.org/docs/pdf/about_the_commission/

ling illegal fishing on the basis of the Food and Agriculture Organization's (FAO) International Plan of Action for Illegal, Unregulated and Unreported Fishing,[21] and inviting non-party states to respect the treaty's objectives.[22]

The treaty binds the parties, but it also requires them to cooperate in deterring tuna fishing by "nationals, residents or vessels of any State or entity not party to this Convention, where such activity could affect adversely the attainment of the objective of this Convention."[23]

The Commission fixed national quotas in 1994.[24] Thereafter, however, it was unable to reach an agreement for updating them. The quotas thus remained unchanged, despite Japan's pressure to increase them.

In 1998 and 1999, Japan undertook an experimental fishing program, which exceeded the limits established by the Commission.[25] In response, Australia and New Zealand initiated arbitration before the appropriate tribunal, as provided by Article 287 and Annex VII of the UNCLOS.[26] The two countries also filed a request for interim measures before the International Tribunal for the Law of the Sea (ITLOS) on the basis of Article 290.5 of the UNCLOS.[27] In addition, in response to the unilat-

---

trade_information_scheme.pdf (regarding the Commission's role in monitoring limitations on trade).

[21] See CCSBT, *Resolution on Illegal Unregulated and Unreported Fishing (IUU) and Establishment of a CCSBT Record of Vessels Over 24 Meters Authorized to Fish for Southern Bluefin Tuna* (Oct. 7-10, 2003), http://www.ccsbt.org/docs/pdf/about_the_commission/resolution_on_authorized_24m_vessel_list.pdf (regarding obligations of the Commission to control illegal fishing).

[22] See CCSBT, *Resolution to Establish the Status of Co-operating Non-Member of the Extended Commission and the Extended Scientific Committee 2*, 2 (Oct. 7-10, 2003), http://www.ccsbt.org/docs/pdf/about_the_commission/Resolution_To_Establish_CooperatingNonMember_Status.pdf (regarding the obligation of the Commission to invite non-members to join the Convention).

[23] See Bluefin Tuna Convention, cit., art. 15, 4.

[24] M. Hayashi, *The Southern Bluefin Tuna Cases*, cit., p. 366-367.

[25] Id. p. 368.

[26] UNCLOS, cit.; M. Hayashi, *The Southern Bluefin Tuna Cases*, cit., p. 362.

[27] UNCLOS, cit., art. 290(5); M. Hayashi, *The Southern Bluefin Tuna Cases*, cit., p. 361-362, p. 371.

eral action by Japan, New Zealand banned Japanese tuna fishing ships from its harbors.[28]

On August 27, 1999, the ITLOS handed down its decision in the Southern Bluefin Tuna Cases (New Zealand v. Japan and Australia v. Japan), ruling that the three countries were not allowed to exceed the fishing limits decided upon by common agreement and that even experimental fishing programs had to respect those limits. It also ordered the parties to resume negotiations.[29] These three countries complied with the ITLOS's order, and negotiations resumed.

In the meantime, the arbitration panel was set up. This tribunal decided to avail itself of the secretariat and chancellery of the International Centre for the Settlement of Investment Disputes (ICSID).[30]

The arbitral tribunal issued its decision on August 4, 2000. It held that without Japan's consent to refer the controversy to the arbitral tribunal, it "lack[ed] jurisdiction to entertain the merits of the dispute brought by Australia and New Zealand against Japan."[31] It acknowledged that the 1994 Convention established "the consensual nature of any reference of a dispute to either judicial settlement or arbitration" and added that "these provisions are meant to exclude compulsory jurisdiction."[32] It thus revoked the provisional measures ordered by the ITLOS but added: "[h]owever, revocation of the Order prescribing provisional measures does not mean that the parties may disregard the effects of that order or their own decisions made in conformity with it."[33] The arbitral tribunal stressed the "possibility of renewed negotiations,"[34] in accordance with

---

[28] C. Bell, *Japanese Tuna Boat Banned from NZ Ports*, in *The Dominion Post*, July 14, 1998, p. 2.

[29] *S. Bluefin Tuna Cases (N.Z. v. Japan; Austl. v. Japan)*, 38 I.L.M. 1624 (Int'l Trib. L. of the Sea 1999). See J. S. Barkin and E. R. DeSombre, "Unilateralism and Multilateralism in International Fisheries Management", in *Global Governance*, 2000, vol. 6, p. 339, for an overview of international fishing and related issues.

[30] International Centre for Settlement of Investment Disputes, http:// www.worldbank.org/ icsid/about/about.htm. Note that this was the first arbitral tribunal established on the basis of Annex VII of the UNCLOS.

[31] *S. Bluefin Tuna Case (N.Z.V. Japan; Austl. V. Japan)*, 39 I.L.M. 1359, 1391 (UNCLOS Arb. Trib. 2000).

[32] Id. p. 1389-1390.

[33] Id.

[34] Id. p. 1392.

Article 16.2 of the 1994 Convention, for which "failure to reach agreement on reference to the International Court of Justice or to arbitration shall not absolve parties to the dispute from the responsibility of continuing to seek to resolve it by any of the various peaceful means referred to in paragraph I above."[35]

In response to this decision, in December 2000, New Zealand revoked the prohibition on Japanese tuna fishing ships in its harbors.[36] Negotiations continued that led to a decision in 2001 to undertake a scientific program to measure the volume of the tuna stock.[37] This program was carried out by independent experts and included placing observers on board fishing ships to control the quantity of tuna fished.

On examination, this case exemplifies all distinctive features of administrative law.[38] There is an organization vested with authoritative powers. It adopts administrative decisions addressed to both constituent parties and other actors. Finally, there are judges empowered to settle disputes between the regulated actors arising out of the organization's decisions.

Once adopted, the global level decision – specifically, the Commission's decision – should be implemented by the States. In this regard, article 117 of the UNCLOS requires that "[a]ll States have the duty to take, or to cooperate with other States in taking, such measures for their respective

---

[35] «Negotiation, inquiry, mediation, conciliation, arbitration, judicial settlement or other peaceful means of their own choice.» Bluefin Tuna Convention, cit., art. 16(1).

[36] New Zealand Backgrounder, cit.

[37] Id.

[38] See generally C. Romano, "The Southern Bluefin Tuna Dispute: Hints of a World to Come...Like it or Not", in *Ocean Development and International Law*, 2001, vol. 32, p. 313; V. Roben, "The Southern Bluefin Tuna Cases: Re-Regionalization of the Settlement of Law of the Sea Disputes?", in *Zeitschrift für ausländisches öffentliches Recht und Völkerrecht*, 2002, vol. 62, p. 61; A. Boyle, "The Southern Bluefin Tuna Arbitration", in *International and Comparative Law Quarterly*, 2001, vol. 50, p. 447; D. J. Devine, "Compulsory Dispute Settlement in UNCLOS Undermined? Southern Bluefin Tuna Case: Australia and New Zealand v. Japan 4 August 2000", in *South African Yearbook of International Law*, 2000, vol. 25, p. 97; C. E. Foster, "The "Real Dispute" in the Southern Bluefin Tuna Case: A Scientific Dispute?", in *International Journal of Marine and Coastal Law*, 2001, vol. 16, p. 571; M. Hayashi, *The Southern Bluefin Tuna Cases*, cit.; J. Peel, "A Paper Umbrella Which Dissolves in the Rain? The Future for Resolving Fisheries Disputes Under UNCLOS in the Aftermath of Southern Bluefin Tuna Arbitration", in *Melbourne Journal of International Law*, 2002, vol. 3, p. 53; L. Sturtz, "Southern Bluefin Tuna Case: Australia and New Zealand V. Japan", in *Ecology Law Quarterly*, 2001, vol. 28, p. 455.

nationals as may be necessary for the conservation of the living resources of the high seas."[39] Yet, even in the top-down phase of implementation, the Commission interacts with members of domestic systems.

Compared to the more familiar State-level administrative law, global administrative law bears some differences. A first difference is the lack of exclusivity among international regimes. The rules governing tuna fishing are rooted in both a specific regime-the treaty for the protection of tuna-and in the general regime of the law of the sea.[40] The Commission for the Conservation of Southern Bluefin Tuna applies not only the norms of the treaty establishing it, but also decisions adopted by another international organization, the FAO.[41] In other words, three different international orders are inter-twined.

A second difference between global and State administrative law is the global law's high degree of self-regulation as regulators and the regulated exist on the same plane. The former collectively decide to submit to shared rules. Invitations to cooperate are used in order to ensure application of the same rules by third parties.

A third difference is that decisions made by independent committees on the basis of scientific criteria and negotiations concluded by agreements play a more important role in global administrative law than in domestic law. In domestic administrative law, decisions made by representative bodies are political decisions, and the unilateral decisions typical of "command and control" prevail.

A fourth difference is that the line between public and private is hardly clear at the global level. Extended members of the Commission include member States as well as fishing entities, which may be sub-State bodies or even private actors.[42]

---

[39] UNCLOS, cit., art. 117.

[40] See *Southern Bluefin Tuna Case (Australia & New Zealand v. Japan)*, ICSID (W. Bank) 91, 91-93, available at http://www.worldbank.org/icsid/bluefintuna/award080400.pdf, (Arbitral Tribunal UN Convention on the Law of the Sea 2000) (deciding to treat the controversy as «a single dispute arising under both Conventions» invoking the «parallelism of treaties» and admitting that «[t]he current range of international legal obligations benefits from a process of accretion and accumulation»).

[41] Food and Agriculture Organization of the United Nations, http:// www.fao.org/.

[42] Neither the treaty norms nor the norms adopted by the organization define the nature of «fishing entities». They must however have ships flying their own flag.

The administrative law inherent in the Bluefin Tuna case may be defined as global[43] even though this qualification may seem unacceptable to those who believe that administrative law cannot be global by definition. Some believe that administrative law is always domestic *par excellence* and that if it is global, then it cannot be administrative law, since global law concerns relations between States.

In this section, I respond to some of the current questions regarding global administrative law. First, how is it structured? Does it operate according to international law by means of negotiation or according to traditional administrative law by "command and control"?

Second, on which grounds does global administrative law rest? National administrative laws are sustained by a constitutional framework that exists above and beyond the State. Beyond the State, there lies a global legal space, which is, at most, a system of "global governance." Can there then be a world administration without a world government?

Finally, what are the relationships between global administrative law and domestic administrative law? Is there a mismatch, an overlap, or integration between the two levels? Does the emergence of global administrative law alter the structure of national public powers?

---

[43] This term calls for an immediate specification. It is the most commonly used. There are, however, two alternative terms: the more traditional «universal law» and «world-wide law» (*droit mondial*) preferred by the French. See, e.g., G. D. Romagnosi, *Diritto pubblico universale* [Universal Public Law] (3rd ed. 1833); M. Delmas-Marty, *Trois défis pour un droit mondial*, Paris, Seuil, 1998. Here the term «international law,» coined by Jeremy Bentham to indicate the relations between sovereign States as unitary actors, is to be avoided. J. Bentham, *An Introduction To The Principles of Morals and Legislation* (1789), p. 6 (J.H. Burns and H.L.A. Hart eds., Oxford University Press, rev. ed. 1996); see generally M. W. Janis, "Jeremy Bentham and the Fashioning of International Law", in *American Journal of International Law*, 1984, vol. 78, p. 405. The expression "international institutional law" has been used to indicate the law of international organizations, but mainly with regard to their internal features (like the relations between international organizations and their employees).

2. THE SPREAD OF GLOBAL REGULATORY SYSTEMS

Global regulatory systems[44] are quite widespread. A quick overview of the areas in which they operate, and of the number and multiplicity of regulators in many sectors, illustrates the density of global regulation.

Trade, finance, the environment, fishing, exploitation of marine resources, air and maritime navigation, agriculture, food, postal services, telecommunications, intellectual property, the use of space, nuclear energy, and energy sources are all subject to global regulation. But global regulation involves many other sectors as well, such as the production of sugar, pepper, tea, and olive oil. It can be said that there is no realm of human activity wholly untouched by ultra-State or global rules.[45]

Goods and functions that escape State control are regulated at the global level.[46] States are not able to control the fishing of migratory fish species, just as they are powerless to unilaterally limit the use of greenhouse effect-producing gases or to prevent the spread of financial crises. When their borders and functions overlap and conflict, as in the case of high seas fishing, States benefit by giving up their regulatory powers to other global, public authorities.

These needs lead to the establishment of global regulatory bodies, called international or intergovernmental organizations. Their current number varies according to the criteria used to define them. According to an assessment based on more restrictive criteria, there were two hundred and forty-five such organizations in 2004; according to surveys based on more open-ended criteria, there were one thousand; and according to a

[44] The term «global regulatory system» is preferable to the frequently used «global governance» (which indicates the activity of governing in the absence of an institution – the government), «international regime» (which depends upon a term to be avoided in this framework, as mentioned above) and «international organization» (descriptive and limited to the structural nature). This section does not examine «regional» bodies, like the European Union, which have developed public powers similar to those of the States, even though they themselves are different from States.

[45] See generally R. Wolfrum and V. Röben (eds.), *Developments of International Law in Treaty Making*, Berlin, Springer, 2005, for an overview of the breadth of global administrative law.

[46] P. G. Cerny, "Globalization and the Changing Logic of Collective Action", in *International Organization*, 1995, vol. 49, p. 595, p. 618.

count based on even more liberal criteria, there exist 7306.[47] To appreciate the meaning of these numbers, consider that there are more of such organizations than there are States (one hundred and ninety-three States belong to the United Nations).[48]

Also interesting is the speed with which these organizations have been established, mostly within the last quarter of a century. In this same period, moreover, the participation of national public authorities in such organizations has tripled.[49] Furthermore, in several sectors, there is more than one regulatory authority, and each body has a different responsibility within the same sector. The International Maritime Organization (IMO)[50] and the International Seabed Authority (ISA)[51] regulate the use of the seas, as does the International Tribunal for the Law of the Sea (ITLOS).[52] The environment is regulated by the World Meteorological Organization (WMO),[53] the United Nations Convention on Climate Change-Clean Development Mechanism (UNFCCC-CDM),[54] the Global Environmental Facility (GEF),[55] and their respective implementation bodies – the United Nations Environment

[47] See Union of International Associations, *Yearbook of International Organizations: Guide to Global and Civil Society Networks 2004-2005*, 2005, vol. 1, p. 2914. See also N. M. Blokker and H. G. Schermers (eds.), *Proliferation of International Organizations: Legal Issues*, The Hague, Kluwer Law International, 2001, pp. 3-4.

[48] Growth in United Nations Membership, 1945-2005, http://www.un. org/Overview/unmember.html.

[49] Union of International Associations, *Yearbook of International Organizations: Guide to Global and Civil Society Networks 2004-2005*, cit., p. 38-39.

[50] See International Maritime Organization, Introduction to IMO, http://www.imo.org/About/mainframe.asp?topic_id=3.

[51] See International Seabed Authority, About the Authority, http://isa.org.jm/en/about/default.htm.

[52] See International Tribunal for the Law of the Sea, General Information: Overview Introduction, http://www.itlos.org/general_information/ overview/intro_en.shtml.

[53] See World Meteorological Organization, About WMO, http://www. wmo.ch/web-en/about.html.

[54] U.N. Framework Convention on Climate Change, May 9, 1992, 1771 U.N.T.S. 165 [hereinafter UNFCCC]. See also UNFCCC, The Mechanisms under the Kyoto Protocol: Joint Implementation, the Clean Development Mechanism and Emissions Trading, http://unfccc.int/kyoto_mechanisms/items/1673.php (last visited Jan. 23, 2006).

[55] Global Environmental Facility, http://www.gefweb.org.

Program,[56] the United Nations Development Program,[57] and the World Bank.[58]

Many bodies are active in the economic and financial area, such as the International Monetary Fund,[59] the World Bank,[60] the Basel Committee on Banking Supervision,[61] the Financial Stability Forum (FSF),[62] the Financial Stability Institute (FSI),[63] the Committee on Payment and Settlement Systems,[64] the Egmont Group,[65] the Financial Action Task Force on Money Laundering (FATF),[66] the International Organization of Securities Commissioners (IOSCO),[67] the International Association of Insurance Supervisors (IAIS),[68] and the International Accounting Standard Board (IASB).[69] The need to coordinate all of these organizations leads to the creation of additional bodies in which several organizations participate, like the Joint Forum, established in 1996 between IOSCO and IAIS under the aegis of the Basel Committee.[70]

To summarize, there are lots of global regulatory systems. The centrality of the State to the notion of public powers has become an optical illusion. This does not mean, however, that the global legal order has supplanted the State, nor that it has become dominant, inasmuch as it

---

[56] U.N. Environment Program, http://www.unep.org.

[57] U.N. Development Program, http://www.undp.org.

[58] The World Bank, http://www.worldbank.org (last visited Nov. 23, 2005).

[59] International Monetary Fund, http://www.imf.org/external/index.htm.

[60] The World Bank, http://www.worldbank.org.

[61] Basel Committee on Banking Supervision, http://www.bis.org/bcbs/.

[62] Financial Stability Forum, http://www.fsforum.org/home/home. html.

[63] Financial Stability Institute, http://www.bis.org/fsi.

[64] Committee on Payment and Settlement Systems Background Information, http://www. bis.org/cpss/cpssinfo0l.htm.

[65] The Egmont Group Financial Intelligence Units, http://www.egmont group.org/about_ egmont.pdf.

[66] The Financial Action Task Force, http://www.fatf-gafi.org.

[67] General information on IOSCO, http://www.iosco.org/about/.

[68] International Association of Insurance Supervisors, http://www.iais web.org/132_ENU_ HTML.asp.

[69] International Accounting Standards Board: History, http://www.iasb.org/about/history. asp.

[70] IAIS - Joint Forum, http://www.iaisweb.org/l34_l343_ENU_HTML.asp.

is also through global regulatory systems that domestic public powers are able to make their voices heard.

This also suggests that the global legal order is a "plural" order in the sense that it lacks unity. Even larger bodies, like the UN family, are not hierarchically superior to the others, nor are they more influential.

3. DEVELOPMENT THROUGH MUTUAL CONNECTIONS

States develop from and around a center. Global administrative institutions develop through mutual connections from peripheral points, in federative or associate forms.

The simplest and most common way that global administrative institutions develop is when States associate in order to establish an ultra-State body; like when the UN international organizations arise from agreements between States but also promote other agreements. For example, the International Maritime Organization has promoted agreements in the areas of security, protection of the marine environment, and the maritime transport of nuclear materials.[71]

In addition to States, sub-State organs may also join to establish international bodies. National bodies for the regulation of financial markets are associated in the IOSCO, national insurance regulating bodies come together in the IAIS, the International Competition Network (ICN) brings together national competition authorities, the Financial Stability Forum (FSI), promoted by the finance ministries and central banks of the G7 countries, brings together finance ministers and heads of the central banks.

A third type of global organization is comprised of neither States, nor of lower level, sub-State entities, but of other global organizations, acting alone or together. For instance, the Commission on Phytosanitary Measures was established by the FAO,[72] and the International

---

[71] See, e.g., Convention for the Safety of Life at Sea (SOLAS), Nov. 1, 1974, http://www. imo.org/home.asp.

[72] Food and Agriculture Organization of the United Nations, http://www.fao.org/documents/ show_cdr.asp?url_fils=/Docrep/W9474T/w9474t 04.htm.

Centre for Settlement of Investment Disputes was established by the World Bank.[73]

In other cases, different global organizations get together to establish another global organization. The Financial Stability Institute (FSI) was set up in 1999 by the Bank for International Settlements and the Basel Committee on Banking Supervision. The *Codex Alimentarius* Commission[74] was established by the FAO and the World Health Organization (WHO). The World Trade Organization (WTO) and the United Nations Conference on Trade and Development (UNCTAD) together established the International Trade Centre.[75]

The horizontal interpenetration of global structures is reinforced by organizational and functional relationships. Examples of organizational ties are the participation of the WTO's Director General on the Executive Board of the UN, the World Bank President's concurrent presidency of the Administrative Council of the International Centre for Settlement of Investment Disputes, the FAO Director General's nomination of the Secretary of the Commission on Phytosanitary Measures, and the appointment of the Secretary of the UNFCC-CDM by the Secretary General of the UN.

Examples of functional relationships are the network of agreements between the World Intellectual Property Organization (WIPO) and the WTO; the close relationship between the Universal Postal Union (UPU), the International Civil Aviation Organization (ICAO), and the International Telecommunication Union (ITU); between the Office International des Epizooties (OIE) and the FAO, WTO, *Codex Alimentarius* Commission, and the WHO; between the Financial Stability Forum (FSF), the IOSCO and IAIS; and between the International Olive Oil Council and the *Codex Alimentarius* Commission.[76]

Even closer are the functional relationships between the WTO and the Commission on Phytosanitary Measures, and between the WTO

---

[73] International Centre for Settlement of Investment Disputes, http://www.worldbank.org/icsid/about/about.htm

[74] *Codex alimentarius*, http://www.codexalimentarius.net/web/index_ en.jsp.

[75] International Trade Centre UNCTAD/WTO, http://www.intracen.org/menus/itc.htm.

[76] See C. Tietje, "Global Governance and Inter-Agency Co-operation in International Economic Law", in *Journal of World Trade*, 2002, vol. 36, p. 501 for a characterization of inter-agency cooperation as a "central element of global economic governance."

and the OIE. The standards set forth by the Commission are not binding in themselves, but have become so within the framework of the WTO because WTO members must establish their phytosanitary measures on the basis of the Commission's standards. The same holds true for the standards of the OIE.[77] Thus, standards established by one organization become binding rules by virtue of the force given to them by another organization.[78]

Finally, the connection between different global regimes is strengthened by the fact that some regimes "lend" their institutions to others for the resolution of disputes. For instance, the International Centre for Settlement of Investment Disputes, instituted for the resolution of controversies regarding World Bank investments, also decides conflicts regarding the North American Free Trade Agreement, the Energy Charter

---

[77] The WTO provides that «Members shall base their sanitary or phytosanitary measures on international standards...»and that «[s]anitary or phytosanitary measures which conform to international standards, guidelines or recommendations shall be deemed to be necessary to protect human, animal or plant life or health, and presumed to be consistent with the relevant provisions of this Agreement and of GATT 1994.» World Trade Org. Agreement on the Application of Sanitary and Phytosanitary Measures art. 3.1-3.2, Apr. 15, 1994, available at http://docsonline.wto.org/ (follow «Browse documents, Frequently Consulted, Legal Texts and Agreements» hyperlink; then follow «Agreement on the Application of Sanitary and Phytosanitary Measures» hyperlink). The OIE, established in 1924, now has 164 members. Office Int'l des Epizooties, What is the OIE? Home Page, http://www.oie.int/eng/OIE/en_oie.htm (last visited Oct. 18, 2005). In 1998 it signed an official agreement with the WTO which provides for cooperation, consultation, participation, exchange of information and documents and joint action concerning the standards, guidelines or recommendations of the OIE. Agreement between the World Trade Org. and the Office Int'I des Epizooties, WTO-OIE, May 4, 1998, http://www.oie.int/eng/oie/accords/en_accord_omc.htm.

[78] See K. Raustiala and D. G. Victor, "The Regime Complex for Plant Genetic Resources", in *International Organization*, 2004, vol. 58, n. 2, p. 277, for a discussion in this vein of the "regime complex," made up of "elemental regimes" which are characterized by a "horizontal, overlapping structure" and the "presence of divergent rules and norms." In other cases, the standards set forth by global bodies become binding by virtue of the decisions of national administrations, as in the case of norms established by the Basel Committee on Banking Supervision, which are given executive force by national central banks. See Basel Committee on Banking Supervision, History of the Basel Committee and its Membership, (Oct. 2004), http://www.bis.org/bcbs/history.pdf. This poses the problem of "private governance regimes," on which, for American law, see H. Schepel, "Constituting Private Governance Regimes: Standards Bodies in American Law", in C. Joerges, I.-J. Sand and G. Teubner (eds), *Transnational Governance and Constitutionalism*, Oxford, Hart, 2004, p. 161.

Treaty, the Cartagena Free Trade Agreement, and the Colonia Investment Protocol of Mercosur.[79]

This system of separate regimes, which are connected into a network by piecemeal ties and cross-references, is not the result of a unitary design and, as we have already seen, does not embody a unitary structure. Instead, it has the following characteristics: it is cooperative and non-hierarchical; it has no center; it does not develop according to a plan, but spontaneously and incrementally; it creates a thick regulatory mass.

Finally, though originating in the States – which continue to keep it under control – this system becomes increasingly less dependent on them as it develops autonomously through voluntary, spontaneous processes.[80] As we shall see ahead, national public powers compensate their relative loss of power by participating in the decision-making processes of global bodies. The incremental and progressive nature of this process advises against attempting a taxonomy. It is instead important to outline its fundamental traits and trace the path of its development.

4. A FLUID ORGANIZATION

As we have seen, the establishment of global regulatory systems is driven by three tendencies: the States' pooling of some of their own tasks in bodies operating at a level other than their own, the need of sub-State bodies to forge relationships with each other, and increased co-operation among international organizations at the global level.

The recurrence of these three factors might suggest that these organizations are constituted according to a homogeneous pattern. On the contrary, their functions vary – there is no real separation of powers

---

[79] See International Centre for Settlement of Investment Disputes, About ICSID, 7 (2005), htpp://www.worldbank.org/icsid/about/about.htm.

[80] C. Moellers, "Transnational Governance without a Public Law?", in *Transnational Governance and Constitutionalism*, cit., p. 327, (observing that there is a "generation of norms as a spontaneous coordination process, normally between formally equal actors").

within them, and the distinctions between participants and non-participants, and between public and private participants, are uncertain.[81]

The most recurrent functions in global regulatory systems are coordination, the promotion of cooperation, harmonization, and standardization. But there are also additional functions, like the allocation of scarce resources (for instance, the allocation of radio frequencies by the International Telecommunication Union),[82] assistance and the provision of services (for example, the work of the International Organization for Migration,[83] the WHO, and the OIE), and protection (for instance, the United Nations High Commissioner for Refugees (UNHCR)).[84]

The organizational structure of global organizations can usually be broken down into four parts: a collegial body, usually referred to as an assembly, in which all of the participants – States, other national organizations, and international organizations – are present; a more restricted collegial body, usually called a council, whose members are elected by the assembly; an executive body, called secretariat, made up of regular employees of the organization; and committees, generally made up of functionaries of national administrations.

The structures vary from one organization to another. There are some, for instance, that do not have their own secretariat. The Basel Committee on Banking Supervision Secretariat is provided by the Bank for International Settlements,[85] and the Paris Club committee (1956) is supported by the French Finance Ministry.[86] Other global organizations have additional regional or decentralized apparatuses. Still others are constituted in the form of a "group." This is the case of the World Bank Group, which is made up of five different institutions – the International

[81] See B. Koremonos, C. Lipson and D. Snidal, "The Rational Design of International Institutions", in *International Organization*, 2001, vol. 55, p. 761 for a discussion on the "flexibility of arrangements" of global institutions.

[82] International Telecommunications Union, Purposes (2004), http:// www.itu.int/aboutitu/ overview/ purposes.html.

[83] The International Organization for Migration was first established in 1951 as the «Intergovernmental Committee for European Migrations.»

[84] United Nations High Commissioner for Refugees, Basic Facts, 1 (2005), http://www/ unhcr.ch/cgi-bin/texis/vtx/basics.

[85] Basel Committee on Banking Supervision, http://www.bis.org/bcbs.

[86] Paris Club, http://www.clubdeparis.org/en/index.php.

Bank for Reconstruction and Development (IBRD), the International Development Association (IDA), the International Finance Corporation (IFC), the Multilateral Investment Guarantee Agency (MIGA) and the International Centre for Settlement of Investment Disputes (ICSID).[87]

While States have a stable division of powers between their different organs, global institutions have, at most, a division of functions between the different organs. And there are even organs that are made up of the same participants but have different capacities and perform different tasks. Within the WTO, this is the case of the General Council, the Dispute Settlement Body, and the Trade Policy Review Body.

The lines distinguishing participants from non-participants and States from private organizations (governmental and non-governmental organizations, to use the common terminology) are also unclear. In the International Civil Defense Organization (ICDO), both affiliated members and associated members without the right to vote participate.[88] In the IAIS, observers such as insurance companies, associations thereof, practitioners, and consultants participate.[89] There are many governmental organizations that admit non-governmental organizations as members: the UPU, ITU, WMO, ILO, WIPO, and the International Civil Aviation Organization (ICAO). In the ICAO, for example, the International Air Transport Association, the Airports Council, the International Federation of Airline Pilots' Associations, and the International Council of Aircraft Owner and Pilot Associations all participate.[90] Finally, many global organizations accept unions of States (mainly the European Union) as a member. The WTO, ICDO, and the International Olive Oil Council all do this.[91]

---

[87] International Bank for Reconstruction and Development, http:// www.web.worldbank. org; International Development Association, http:// www.web.worldbank.org; International Centre for Settlement of Investment Disputes, http://www.worldbank.org/icsid/about/about. htm; International Finance Corporation, http://www.ifc.org/about; Multilateral Investment Guarantee Agency, http://www.miga.org.

[88] International Civil Defense Organization, About ICDO Membership (2005), http://www. icdo.org/conmem.htm.

[89] International Association of Insurance Supervisors, About IAIS (2005), http://www. iaisweb.org/l32_ENU_HTML.asp.

[90] International Civil Aviation Organization, How it Works (2005), http://www.icao.int/cgi/ goto_m.pi?/icao/en/howworks.htm.

[91] See e.g., Understanding the WTO: The Organization (2005), http://www.wto.org/English/ thewto_e/whatis_e/tif_e/org6_e.

As we move farther away from the State, the line between public and private becomes more and more unclear. From the organizational standpoint, the global legal order does not follow a single model. It is instead an example of "ad-hoc-cracy," in the sense that it adapts to the functions to be performed, sector by sector. Functions, organizations, the internal balance of powers, and the relationship between public and private all vary according to specific needs.

5. THE JOINT DECISION-MAKING TECHNIQUE

The above examination of global organizations suggests that global administration does not exist in isolation from the national level. Examining their decision-making processes confirms this diagnosis. Global administrations are inspired by the techniques of joint action, mutual conditioning, composition and balancing, and progressiveness.[92]

It is just as misguided to argue that States have an exclusive hold on the reins of global power, as it is to think that global decisions escape their power.[93] There is a mixed, gray area between global regulatory systems and national regulators. This can serve the States and the global system, and sometimes both at the same time-States in making their voices heard in the global system, and the global system in penetrating States to reach civil society and local actors, even if this reach is generally lacking in global public powers. The global legal order is a saprophyte order unable to live on its own; it is necessarily related with others, and it makes them permeable, while reinforcing them at the same time. In contrast with international law, in global law, the two levels come together.

The committees of global organizations comprised of national representatives, the mixed (global-domestic) network of offices, and the

---

[92] Note that according to Bentham, international law and national law are independent of each other, and the question of whether an international law norm applies to national law depends on whether this norm has been accepted into national law. J. Bentham, *An Introduction To The Principles of Morals and Legislation* (1789), cit., p. 296. See also M. W. Janis, *Jeremy Bentham and the Fashioning of International Law*, cit., p. 408.

[93] For a discussion of the different roles and functions of international organizations, see A. Caffarena, *Le organizzazioni internazionali*, Bologna, il Mulino, 2001, pp. 36-43.

national implementation of global decisions all constitute elements of the gray area in which global and domestic regulatory systems co-operate to pursue a common interest, even if for different reasons.

Global regulatory systems relive the States' formative experience of "polysynody."[94] There is a panoply of committees, mainly consultative, in which proposals are elaborated. These committees are made up of national civil servants or experts, or representatives of national interests. The distribution of work is clear. Representatives of domestic political bodies sit in the highest bodies of the global administrations. To see how this works, take the examples of the WMO, the Commission on Phytosanitary Measures, the *Codex Alimentarius* Commission, and the IAIS.

This polysynody addresses the need for specialization, but it mainly serves the purpose of communicating with national administrations and civil society. In fact, it is through the committees that global regulators are able to stretch their own scope of action within States, to listen to their needs, and to acquire information. At the same time, committees serve States and national interests in making their voices heard at the global level, and in keeping global decision making processes under control. The conditioning is mutual.

Joint decision making also occurs in the sharing of functions between national offices and the offices of global regulatory systems. An example of this is the tuna fishing case, in which the Commission has direct relations with the States and with fishing entities. Likewise, in most other cases, the global organization has relationships with both member States and the national offices. These offices are directly designated by the international organization concerned, and usually operate on the basis of orders by, and respond to, the same organization. For instance, the OIE has direct relations with the State sectoral offices of the different

---

[94] On this matter see the pivotal work by C.I. De Saint-Pierre, *Discours sur la Polysynodie* (1718), Italian translation in C.I. De Saint-Pierre, *Scritti politici. Per la pace perpetua e sulla polisinodia*, Lecce, Milella, 1996. Saint-Pierre's ideas were subsequently discussed by Rousseau. The plurality of councils was supposed to help the king by placing competent persons at his side, in order to provide counsel and information. The polysynody was opposed to the absolute power, defined as "vizery." This is one of the first theories of bureaucracy as a stable body of experts.

countries.[95] Article IV of the International Plant Protection Convention established the Commission on Phytosanitary Measures and provided that each contracting party shall establish a national plant protection organization, corresponding to the global institution,[96] set forth the tasks to be assigned to it, and required that such organization cooperate at the international level.[97] Furthermore, Article VIII.1 provides that member States undertake to cooperate with one another in establishing regional (meaning pluri-State) plant protection organizations in appropriate areas.[98]

The global and domestic administrative levels depend on each other in the sense that decision-making processes begin at the global level, either with preliminary examination or a decision, and they conclude at the national level, either with a decision or with the implementation of the global decision. In the first case, the domestic decision depends on preliminary examination, carried out by the international organization. In the second case, the effectiveness of the decision adopted by an international organization depends on the implementation by national offices.

An example of the first type of decision making process is that provided and regulated by the Patent Cooperation Treaty. This provides that a patent application can be submitted to the international organization, which carries out a preliminary examination and then transfers the procedure to the national office specified by the applicant. The national office carries out further examinations and makes a decision.[99]

Much more frequent is the second type of decision-making process, where enforcement lies with member States. This is because, with a few exceptions, global regulatory systems lack executive apparatuses. For

---

[95] International Agreement for the Creation at Paris of an International Office for Epizootics, Annex, art. II, Jan. 17, 1925, 57 L.N.T.S. 135.

[96] The norm provides that «[e]ach contracting party shall make provision, to the best of its ability, for an official plant protection organization with the main responsibilities set out in this Article.» International Plant Protection Convention art. IV, Dec. 6, 1951-May 1, 1952, 23 U.S.T. 2767, 150 U.N.T.S. 67.

[97] Id. art. Xl.

[98] Id. art. IX.

[99] Patent Cooperation Treaty, arts. 31-42, June 19, 1970, 28 U.S.T. 7645, 7677-87, 1160 U.N.T.S. 231, 247-52.

example, according to Annex C (control, inspection and approval procedures) of the Agreement on the application of sanitary and phytosanitary measures, WTO members must ensure procedures to fulfill global sanitary and phytosanitary measures.[100]

In both cases, global administrative functions condition domestic administrative functions, and global administrations eventually appropriate some of the States' own tasks.

Both when global administrative acts are non-binding and when compliance is voluntary,[101] and when they are binding but depend on national offices for their implementation, global regulatory systems compensate for their weakness by keeping execution under their control. For example, the WIPO provides for an Advisory Committee on Enforcement of Industrial Property Rights, which elaborates best practices and implementation procedures.[102] Other organizations check up on implementation, or make use of the assistance of national offices or enable private actors to call their attention to implementation gaps. In this way, the acts are non-binding, while the procedures implementing them are binding.[103]

The mixture of global and national is, in these cases, particularly strong and complex. Domestic administrations that have collaborated to reach a decision must collaborate again, this time individually, to ensure implementation. Mediation at the national level is fundamental. The decision-making process is mixed, and cannot be labeled as exclusively global or national. Therefore, there is no clear separation between global law and domestic law. Joint decision-making renders national legal systems porous. It disaggregates them, undermining the paradigm of the State as a unity, as when, for instance, it is the global regulatory system

[100] Agreement on Sanitary and Phytosanitary Measures Annex C, Apr. 15, 1994, Marrakesh Agreement Establishing the World Trade Organization, Annex 1A, available at http://www.wto.org/English/docs_e/legal_e/legal_e.htm.

[101] This is the case with many standards. See, e.g., S. A. Shapiro, "International Trade Agreements, Regulatory Protection, and Public Accountability", in *Administrative Law Review*, 2002, vol. 54, p. 435 and 438-440.

[102] Press Release, WIPO, Advisory Committee on Enforcement Holds Inaugural Meeting (June 16, 2003), http://www.wipo.int/wilma/pressinfo-en/ 200306/msg00001.html.

[103] F. Morgenstern, *Legal Problems of International Organization*, Cambridge, Cambridge University Press, 1986, p. 125.

that designates the competent national office to maintain direct relations with it. It penetrates into the national systems, which thus lose their impermeability or exclusivity and are required to cooperate with the higher level. It by-passes the States, insofar as it directly addresses national citizens, organizations and corporations, which become the targets of global decisions. Finally, it fosters the lateral opening of national systems, which become able to communicate with each other by means of equivalence agreements. These render arbitrage between national legal systems possible. As a result, the boundary between the State and the global is blurred.[104]

Similarly, in the opposite direction, there is a continuous exchange from the State level to the global one, in that the global level absorbs principles common to domestic systems like a sponge, but this creates additional problems. The national models in circulation are in fact those of the dominant countries or at least those of States with an evolved administrative law. But these do not easily fit other countries, as is demonstrated by the principle of open bidding for the tender of public contracts, which encounters difficulties in those countries in which public contracts are used for the pursuit of other public ends, such as the development of particular zones, and ad hoc, preferential, regimes are set up to favor this.

In conclusion, the porousness of national legal orders and the sponge-like nature of the global one make mutual conditioning possible. If the States can capture global organizations, global organizations, in turn, can also capture the States.[105]

---

[104] S. Sassen, "The Participation of States and Citizens in Global Governance", in *Indiana Journal of Global Legal Studies*, 2003, vol. 10, p. 5, 8.

[105] On «integrated decision-making,» see J. C. Dernbach, "Achieving Sustainable Development: The Centrality and Multiple Facets of Integrated Decisionmaking", in *Indiana Journal of Global Legal Studies*, 2003, vol. 10, p. 247, 279-280. On regulatory agencies becoming captives of the regulated industry and the "capture" theory, see M. H. Bernstein, *Regulating Business by Independent Commission*, 157 (1955); J. Q. Wilson, "The Politics of Regulation", in J. Q. Wilson (ed.), *The Politics of Regulation*, New York, Basic Books, 1980, p. 357- 360.

6. THE GLOBAL AND THE DOMESTIC ARE NOT TWO SEPARATE LEVELS

We have seen that between the global and the domestic spheres there is a gray area of mixed bodies and procedures, joint decisions and parasitical systems. All of this enables us to understand that there is no clear line of separation between the global and the national.

In these cases, the distinction between international and domestic law does not hold. The weakness of the recurring metaphor of levels is also clear. According to this metaphor, public powers are set up on such different levels: regional, national, and global.

The continuity between the two orders under examination here – the national and the global[106] – is clear if we consider the relationships between citizens (or better yet, nationals, in the sense of persons belonging to a nation) and global administrations. Global administrative law ascribes two fundamental rights to citizens, and these are derived from domestic administrative law: the right to participation and the right to defense. The former consists of the chance to intervene in the course of a global or mixed administrative proceeding; the latter implies a citizen's right to appeal to a global judicial authority for the review of national (or global) decisions.

An example of participation in an individual administrative proceeding (and thus of adjudication) is in the abovementioned Patent Cooperation Treaty. This provides that, during the International Preliminary Examination, the applicant has "a right to communicate orally and in writing" with the "International Preliminary Examining Authority," which must, in turn, issue a written opinion, to which the applicant may respond.

The participation in an administrative proceeding in which multiple parties are interested, and that thus has a general character, is provided for in the projects financed by the IBRD and the IDA. Interested parties may request the partially independent World Bank Inspection Panel for an opinion.[107]

---

[106] An analogous examination of the relations between the regional and global level ought to be undertaken.

[107] See, e.g., The Inspection Panel, India: Mumbai Urban Transport Project (2004). See also B. Kingsbury, N. Krisch and R. B. Stewart, *The Emergence of Global Administrative Law*, p. 20-21 (N.Y.U. School of Law Inst. far Int'l Law and Justice, Working Paper No. 1, 2004),

A genuine administrative judicial system has thus evolved in the global legal system. We will turn to this later. It is interesting now to underscore the quantity and the variety of the relationships being established between national citizens or businesses, global adjudicating bodies, and domestic administrations.

Disputes between the corporations of one State and the public authorities of another may be brought before the ICSID, a global organization with the task of conciliation and arbitration.[108] Likewise, chapter 19, Article 1904 of the NAFTA treaty empowers a Bi-national Review Panel to review the decision of a national administrative body, on the basis of the national law of that State and upon the application of a private business from another State.[109]

The World Intellectual Property Organization Arbitration and Mediation Center (WIPO) can hear disputes between a domain name registrant and a third party holding the same registration in the context of country code top-level domain names, like ".fr" or ".ro" The question is brought before a Dispute Resolution Service Provider approved by the Internet Corporation for Assigned Names and Numbers (ICANN), which then names an administrative panel to rule upon the application. The decision then must be implemented by the national registration administrator, which in many countries has a public character.[110] The "WTO Dispute Settlement Body also has the job of reviewing the deci-

---

available at http://www.iilj.org/global_adlaw/documents/10l20502_KingsburyKrischStewart. pdf.

[108] Convention on the Settlement of Investment Disputes Between States and Nationals of Other States of 1966 art. 25, Aug. 27, 1965, 17 U.S.T. 1270, 575 U.N.T.S. 159 (entered into force Oct. 14, 1966). See also *Tokios Tokeles v. Ukraine*, Case No. ARB/02/18, Decision on Jurisdiction (Int'l Ctr. For Settlement of Inv. Disputes 2004) (action by Lithuanian business enterprise against government of Ukraine).

[109] For an example of a Panel decision conducted pursuant to Article 1904, see In the Matter of: Certain Iodinated Contrast Media Used for Radiographic Imaging, Originating in or Exported from the United States of America (including the Commonwealth of Puerto Rico), CDA-USA-2000-1904-02 (Binational Panel Pursuant to the N. Am. Free Trade Agreement 2003). See also G. R Winham, "NAFTA Chapter 19 and the Development of International Administrative Law - Applications in Antidumping and Competition Law", in *Journal of World Trade*, 1998, vol. 32, p. 65, 70-71 (describing general details of Chapter 19).

[110] See generally WIPO, *WIPO Arbitration and Mediation Rules*, Pub. No. 446 (E) (effective Oct. 1, 2002), http://arbiter.wipo.int/center/publications/e446.pdf. For an example of a WIPO decision, see Casio Keisanki Kabushki Kaisha v. Fulviu Mihai Fodoreanu, No. DRO2003-0002.

sions of national administrations. For instance, it reviews whether or not a national body has fulfilled its duty to give a "reasoned and adequate explanation."[111]

These examples are paradigmatic in explaining the continuity between the domestic administrative order and the global one. Actors belonging to a given national administrative system appeal to global judicial organs for the review of contested decisions in disputes with the public organs of States other than those of which they are nationals. As we have seen, this does not unfold in a stereotypical way according to fixed and conventional models. Some global judicial organs decide according to global law, others according to domestic law. Sometimes they handle disputes between a private actor and the public body of another domestic system; other times they adjudicate controversies between two private actors that also, albeit indirectly, involve a domestic administrative authority.

As we have seen, the quantity and variety of these intersecting ties between the "two levels" demonstrates that there is continuity – not cleavage – between them.

7. AN ADMINISTRATION WITH NO CONSTITUTIONAL FOUNDATION

Administrative law has thus moved beyond its natural domain of the State into a territory where it was formerly denied citizenship. It has developed rapidly, quickly losing its embryonic character and developing unique features, distinct from those of State administrative law. But in contrast to the State legal system, in the global legal order, administrative law does not have a constitutional foundation.

The constitutional framework holding up domestic administrative law is lacking in the global arena. Here, there is no government or higher institution, but just a body of sectoral sub-governments. There are, however, signs that international law is beginning a process of con-

---

(WIPO July 22, 2003), http://arbiter.wipo.int/domains/decisions/html/2003/dro2003-0002.html.

[111] Appellate Body Report, United States - Definitive Safeguard Measures on Imports of Certain Steel Products, 5, WT/DS248/AB/R (Nov. 10, 2003).

stitutionalization.[112] The recognition of human rights, rules governing the sources of law, and the rise of a penal system are preliminary signs. But these are still rudimentary and, in any case, less developed than the rules and principles of national administrative law. For this reason, global administrative law is known as a "private law framework of public institutions."[113]

The absence of a constitutional foundation to global administration and administrative law raises the much-discussed issue of their accountability.[114] This is because, unlike in the States, there is no intermediary between a representative body and the executive – that is, the government or cabinet. The following argument is commonly advanced: the State is the locus of democracy. If we escape from the State, democracy will be eroded, and we will have a global technocracy, capable of dialogue only with national bureaucracies.[115]

Yet, the absence of an executive vertex, accountable before a representative body, actually increases the pressure on global adminis-

[112] See generally D. Z. Cass, "The 'Constitutionalization' of International Trade Law: Judicial Norm-Generation as the Engine of Constitutional Development in International Trade", in *European Journal of International Law*, 2001, vol. 12, p. 39 (arguing that 'constitutionalization' results from the generation of constitutional-type norms and structures by the decision-making of the Appellate Body of the World Trade Organization); B.-O. Bryde, "Konstitutionalisierung des Voelkerrechts und Internationalisierung des Verfassungsrechts", in *Der Staat*, 2003, vol. 42, p. 61-75 (discussing the constitutionalization of international law and the internationalization of constitutional law as related processes that have a common source in twentieth century thought that only accepts political authority as legitimate when it protects human rights).

[113] C. Moellers, *Transnational Governance without a Public Law?*, cit., p. 327. See also P. G. Cerny, *Globalization and the Changing Logic of Collective Action*, cit., p. 618.

[114] This issue is rooted in some questionable assumptions. One holds that democracy is the only form for the legitimation of power (law is another form of legitimation). Another is the assumption that democracy in global institutions ought to take the same form as in national legal systems (but must global institutions adapt to the democracy of the States, or should democracy instead adapt to global institutions?).

[115] See M. Shapiro, *"Deliberative," "Independent" Technocracy v. Democratic Politics: Will the Globe Echo the E.U.?*, p. 5-7 (N.Y.U. School of Law Inst. for Int'l Law and justice, Working Paper No.5, 2004), available at http://www.iilj.org/papers/2004/2004.5.htm; cf. R. W. Grant and R. O. Keohane, *Accountability and Abuses of Power in World Politics*, p. 12-13 (N.Y.U. School of Law Inst. for Int'l Law and justice, Working Paper No.7, 2004), available at http://www.iilj.org/papers/2004/2004.7.htm (arguing that we must look beyond democracy for accountability at the global level).

trative law towards greater openness, participation and transparency. These features may make up for the democratic deficit caused by the absence of a constitutional foundation to global administrative law. Insofar as the global legal order lacks top-down legitimacy, it could be, at least partially, compensated by means of reinforced guarantees for civil society. The need for such guarantees magnifies the problem of asymmetric participation by private actors in the adoption of global administrative (either general or individual) decisions. The issue is particularly sensitive in those countries in which public administrations accord wide space to private interests – for example, in the United States, where the "interest representation model" applies. Shifting decision-making from the national to the global level deprives citizens and corporations of these participatory rights. Hence, there should be greater participation in the formation of the national position ahead of global administrative negotiations, or actual participation in these negotiations, directly or through (similarly global) non-governmental organizations.[116]

---

[116] For a discussion of the problem, see S. A. Shapiro, *International Trade Agreements*, cit., p. 449-453.

As mentioned above, the forms of participation are different. Some of these forms are organic: actors not belonging to the organization are admitted to the body with observer status. See, e.g., *Codex Alimentarius* Commission, Codex Alimentarius Commission: 14Th Procedural Manual 12-13 (2004), http://www.codexalimentarius.net/web/procedural_manualJsp. Other forms are procedural, in the sense that non-members are informed of decisions affecting them and are able to submit observations. For example, the Financial Action Task Force informs Non-Cooperative Countries and Territories of evaluations regarding them and permits them to present comments. Financial Action Task Force, *Annual and Overall Review of Non-Cooperative Countries or Territories*, p. 3-4 (2005), http://www.fatf-gafi.org/dataoecd/41/26/34988035. pdf.

For a discussion of the importance of dialogue with civil society, see Report by the Consultative Board to the Director-General S. Panitchpakdi, *The Future of the WTO: Addressing institutional challenges in the new millennium*, p. 53 (prepared by Peter Sutherland, Jagdish Baghwati et al.), available at http://www.wto.org/english/thewto_e/10anniv_e/future_wto_e.pdf and the analysis by F. Bignami, "Civil Society and International Organizations: A Liberal Framework for Global Governance", Duke Law Faculty Scholarship Paper n. 1126/2007.

8. THE LEGALIZATION OF GLOBAL ADMINISTRATIVE NET-WORKS: TOWARDS A UNIVERSAL RULE OF LAW?

Economic globalization, while often opposed in the name of domestic rights, also creates rights. These rights do not only concern the private sphere (eliminating, for instance, trade barriers in order to sell in wider markets) but also the public sphere (for instance, norms on the relations between national offices and global organizations, or between national legal subjects and the global legal order). It might be argued that the universalization of rights, rather than the universalization of the market, is the most characteristic feature of globalization.

Up until about twenty years ago, one could rightfully lament the inadequacy of the law applying to international organizations.[117] But as we have seen in the last quarter-century, the global legal order has made great strides, so that law now plays a decisive role in the global arena.

The global legal order is held up by a complicated system of norms. There are norms arising out of treaties, unilateral norms, externally imposed norms, and norms created by the institutions themselves.[118] There are global norms and national norms that apply to global institutions (for instance, those of the country hosting the organization's headquarters), as well as hard law and soft law. As noted above, the body that creates the norms is not always the same one that gives them binding force. There is no precise hierarchical order of norms. Finally, these norms are not uniformly applied: for example, the Government Procurement Agreement of the WTO provides for access to sub-central government organs on the condition that others make an equal offer.[119] Obligations are not always applied in a uniform fashion.

---

[117] F. Morgenstern, *Legal Problems of International Organization*, cit., p. 136.

[118] Some of which are directed outwards, others of which address components of the institution that issued them; an example of this latter kind of norm is provided by the World Bank Group's Code of Professional Ethics, which applies to the Group's staff of managers, consultants and temporary employees. Prof'l Ethics Office, World Bank Group, Code of Professional Ethics 5 (1999), http://wbln0018.worldbank.org/crn/ope/ethics.nsf/(BillboardPictures)/ code/$-FILE/ code.pdf.

[119] Agreement on Government Procurement, Apr. 15, 1994, Marrakesh Agreement Establishing the World Trade Organization, Annex 4(b), available at http://www.wto.org/english/docs_e/legal_e/gpr-94_e.pdf. See also V. Mosoti, "The WTO Agreement on Government Pro-

As we have seen, a body of general principles is being consolidated in the global arena: the principle of legality, the right to participate in the formation of norms ("notice and comment," as recognized by the OIE), the duty of consultation (imposed by the World Bank on domestic administrations in the context of the Heavily Indebted Poor Countries Initiative),[120] the right to be heard ("procedural participation" recognized by the FATF and the WTO Appellate Body),[121] the right to access administrative documents, the duty to give reasons for administrative acts (the duty to give a reasoned decision, affirmed by the WTO Appellate Body[122]), the right to decisions based upon scientific and testable data, and the principle of proportionality.[123]The global development of these principles are rooted in traditional administrative law rights (participation, transparency, reasoned decision, proportionality, reasonableness), which creates a paradox. On the one hand, the greater the weight of civil society and the direct relations between private actors and global

---

curement: A Necessary Evil in the Legal Strategy for Development in the Poor World?", in *University of Pennsylvania Journal of International Economic Law*, 2004, vol. 25, p. 593.

[120] See International Monetary Fund, Debt Relief Under the Heavily Indebted Poor Countires (HIPC) Initiative, http://www.imf.org/external/np/exr/facts/hipc.htm (last visited Jan. 31, 2006).

[121] See Appellate Body Report, *United States - Restrictions on Imports of Cotton Man-made Fibre Underwear*, p. 21, WT/DS24/AB/R (Feb. 10, 1997). See also S. Charnovitz, "Transparency and Participation in the World Trade Organization", in *Rutgers University Law Review*, 2004, vol. 56, p. 927.

[122] See Appellate Body Report, *Mexico - Antidumping Investigation of High Fructose Corn Syrup (HFCS) From the United States*, 106, WT/DS132/AB/RW (Oct. 22, 2001). See also Understanding on Rules and Procedures Governing The Settlement of Disputes, Apr. 15, 1994, Marrakesh Agreement Establishing the World Trade Organization, Annex 2, available at http://www.wto.org/english/docs_e/legal_e/legal_e.htm.

[123] Some of these principles directly apply to citizens, others to Member States, and others to international organizations, often in a contradictory way, such as when global judges apply to States principles that do not apply to global organizations themselves (for instance, the principle of transparency is obligatory for the Member States of the WTO, but not for the WTO itself). See, e.g., General Agreement on Trade in Services and Annexes, Apr. 15, 1994, Marrakesh Agreement Establishing the World Trade Organization, Annex lB, 33 I.L.M. 1129 (1994). For opposing views on the process of legalization, compare J. Goldstein, M. Kahler, et al., *Introduction: Legalization and World Politics*, in *International Organization*, 2000, vol. 54, p. 385 (discussing the global movement towards law as a resolving force in many issues) with P. Sands, *Lawless World: America and the Making and Breaking of Global Rules*, London, Penguin, 2004, p. 18-19 (discussing the U.S.-led trend towards deregulation and the enhancement of the role of private enterprise in governing international relations).

organizations, the greater the need to introduce and respect such principles. On the other hand, the spread of these principles highlights their meagerness compared to the richer panoply of rights recognized by national legal systems, a difference accentuated by asymmetries in the different national legal and administrative traditions.[124]

The third important aspect of the penetration of law into the global arena concerns judicial review. Global administrative decision making raises the following problems: who ensures legal protection for those affected by such decisions? National courts or judicial bodies belonging to the global legal system? If it is the latter, does the complainant have the same rights as it would in a national court? What relationship ought to be established between national courts and global tribunals, when global administrative decisions are not the exclusive product of global institutions, but originate in joint, global-national, decisions? It is in this area that we face the biggest issues of global administrative justice.

Until now, the global legal order has given diverse answers to these questions. There are, first of all, global institutions, like the ICDO and the WMO, in which there is no need for dispute resolution mechanisms. In other cases, national courts review the decisions of global institutions.[125]

The most interesting phenomenon, however, is the increase of global administrative courts. We do not need to dwell on names here (they are often called "panels"), but rather observe that they decide disputes through adversarial procedures and are required to be independent. There are many adjudicating bodies, and some have already been mentioned above: the Dispute Settlement Body of the WTO, the International Tribunal for the Law of the Sea, NAFTA's Dispute Set-

---

[124] This is a general phenomenon but it is particularly felt in the United States, where the domestic rules governing participation in administrative proceedings (in the context of both rule-making and adjudication) are more developed. See G. Silverstein, "Globalization and the Rule of Law: 'A Machine that runs of itself?'", in *Journal of Constitutional Law*, 2003, vol. 1, p. 427.

[125] B. Kingsbury et al., *The Emergence of Global Administrative*, cit., p. 20-21; see also A. Reinisch, *International Organizations Before National Courts*, Cambridge, Cambridge University Press, 2000, p. 323 (discussing the appropriateness of national courts' rulings on disputes involving decisions made by international organizations); cf. C. McCrudden and S. G. Gross, "WTO Government Procurement Rules and the Local Dynamics of Procurement Policies: A Malaysian Case Study", in *European Journal of International Law*, 2006, vol. 17, p. 151 ff.

tlement Panels, the International Centre for the Settlement of Investment Disputes (ICSID), the WIPO's Arbitration and Mediation Center, the World Bank Inspection Panel, and the Subsidiary Body on Dispute Settlement of the Commission on Phytosanitary Measures. Many other international bodies have mechanisms or procedures in place, such as arbitration, for dispute resolution. The UPU is one such organization.[126] Sometimes States have access to these courts; sometimes private actors do. Some of these courts have jurisdiction over decisions adopted by national administrations – such as the Dispute Settlement Body of the WTO – others over administrative decisions adopted by global authorities. These adjudicating bodies are characterized by the fact that they resolve disputes between States (and thus resemble international law), which are, at the same time, transnational conflicts[127] (which thus resem-

---

[126] The phenomenon of the multiplication of tribunals at the global level is examined here with an eye to only those tribunals operating in the field of administrative law, even if it is hard to distinguish those having an administrative jurisdiction from those having jurisdiction over trade or other areas.

There is a rich body of recent literature on the spread of tribunals. A. Fischer-Lescano argues in *Die Emergenz der Globalverfassung* that at the core of the global legal system there are "global remedies", in *Zeitschrift für ausländisches öffentliches Recht und Völkerrecht*, 2003, vol. 63, p. 717 ff. See A. Del Vecchio, *Giurisdizione internazionale e globalizzazione: i tribunali internazionali tra globalizzazione e frammentazione*, Milan, Giuffrè, 2003 (analyzing the tribunals and their jurisdiction). For a study of judicial globalization, see generally Sir D. Williams, *Courts and Globalization*, in *Indiana Journal of Global Legal Studies*, 2004, vol. 11, p. 57; R. O. Keohane et al., *Legalized Dispute Resolution: Interstate and Transnational*, in *International Organization*, 2000, vol. 54, p. 457; A.-M. Slaughter, *Judicial Globalization*, in *Vanderbilt Journal of International Law*, 2000, vol. 40, p. 1103; A.-M. Slaughter, *A New World Order* 65-103 (2004); A. Stone Sweet, *Judicialization and the Construction of Governance*, in *Comparative Political Studies*, 1999, vol. 32, p. 147; A. Stone Sweet, *Islands of Transnational Governance* (Ctr. for European and German Studies, Univ. of Cal. Berkeley, Political Relations and Inst. Research Group, Working Paper No. 2.89, 2001). Regarding the WTO dispute resolution mechanism, see generally G. della Cananea, "Il diritto amministrativo globale e le sue corti", in F. Manganaro and A. Romano Tassone (eds), *Dalla cittadinanza amministrativa alla cittadinanza globale*, Milan, Giuffrè, 2005, 125, 125-41; C.-D. Ehlermann, *Some Personal Experiences as Member of the Appellate Body of the WTO*, p. 3-4 (The Robert Schuman Ctr. For Advanced Studies, European Univ. Inst., Policy Paper 02/9, 2002); M. Melloni, "L'intesa sulla soluzione delle controversie dell'organizzazione mondiale del commercio: problemi emersi nei primi otto anni di attività e prospettive di soluzione", in *Il diritto dell'economia*, 2003, nn. 2/3, p. 427.

On the ICSID, see generally S. Flogaitis, "Administrative Law of International Organizations": the World Bank, in *Essays In Honour of G. I. Kassimatis*, Bruxelles, Bruylant, 2004, p. 604.

[127] Meaning that they involve relationships that cross national borders, in which at least one party is not a State or public entity.

ble administrative law). Moreover, they make decisions backed up by a system of sanctions, like the retaliation and cross-retaliation authorized by WTO panels.[128]

In conclusion, the large number of norms, the development of rules and principles, and the rise of courts all confirm the high degree of institutionalization (or legalization, as American scholars like to say) of the global administrative system. This stands in direct relation to the greater efficacy of global decisions in targeting national citizens, organizations, and corporations.

The more that global organizations widen their scope of action beyond States and domestic public organizations, the more that it becomes important to ensure respect for the rule of law, the principle of participation, and the duty to give a reasoned decision. These procedures are important in order to ensure the protection of citizens, organizations, and corporations, not only in their relations with States and other national public powers, but also in their relations with the new global public powers.

II. IS THERE A GLOBAL ADMINISTRATIVE LAW?*

1. AN IMPORTANT INTELLECTUAL EXERCISE

We are currently engaged in a very important intellectual exercise - no less important, indeed, than that undertaken by the nineteenth-century "founding fathers" of public law, such as Laferrière in France, Gerber, Laband and Mayer in Germany, and Orlando and Romano in Italy. Scholars in New York, Rome, Heidelberg and elsewhere are working on a new area of legal theory and practice: that of global law.

---

[128] *The Future of the WTO: Addressing institutional challenges in the new millennium*, cit., p. 53.

* This section offers some reflections on Armin von Bogdandy's piece, "General Principle of International Public Authority: Sketching a Research Field", in *The Exercise of Public Authority by International Institutions*, Heidelberg, Springer, 2010. Thanks are due to Euan Mac-Donald, Mariangela Benedetti, Lorenzo Casini, Elisabetta Morlino, and Gianluca Sgueo for their comments.

This scholarly work[129] has three main features. It is, firstly, a truly global effort. Jurists from all over the world are engaged in such research, some providing in-depth analyses of individual global regimes, while others seek to deduce from the many and varied governance experiences a body of common principles and rules.

It is worth noting that a scholarly endeavor of this sort has not been undertaken since the seventeenth-century Indeed, ever since the attack from legal positivism led to the collapse of natural law approaches to the discipline, law has been conceived of as exclusively the product of nation-States, with international law conceptualized mainly on the basis of "contractual" relations between them. As a consequence, the study of each national system of law has become for the most part limited to national "schools" of lawyers, with occasional raids into foreign legal systems permitted to scholars of a more comparative bent.

Secondly, this endeavor deals with an entirely new subject-matter; one that has developed only relatively recently, chiefly in the last twenty years. It encompasses a vast array of different treaties, rules, standards, institutions, and procedural arrangements established beyond national frontiers either by States themselves, or by other global institutions, in order to deliver services, establish further standards, monitor compliance, or act as "clearing houses" more generally.

This body of law is confusing, at least when viewed through the lens of traditional conceptual criteria. It is law, but in most cases non-binding. It does have established institutions, but these can most often proceed only tentatively at best, because their authority is not yet widely recognized.

Thirdly, in the study of this field one cannot rely upon the usual paradigms of public law. These have been developed in national contexts as a set of values, principles, and rules necessary to the proper functioning of domestic institutions. For example, regular elections at the national and local levels serve the purpose of democracy; and the due process of

[129] See the Global Administrative Project launched by New York University in 2005 (http://www.iilj.org/GAL/default.asp), the research on Global Administrative Law led by the Institute for Research on Public Administration (IRPA) in Rome (http://www.irpa.eu/index.asp?idA=161), and the Project on The Exercise of Public Authority by International Institutions at the Max-Planck Institut für ausländisches öffentliches Recht und Völkerrecht at Heidelberg (http://www.mpil.de).

law is instrumental to the protection of fundamental rights. But can they be transposed mechanically to an entirely new environment, beyond the State? Can new wine be poured into old wineskins?

2. BOGDANDY ON THE LEGAL NATURE AND PRINCIPLES OF THE GLOBAL ARENA

Armin von Bogdandy's paper on "Principles of International Public Authority" is a very rich and complex contribution to this new field. It examines not only the principles of international public authority, but also the legal nature of the global arena more generally.

Von Bogdandy's argument rests upon the following five basic assumptions:

1. to exercise public authority means to unilaterally govern the conduct of third parties, even without their consent;

2. there exists no one single and unitary body of law, nor a proto- federal legal order, nor a legal space, that can be called "global";

3. the direct exercise of authority by international institutions over individuals is extremely rare, and in the global arena there is thus, for the most part, neither direct effect nor supremacy of global norms; as a rule, the decisions of international institutions do not unilaterally affect private parties, but are addressed to national administrations;

4. the relationship between international institutions and national legal systems can be understood as based on two principles: the principle of autonomy (or independence) and the principle of delegation;

5. international institutions are subject to the principle of attributed competence: they cannot acquire powers on their own initiative; rather, their competences are attributed to them by national governments.

Von Bogdandy ends with five main conclusions:

1. while there is little evidence of the development of overarching principles at the international level, some principles regulating international public authority are emerging;

2. a hierarchy of sources of law is establishing itself in the operation of
   international institutions; in each regulatory regime, the founding
   treaty of each institution operates as the framework for the law that
   it produces;

3. international institutions are subject to the principle of cooperation
   in their relations both with national governments and with other
   global bodies, and to specific procedural duties (the duty to inform
   affected parties, their right to be heard, etc.);

4. the protection afforded to individuals against action taken in violation of their rights by international institutions is at present unsatis-
   factory, although this is beginning to change;

5. the relevant global legal principles remain under-developed, due to
   the fact that only a few international institutions are subject to direct
   judicial review.

3. WHAT IS LAW IN THE GLOBAL ARENA?

The first point that I want to discuss here concerns the very concept
of law in the global arena, and the related concepts of binding force and
authority.

In domestic legal orders there is a clear-cut dichotomy between legal
and non-legal prescriptions; and this is because there is a higher authority that establishes the dividing line between what is and what is not law.
This picture, however, changes as we move into the global arena. There,
we are confronted by a world that is highly formalized, but not in strictly
legal terms.

For example, many World Bank "legal" instruments are simply
referred to as "policy" documents; yet in many cases these can scarcely be
considered less important than statutes passed by national parliaments.
They regulate important aspects of the Bank's activity, such as the duty

to perform an environmental impact assessment and all of the procedural requirements related to this.[130] Private parties in India or South Africa can appeal to these standards, and ask that global and national governance bodies comply with them. Must we concede that anything that is not binding is, *ipso facto*, not law? If there is an area of law in which the Latin motto *"ubi societas, ibi ius"* holds true, then surely it must be the global arena.

At this point, a second dichotomy emerges, related to the first: that between binding ("hard") and non-binding ("soft") law. The basic question that we might pose in this regard is as follows: is a formally binding commitment to obey a rule the only means of producing rule-conforming behavior?

Even in domestic legal orders, not all rules are binding or compulsory. National legislation also establishes incentives and issues guidelines; it seeks not only to compel, but also to promote, to correct, to educate, and so on.

An example from the global arena is provided by the standards generated by the *Codex Alimentarius* Commission. These are not, in and of themselves, compulsory; they are, however, in effect given binding force by the World Trade Organization.[131] One authority produces rules;

---

[130] Elsewhere, I have defined the World Bank's operative policies as «ad hoc international administrative norms»: see S. Cassese, "Global Standards for National Administrative Procedures", in *Law & Contemporary Problems*, vol. 68, 2005, p. 109. Moreover, NGOs and local communities have increasingly been addressing the World Bank's policies within the context of global compliance mechanisms; see, for instance, M. Circi, "The World Bank Inspection Panel: The Indian Mumbai Urban Transport Project Case", in S. Cassese, B. Carotti, L. Casini, M. Macchia, E. MacDonald and M. Savino (eds), *Global Administrative Law: Cases, Materials, Issues*, 2008, p. 55 ff.; a broader analysis of the World Bank social policies can be found in A. Vetterlein, "Economic Growth, Poverty Reduction, and the Role of Social Policies: The Evolution of the World Bank's Social Development Approach", in *Global Governance*, 2007, vol. 13, p. 513. See also K. Tomasevski, "The Influence of the World Bank and IMF on Economic and Social Rights", in *Nordic Journal of International Law*, 1995, vol. 64, p. 385; M. Nesbitt, "The World Bank and de facto Governments: A Call for Transparency in the Bank's Operational Policy", in *Queens Law Journal*, 2006-2007, vol. 32, p. 641; K.W. Simon, "World Bank Wants a New Approach to Consultations with Civil Society", in *International Journal of Civil Society*, 2003, vol. 1, p. 41.

[131] See, for a general overview of the *Codex Alimentarius* Commission within the World Trade Organization, J. Vapnek, "Legislative Implementation of the Food Chain Approach", in *Vanderbilt Journal of Transnational Law*, 2007, vol. 40, p. 987; J. Kurtz, "A Look behind the Mirror: Standardisation, Institutions and the WTO SPS and TBT Agreements", in *University*

another endows them with binding force. The rule is not binding from its inception, only becoming so because another authority imposes conformity upon those under its jurisdiction. Therefore, in this case the rule is binding in the field of global trade, but not in other areas, creating a "dédoublement".

A third point, again related, concerns the concept of authority. Power, not authority, is central in the global arena. Power can be exercised through authoritative means (such as the «command and control» models familiar from domestic administrative systems), but also through agreements, contracts, incentives, standards and guidelines.

4. THE GLOBAL LEGAL SPACE

The area beyond the State is not only "global" from an economic point of view; rather, there also exists a global legal space, encompassing a vast number of different regulatory bodies, a mass of rules, a great quantity of procedures, and a complex array of links both to national bureaucracies and civil society.

What is missing is one general and unitary body of global law. Instead, there are numerous (at least two thousand) global regimes.

---

of New South Wales Law Journal, 2007, vol. 30, p. 504; T.P. Stewart and D.S. Johanson, "The SPS Agreement of the World Trade Organization and International Organizations. The Roles of the Codex Alimentarius Commission, the International Plant Protection Convention, and the International Office of Epizootics", in *Syracuse Journal of International Law & Commerce*, 1998-1999, vol. 26, p. 27. An analysis of the complex relationship between the global standards of the *Codex Alimentarius* Commission and domestic States is provided by D. Livshiz, "Updating American Administrative Law: WTO, International Standards, Domestic Implementation and Public Participation", in *Wisconsin International Law Journal*, 2006-2007, vol. 24, p. 961. A more general overview is provided by K. Claire, "Power, Linkage and Accommodation: The WTO as an International Actor and Its Influence on Other Actors and Regimes", in *Berkeley Journal of International Law*, 2006, vol. 24, p. 79. A further analysis of the *Codex Alimentarius* standards and their connection to the FAO and WTO is given by M.D. Masson-Matthee, *The Codex Alimentarius Commission and Its Standards*, The Hague, T.M.C. Asser Press, 2007. It is worth noting that the standards can also diverge. See, for instance, E. D'Alterio, *Relations between Global Law and EU Law*, in S. Cassese, B. Carotti, L. Casini, M. Macchia, E. MacDonald and M. Savino (eds), *Global Administrative Law: Cases, Materials, Issues*, cit., p. 105; H.S. Shapiro, "The Rules That Swallowed Exceptions: The WTO SPS Agreement and Its Relationship to CATT Articles XX and XXI - The Threat of the EU-GMO Dispute", in *Arizona Journal of International & Comparative Law*, 2007, vol. 24, p. 199.

However, both the administrative actors and the judicial bodies (where these exist) within each individual regime establish links to, and rules of engagement with, other regimes. Cooperation, division of labor and dialogue are common among global regimes and their constituent institutions. This law is generated through a process of accretion and accumulation, and the cooperative dialogue between regimes means that the principles of each should not be interpreted and applied in a vacuum. It is in this process that some have recognized the emergence of a general body of law at the global level.[132]

Moreover, each national legal order has developed a certain number of common rules, and these now provide core standards that can be shared and even codified at a supranational level (take, for example, the Council of Europe's codification of rules on administrative procedure).[133]

Given that the global legal order is fragmented (or, perhaps more accurately, that there is not one unitary legal order at the global level, but rather many different and self-contained legal regimes), there are no general legal principles common to all. But some common understandings are developing: the duty to respect human rights and the rule of law; the obligation to inform and to hear interested parties before a decision is taken (as held, for example, in the *Juno Trader* case before the International Tribunal of the Law of the Sea);[134] and substantive

---

[132] «The current range of international legal obligations benefits from a process of accretion and cumulation» (Arbitral Tribunal, *Southern Bluefin Tuna* case, n. 52, 14 August 2000). "[...] the principles underlying the Convention [on Human Rights] cannot be interpreted and applied in a vacuum" (European Court of Human Rights, *Bankovic v. Belgium and others*, 12 December 2001). "The scope of special laws is by definition narrower than that of general laws. It will thus frequently be the case that a matter not regulated by special law will arise in the institutions charged to administer it. In such cases, the relevant general law will apply." (UN Study Group on the Fragmentation of International Law, *Conclusions*, 2006).

[133] Council of Europe, *The Administration and You. Principles of Administrative Law Concerning the Relations Between Administrative Authorities and Private Persons*, Strasbourg, 1996.

[134] International Tribunal of the Law of the Sea, The *"Juno Trader" Case* (*Saint Vincent and the Grenadines v. Guinea-Bissau*), case no. 13, December 18, 2004 (www.itlos.org/cgi-bin/cases/case_detail.pl?id=13&lang=en); see D. Agus and M. Conticelli, "The International Tribunal for the Law of the Sea (JTLOS): The Juno Trader Case", in S. Cassese, B. Carotti, L. Casini, M. Macchia, E. MacDonald and M. Savino (eds), *Global Administrative Law: Cases, Materials, Issues*, cit.

duties relating to principles of fairness and reasonableness, amongst others.

5. THE GLOBAL LEGAL SPACE AS A "MARBLE CAKE": SHARED POWERS

The widely-used expression "multilevel governance" is misleading, insofar as there is no clear-cut separation of competences between national governments and global institutions, structured within a definite hierarchy, of the type that this expression seems to suggest. Rather, the global arena is characterized by the spread of powers between the global and the national levels of government. For instance, environmental protection is at once a global and a national task, and competencies in this field are not merely shared by global and national bodies; rather, areas of jurisdiction overlap and compete with each other. The line between the national and the international is becoming increasingly blurred (see, for example, the Cybersquatting cases before the dispute resolution panels of the World Intellectual Property Organization).[135] In the case of shared powers of this sort, the rule is not strict separation and rigid hierarchy, but rather permeability, intermingling, interpenetration.

Global institutions derive their jurisdiction and their powers from national governments. It does not necessarily follow, however, that of all their powers originate in a direct delegation by States. For example, there are international institutions that were not established by national governments, but by other international bodies (for example, the *Codex Alimentarius* Commission).[136]

---

[135] See, for example, World Intellectual Property Organization, Arbitration and Mediation Center, Administrative Panel Decision, decision of 22 July 2003 *Keisanki Kabushki Kaisha, dba Casio Computer Co., Ltd v. Fulviu Mihai Fodoreanu*, Case No. DRO2003-0002 ("Casio"); decision of 4 August 2000; *Excelentisimo Ayuntamiento de Barcelona v. Barcelona.com Inc.*, Case No. D2000-0505. Decisions are available at: http://arbiter.wipo.int/domains/ decisions/index-cctld. html.

[136] See M.D. Masson-Matthee, *The Codex Alimentarius Commission and Its Standards*, cit. Further information is available in J.A. Bobo, "The Role of International Agreements in Achieving Food Security: How Many Lawyers Does It Take to Feed a Village?", in *Vanderbilt Journal of Transnational Law*, 2007, vol. 40, p. 937.

Moreover, cooperation in the global arena does not occur only between international institutions and national governments, but also among international institutions themselves. The global order can be illustrated by the well-known metaphor of the marble cake, as there are no clear dividing lines between layers (national and global) and (global) sectoral regimes; rather, the two worlds are linked both vertically and horizontally through a complex array of relations and networks.

6. LEGITIMACY THROUGH THE LAW

There exists no cosmopolitan democracy, no planetary constitution, no global parliament. Is this cause for concern?

Here again it is necessary to return to certain basic questions. Why do we want national governments to be legitimate? Simply put, the answer might run as follows. National governments exercise their power through authority: they oblige and impose. Therefore, they must be run on the basis of the consent of the governed. Through recurrent elections, politicians are chosen and kept under control by the people.

A number of differences emerge, however, when we move from the national to the global context. Firstly, global bodies do not normally exercise power through authority: they do not seek to simply impose their will, but rather to influence the behavior of national bureaucracies and private parties through a variety of different mechanisms.

Secondly, global bodies are usually established in order to keep national governments under control, or to provide services or pursue goals that governments alone are unable to. Therefore, they put limits on the activities of national executives. In this regard, we might suggest, they are on the same "side" as the people, formally speaking at least.

Thirdly, periodic elections are not the only means of legitimizing public power. Global institutions seek to forge their legitimacy through ensuring openness, dialogue and the participation of private parties ("*Legitimation durch Verfahren*")[137] in the decision-making process. Examples of this abound within global regimes: consider, for instance, the

---

[137] N. Luhmann, *Legitimation durch Verfahren*, Neuwied, Luchterhand, 1969.

International Preliminary Examination procedure for the protection of inventions, established by the Patent Cooperation Treaty; or the complaints procedure before the World Bank Inspection Panel.

Judicial protection is not guaranteed by every global regulatory regime. However, many do establish mechanisms that can act as a surrogate for formal judicial protection, for example granting "ex ante" participation rights to affected private parties or national governments, establishing quasi-judicial procedures and ensuring some degree of independence from decision-making bodies.

Finally, there are now around a hundred and twenty extra-national courts around the world (most of them with jurisdiction in criminal matters).[138] Technical and scientific expertise often play an important role in the controversies brought before these courts (see, for example, the Apples and Fire Blight case before the World Trade Organization Dispute Settlement Body[139] and the Southern Blue Fin Tuna case before the Arbitral Tribunal of the United Nations Convention on the Law of the Sea[140]). There also exist some internationalized forms of administrative review of domestic agencies (for example, the NAFTA Chapter 19 Panels[141]); and

---

[138] See the Project on International Courts and Tribunal International (PICT) and the synoptic chart, available at: http://www.pict-pcti.org/publications/synoptic_chart/Synop_C4.pdf.

[139] The relevant decisions in this case are Panel Report, Japan - Measures Affecting the Importation of Apples, WT/DS245/R, 15 July 2003 and Report of Appellate Body, Japan - Measures Affecting the Importation of Apples, WT/DS245/AB/R, AB-2003-4, 26 November 2003: see A. Albanesi, "The WTO 'Science-Fest': Japan Measures Affecting the Importation of Apples", in S. Cassese, B. Carotti, L. Casini, M. Macchia, E. MacDonald and M. Savino (eds), *Global Administrative Law: Cases, Materials, Issues*, cit., p. 178 ff.

[140] Arbitral Tribunal established under Annex VII of the United Nations Convention on the Law of the Sea, Australia and New Zealand v. Japan, Award on Jurisdiction and Admissibility, 4 August 2000. See also B. Carotti and M. Conticelli, "Settling Global Disputes: The Southern Bluefin Tuna Case", in S. Cassese, B. Carotti, L. Casini, M. Macchia, E. MacDonald and M. Savino (eds), *Global Administrative Law: Cases, Materials, Issues*, cit., p. 145 ff.

[141] NAFTA Article 1904 establishes a mechanism that provides an alternative to judicial review by domestic courts of final determinations in antidumping and countervailing duty cases: the Binational Panel system. This system uses panels consisting of US and Canadian or Mexican panelists to review antidumping and countervailing duty decisions taken by national administrative authorities. The Panel may uphold or remand the national administrative action, and its decisions are binding. The Binational Panel system represents an internationalized form of administrative judicial review of domestic agencies: it reviews decisions of domestic agencies; its decisions are based on domestic law, not international trade rules; and the private parties involved (e.g. firms) have a right to initiate panel review. For an overview on this topic, see

there are many more bodies that provide some sort of judicial review by acting as quasi-independent courts, open to the petitions of the affected citizens, and following adversarial or quasi-adversarial procedures. These are often referred to as, for example, "compliance committees"[142] or "inspection panels".[143] In many regards, these latter bodies resemble

---

G.R. Winham and A. Heather, "Antidumping and Countervailing Duties in Regional Trade Agreements: Canada-US. FTA, NAFTA and Beyond", in *Minnesota Journal of Global Trade*, 1994, vol. 3, p. 1; G.R. Winham and G.C. Vega, "The Role of NAFTA Dispute Settlement in the Management of Canadian, Mexican and U.S. Trade and Investment Relations", in *Ohio Northern University Law Review*, 2001-2002, vol. 28, p. 651; E.J. Pan, "Assessing the NAFTA Chapter 19 Binational Panel System: An Experiment in International Adjudication", in *Harvard International Law Journal*, 1999, vol. 40, p. 379. See also M. Macchia, "Reasonableness and Proportionality: The NAFTA Binational Panel and the Extension of Administrative Justice to International Relations", in S. Cassese, B. Carotti, L. Casini, M. Macchia, E. MacDonald and M. Savino (eds), *Global Administrative Law: Cases, Materials, Issues*, cit., p. 86 ff.

[142] The term «compliance committee» is used in multilateral environmental agreements (MEAs). See Convention on Biological Diversity, COP-MOP 1 Decision BS-I/7, *Establishment of Procedures and Mechanisms on Compliance under the Cartagena Protocol on Biosafety*, Kuala Lumpur, 23-27 February 2004; Meeting of the Parties to the Convention on Access to Information, Public Participation in Decision-making and Access to Justice in Environmental Matters, Report of the First Meeting of the Parties, Addendum, *Decision 1/7 Review of Compliance* adopted at the first meeting of the Parties held in Lucca, Italy, on 21-23 October 2002, ECE/MP.PP/2/Add.8, 2 April, 2004; Commission for environmental cooperation, *Adoption of the Revised Guidelines for Submissions on Enforcement Matters Under Articles 14 and 15 of the North American Agreement on Environmental Cooperation*, 28 June 1999, Council resolution 99-06.

[143] The term «inspection panel» is used by the Multilateral Development Banks (MDBs, consisting of the World Bank Group and the four Regional Development Banks: The African Development Bank, The Asian Development Bank, The European Bank for Reconstruction and Development, The Inter American Development Bank Group). See International Bank for Reconstruction and Development, I.B.R.D. Res. 93-10 (Sept. 22, 1993); International Development Association, IDA Res. 93-6, Sept. 22, 1993 (the two Resolutions are identical and are reprinted in World Bank, *World Bank Operational Manual: Bank Procedures*, 17.55, annex A, 1997); Asian Development Bank, *Establishment of an Inspection Function*, ADB Doc. R225-95 (Nov. 10, 1995); IFC/ MIGA's Office of the Compliance Advisor/Ombudsman, (see also Compliance Advisor/Ombudsman – CAO, *Operational Guidelines*, April 2004); European Bank for Reconstruction and Development – EBRD, *Independent Recourse Mechanism: As Approved by the Board of Directors on 29 April 2003* (2003), (see also *Independent Recourse Mechanism Rules of Procedure: As Approved by the Board on 6 April 2004*); Inter-American Development Bank (IDB), *IDB's Independent Investigation Mechanism (IIM)*, (see also the rules and procedures of IDB's IIM); African Development Bank, Board of Director, *Enabling Resolution* B/BD/2004/9-F/BD/2004/7-B/BD/2004/10, June 30, 2004. Asian Development Bank, *Review of the Inspection Function: Establishment of a New ADB Accountability Mechanism*, May 2003. For an overview, see E. Suzuki and S. Nanwani, "Responsibility of International Organizations: The Accountability Mechanisms of Multilateral Development Banks", in *Michigan Journal of Inter-*

the French *Conseil d'État* in the period between 1800 and 1872, when the Council was not legally recognized as a judicial body despite the fact that it was exercising de facto judicial review.

7. IS THERE A GLOBAL ADMINISTRATIVE LAW?

Finally, let me return to the question contained in the title of this contribution: is there a global administrative law?

This question must, in my view, be answered in the affirmative. This law has the following features.

1. Notwithstanding some areas of overlap, global administrative law should be distinguished from traditional international law. *"Ius gentium"*, *"Ius inter gentes"* and "the law of the nations" refer to the law established between the governments of States to regulate relations between States as legal entities. Despite displaying some features to the contrary, this law is still largely non-hierarchical, voluntaristic and contractual in nature. Global law, on the other hand, consists in large part of the rules produced by international organizations of various different kinds.

2. International law is mainly based on transactions, while global law has developed a more robust hierarchy of norms. This hierarchy has developed within each individual regulatory regime; it is now emerging among the different regulatory regimes as well (for example, the European Court of Justice, in the *Kadi* case,[144] has recognized the primacy of United Nations law over European law).

---

national Law, 2006, vol. 27, p. 177; N. Wahi, "Human Rights Accountability of the IMF and the World Bank: A Critique of Existing Mechanisms and Articulation of a Theory of Horizontal Accountability", in *University of California Davis Journal of International Law & Policy*, 2005-2006, vol. 12, p. 331.

[144] Judgment of the Court (Grand Chamber) 3 September 2008, joined cases C-402/05 P and C-415/05 P. See also A. Sandulli, "Caso Kadi: tre percorsi a confronto"; S. Cassese, "Ordine comunitario e ordine globale"; E. Chiti, "I diritti di difesa e di proprietà nell'ordinamento europeo"; M. Savino, "Libertà e sicurezza nella lotta al terrorismo: quale bilanciamento?"; G. Vesperini, "Il principio del contraddittorio e le fasi comunitarie di procedimenti globali"; and G. della Cananea, "Un nuovo nomos per l'ordine globale", in *Giornale di diritto amministrativo*, 2008, p. 1088-1104.

3. As already noted, there currently exist around two thousand international organizations,[145] which are often capable of reproducing other such organizations (in fact, many of them were themselves established by other global bodies). They conclude treaties and make rules, and can no longer be considered as the mere agents of States. Indeed, they can even create standards that are aimed at transforming the internal structure of national governments.

4. Perhaps the most important global bodies are those that carry out a standard-setting function. These standards are generally addressed to national governments; but this does not mean that private parties are not affected by them. For example, the food that we eat is subject worldwide to the standards of the *Codex Alimentarius* Commission.[146] The standards established by the Forced Labour Convention (1930) are addressed to national governments, but affect private individuals (see, for example, the case of Myanmar and the International Labour Organization[147]).

5. Such bodies are at the top of many sectoral regimes. These regimes do not, however, exist entirely independent of each other, but rather are linked in myriad different ways – either in relatively structured "regime complexes" –[148] or simply through the significant areas of

---

[145] Union of International Associations, *Yearbook of International Organizations*, München, Saur, 2005.

[146] See J. Kurtz, *A Look behind the Mirror*, cit.; D. Livshiz, *Updating American Administrative Law*, cit. See, with particular reference to the interactions with the US system, D.M. Strauss, "International Regulation of Genetically Modified Organism: Importing Caution into the U.S. Food Supply", in *Food and Drug Law Journal*, 2006, vol. 61, p. 167; also, S. Keane, "Can a Consumer's Right to Know Survive the WTO: The Case of Food Labeling", in *Transnational Law & Contemporary Problems*, 2006-2007, vol. 16, p. 291.

[147] Commission of Inquiry, ILO, *Forced Labor in Myanmar (Burma), Report of the Commission of Inquiry Appointed Under Article 26 of the Constitution of the International Labor Organization to Examine the Observance by Myanmar of the Forced Labor Convention, 1930* (No. 29), Geneva, 2 July 1998. See also E. Morlino, "Labor Standards: Forced Labor in Myanmar", in S. Cassese, B. Carotti, L. Casini, M. Macchia, E. MacDonald and M. Savino (eds), *Global Administrative Law: Cases, Materials, Issues*, cit., p. 1 ff.

[148] A regime complex can be defined as «an array of partially overlapping and non hierarchical institutions governing a particular issue-area ... [R]egime complexes, are marked by the existence of several legal agreements that are created and maintained in distinct fora with participation of

overlap in their respective fields of jurisdiction (e.g. trade and labor; trade and human rights; environmental protection and human rights; etc.).[149]

6. The global and the national levels interact in a number of different ways: for example, national governments act as law-makers at the global level, but are also the addressees of global substantive and procedural standards.

7. A global administrative law has thus developed, in terms of which global regimes are encouraged, and sometimes compelled, to ensure and promote the rule of law and procedural fairness, transparency, participation, and the duty to give reasons throughout all areas of their activity.

---

different sets of actors. The rules in these elemental regimes functionally overlap, yet there is no agreed upon hierarchy for resolving conflicts between rules. Disaggregated decisionmaking in the international legal system means that agreements reached in one forum do not automatically extend to, or clearly trump, agreements developed in other forums.»; see K. Raustiala and V. David, "The Regime Complex for Plant Genetic Resources", in *International Organization*, 2004, vol. 2, p. 279.

[149] The many linkages between protection of human rights and protection of the environment have long been recognized. Principle 1 of the 1972 United Nations Conference on the Human Environment (Stockholm Declaration) declared that man has a fundamental right to freedom, equality and adequate conditions of life, in an environment of a quality that permits a life of dignity and well-being. It also recognized the responsibility of each person to protect and improve the environment for present and future generations. Almost twenty years later, in Resolution 45/94, the UN General Assembly recalled the language of Stockholm, stating that all individuals are entitled to live in an environment adequate for their health and well-being. The resolution called for enhanced efforts towards ensuring a better and healthier environment. In contrast to the earlier documents, the 1992 Rio de Janeiro Conference on Environment and Development formulated the link between human rights and environmental protection largely in procedural terms (see Principle 10). This angle was further developed in 1998, with the conclusion of the Convention on Access to Information, Public Participation in Decision-making and Access to Justice in Environmental Matters (Aarhus Convention). The Convention focused on the same issues as Principle 10 of the Rio Declaration and Principle 1 of the Stockholm Declaration, but in a more concrete manner, which strengthens the areas of overlap between human rights and environmental issues. For a comment on the Aarhus Convention, see M. Macchia, "Legality: The Aarhus Convention and the Compliance Committee", in S. Cassese, B. Carotti, L. Casini, M. Macchia, E. MacDonald and M. Savino (eds), *Global Administrative Law: Cases, Materials, Issues*, cit., p. 71 ff.

8. Dispute settlement by mandatory adjudication remains, as yet, the exception rather than the rule within the global legal order. Traditional diplomatic relationships and negotiations survive and operate side by side with compulsory and binding adjudication by supranational courts and the non-binding decisions of different *quasi-judicial* bodies.

9. Global regulatory regimes become effective through various means. For example, within the WTO, a number of different mechanisms are used to ensure that the rules of the regime are enforced: mutual support, dumping/antidumping, subsidies/countervailing measures, non-implementation of WTO judicial decisions/retaliation, etc.[150]

10. As there are no periodic elections at the global level, procedural accountability plays a dominant role in making global bodies responsible to global society.

11. Membership in multicultural institutions can also enhance democracy at the national level: "as international bodies come into interaction with national centers of power, they can check abuses by those national centers [...] and force them into a better level of democratic

---

[150] On the retaliation principle and on countervailing measures, see K. Anderson, "Peculiarities of Retaliation in WTO Dispute Settlement", in *World Trade Review*, 2002, vol. 2, p. 123; T. Giannakopoulos, "Safeguarding Companies' Rights in Competition and Antidumping/Antisubsidies Proceedings", in *Common Market Law Review*, 2006, vol. 43, p. 268; T. Jurgensen, "Crime and Punishment: Retaliation under the World Trade Organization Dispute Settlement System", in *Journal of World Trade*, 2005, vol. 39, p. 327; Y.H. Ngangjoh and R.R. Herran, "WTO Dispute Settlement system and the Issue of Compliance: Multilateralizing the Enforcement Mechanism", in *Manchester Journal of International Economic Law*, 2004, vol. 1, p. 15; J. Pauwelin, "Enforcement and Countermeasures in the WTO: Rules are Rules –Toward a More Collective Approach", in *The American Journal of International Law*, 2000, vol. 94, p. 335. In this regard, an important case arose before the WTO Appellate Body with reference to the reactions of WTO Member States against the Continued Dumping and Subsidy Offset Act of 2000 (also known as the "Byrd Amendment") approved by the US Senate. See WTO Appellate Body Report, *United States - Continued Dumping and Subsidy Offset Act of 2000 ("Byrd amendment")*, WT/DS217, 234/AB/R, 27 January 2003 and Panel Report, *United States - Continued Dumping and Subsidy Offset Act of 2000*, WT/217/R, WTDS234/R, 16 September 2002. For an analysis of the case, see M. Benedetti, "EU Countermeasures against the U.S. Byrd Amendment", in S. Cassese, B. Carotti, L. Casini, M. Macchia, E. MacDonald and M. Savino (eds), *Global Administrative Law: Cases, Materials, Issues*, cit., p. 185 ff.

performance".[151] Perhaps the clearest example of this phenomenon in practice is provided by the European Convention on Human Rights, which provides for individual complaints to be brought before the European Court of Human Rights, which in turn has compulsory jurisdiction over its Member States.[152] These two features "give rise to a potentially expansive process of transnational dispute resolution".[153]

III. GLOBAL STANDARDS FOR NATIONAL ADMINISTRATIVE PROCEDURE*

1. INTRODUCTION

In 1989, the United States imposed an embargo on the importation of shrimp from countries that used fishing methods harmful to marine turtles. The shrimp were not a protected endangered species, but the marine turtles were. The embargo was thus motivated by the rightful concern to protect an animal species from extinction. Claiming this embargo to be a violation of Article XI of the General Agreement on Tariffs and Trade 1994 (GATT 1994), which provided for the general

[151] R.O. Keohane, S. Macedo and A. Moravcsik, *Democracy-Enhancing Multilateralism*, IILJ Working Papers, Global Administrative Law Series, 2007/4, available at: http://iilj.org/publications/documents/2007-4.GAL.KMM.web. pdf.

[152] Council of Europe, Convention for the Protection of Human Rights and Fundamental Freedoms, as amended by Protocol No. 11, Art. 34.

[153] R. Keohane et al., *Democracy-Enhancing Multilateralism*, cit., p. 27.

* I thank Professors Stefano Battini, Francesca Bignami, Armin von Bogdandy and Paolo Picone for their comments. In the course of this paper's presentation on 12 April 2004, at New York University School of Law (Hauser Global Law School Program), I received valuable comments from Nico Krisch, Nathan G. Alley, Ofer Eldar, Chaim Koch, and David Livshiz, as well as from the other participants in the seminar. This second version has benefited from the help of Alessandra Battaglia, Lorenzo Casini and Maurizia De Bellis, as well as from Antonella Albanesi and Stefania Corsi, who helped me correct further documentation. Dr. Luigi Tonini, of the Ministry of Foreign Affairs, and Drs. Francesco di Stefano and Pietro Rosi, of the "Consiglio nazionale dei ragionieri e dei periti commerciali" kindly provided me with information and documentation.

elimination of quantitative restrictions on trade, India, Malaysia, Pakistan, and Thailand commenced proceedings on the basis of the Dispute Settlement Understanding (DSU) of the World Trade Organization (WTO).

In *United States—Import Prohibition of Certain Shrimp and Shrimp Products (Shrimp–Turtle)*,[154] the WTO Appellate Body concluded that Section 609 of Public Law 101-162[155] "has been applied by the United States in a manner which constitutes arbitrary and unjustifiable discrimination between Members of the WTO... [:]"[156]

> [W]ith respect to neither type of certification under Section 609(b)(2) is there a transparent, predictable certification process that is followed by the competent United States government officials. The certification processes under Section 609 consist principally of administrative *ex parte* inquiry or verification by staff of the Office of Marine Conservation in the Department of State with staff of the United States National Marine Fisheries Service. With respect to both types of certification, there is no formal opportunity for an applicant country to be heard, or to respond to any arguments that may be made against it, in the course of the certification process before a decision to grant or to deny certification is made. Moreover, no formal written, reasoned decision, whether of acceptance or rejection, is rendered on applications for either type of certification, whether under Section 609(b)(2)(A) and (B) or under Section 609(b)(2)(C). Countries which are granted certification are included in a list of approved applications published in the Federal Register; however, they are not notified specifically. Countries whose applications are denied also do not receive notice of such denial (other than by omission from the list of approved applications) or of the reasons for the denial. No procedure for review of, or appeal from, a denial of an application is provided.[157]

---

[154] WTO Appellate Body, United States—Import Prohibition of Certain Shrimp and Shrimp Products, WT/DS58/AB/R, Doc. No. 98-3899 (Oct. 12, 1998) [hereinafter *Shrimp–Turtle*].

[155] Departments of Commerce, Justice, and State, the Judiciary, and Related Agencies Appropriations Act, 1990, Pub. L. No. 101-162, 103 Stat. 988 (1989) (codified at 16 U.S.C. § 1537 (2000)).

[156] *Shrimp–Turtle*, cit., p. 55, ¶ 186.

[157] *Id.* p. 54 ¶ 180 (citations omitted). Many have commented upon this decision. See, e.g., R. Howse, "The Appellate Body Rulings in the Shrimp/Turtle Case: A New Legal Baseline for

This decision was made pursuant to Article XX of the GATT 1994, according to which "such measures are not [to be] applied in a manner which would constitute a means of arbitrary or unjustifiable discrimination between countries where the same conditions prevail, or a disguised restriction on international trade ... ".[158] It follows that for States to respect the prohibition on arbitrary discrimination between countries where the same conditions prevail, as required by the GATT norm, they must respect the principle of due process. Though usually established by national laws, the principle of due process can also enter national administrative law through another door: being established at the international level and then applied at the national one.

The *Shrimp–Turtle* case concerning the U.S. import prohibition is not the only case in which an international treaty or international organization imposed procedural principles upon State administrations.[159] This section will examine some of these principles and evaluate how they operate in the global context.

This topic illustrates the degree to which global law penetrates national legal systems by dictating principles and criteria that national administrations must respect and that private actors may wield in their own interest. Though belonging to different national legal systems, these rules are nevertheless subject to the global system. We have come to expect and accept international organizations that set *substantive* standards (establishing, for example, legal levels of pollution or limiting the genetic manipulation of agricultural products), so it is easy to argue that national administrations ought to respect global substantive goals, standards, and criteria. More interesting, however, are examples of *procedural* principles and criteria. These usually are established at the national

---

the Trade and Environment", in *Columbia Journal of Environmental Law*, 2002, vol. 27, p. 491.

[158] General Agreement on Tariffs and Trade, Art. XX, Oct. 30, 1947, 55 U.N.T.S. 194, 262, *available at* http://www.wto.org/english/docs_e/legal_e/gatt47_e.pdf (last visited Feb. 23, 2005) [hereinafter GATT] (incorporated into General Agreement on Tariffs and Trade 1994, Apr. 15, 1994, Marrakesh Agreement Establishing the World Trade Organization [hereinafter WTO Agreement], Annex 1A, The Legal Texts: The Results of the Uruguay Round of Multilateral Trade Negotiations 17 (1999), 1867 U.N.T.S. 190 [hereinafter GATT 1994]).

[159] See G. della Cananea, "Beyond the State: The Europeanization and Globalization of Procedural Administrative Law", in *European Public Law*, 2003, vol. 9, p. 563-578 (identifying and discussing two trends: an increasing Europeanization of administrative procedures and a globalization of administrative procedures due to the influence of new international organizations).

level, by courts or laws like the United States Administrative Procedure Act (APA)[160] or equivalent laws in Spain, Germany, and Italy.[161] It is more difficult to affirm that national administrations ought also to respect global constraints regarding the procedural aspects of their activity and to recognize that global standards effectively limit the purely national scope of administrative laws and increase the degree to which national administrations are subject to the rule of law, both national and global. This difficulty arises in part because recognizing such duties as those of consultation, transparency, due process, and judicial review means recognizing globally established private rights against national public administrations, the exercise of which cannot be limited only to national citizens, as is generally the case with nationally established procedural rights. The global legal order grants the rights of consultation and intervention in national administrative procedures to the citizens of other States as well as nationals, as will be seen in greater detail below.

Global procedural standards are particularly sophisticated in the area of trade in services. It cannot be said for this area that the opening of national frontiers by global law—and the concomitant procedural constraints—have been driven by the interests of multinational corporations and the most developed nations. Rather, the rule of law and the principles of participation, transparency, due process, and judicial review, well developed in most domestic laws, provide "rules of the game" that do not necessarily favor those constituencies.

After a preliminary discussion of administrative law as State law, this section identifies the global regulatory regime characterized by permanent rules and briefly describes the characteristics common to different instruments in this system. It then turns to the peculiarities of this global regime, organizing them into four categories: the regulators, the regulated, the regulatory process, and the legal status of the rules. This section will analyze three issues with respect to the regulators: (1) regulation set forth by international treaties and regulations set forth

---

[160] Administrative Procedure Act, Pub. L. No. 79-404, 60 Stat. 237 (1946) (codified as amended in scattered sections of 5 U.S.C. (2000)).

[161] See the Ley de Procedimiento Administrativo (B.O.E. 18.07.1958); Verwaltungsverfahrensgesetz, v. 25.5.1976 (BGBl. I S.1253); and Nuove norme in materia di procedimento amministrativo e di diritto di accesso ai documenti amministrativi, Law no. 241 of Aug. 7, 1990 (It.), Gazzetta Ufficiale della Repubblica Italiana (Gazz. Uff.) No. 192 (Aug. 18, 1990), respectively.

by secondary regulators, like the committees of international organizations; (2) the schism between the authors of the regulation and the authorities overseeing national compliance with it; and (3) the disintegration of the States produced by national authorities that act as partners with the international authorities. As for the regulated, this section considers the regulations' "vertical" effect between international organizations and States and their "horizontal" effect between the States themselves, as well as other relationships between States and interested parties established by the international legal order. In the discussion of the regulatory process itself, this section examines the peculiarity of voluntary, self-imposed mutual recognition and the characteristics of the notice and comment procedure as applied to interstate relations and to the relations between States and private parties. Finally, in considering the legal status of these international administrative measures, this section examines both their non-binding character and the source of their effectiveness.

This section does not consider the ways in which domestic legal systems react upon contact with international administrative law. Thus, it does not address whether the institutions governed by this law are altered and adapted to the national context, whether international institutions spread as contagious infections, or whether national legal systems instead resist and reject international norms (and at what cost). Neither does it examine whether global principles and standards conflict with national ones, creating potential asymmetries between sectors governed only by national law and those tied to global law. Finally, this section does not consider whether the national application of global (and thus non-indigenous) procedural principles is merely ritualistic, slows down State action, or benefits the particular groups that make instrumental use of it.

2. ADMINISTRATIVE LAW AS STATE LAW

Historically, administrative law has sprung from national States. Public administrations belong to a national community, and they depend structurally on national, or State, governments. Because of the principle of legality, these administrations are subjected to laws and regulated by them. Administrative law is thus fundamentally State law.

History thus suggests the impossibility of international administrative law, because public administrations are exclusively national phenomena. And history suggests the impossibility of global governance of national administrative laws, because only within the State can there be an administration that enjoys a monopoly of executive power, and only within the State can there be the authority-versus-liberty dialectic that characterizes administrative law.[162] A global system governing national administrative law cannot exist, in short, because administrative governance finds its source exclusively in national law. As Otto Mayer, one of the founders of German administrative law, observed, the national public power is the lord of its own domain, to the exclusion of all others; therefore, the action of a foreign power on the territory of a foreign State can be considered valid only in exceptional situations.[163] If international obligations exist, they must pass through the filters of national law, which transform them into national rules.

Two developments have called this traditional perspective into question. The first is the rise of an international administrative law tied to global administrations rather than to the State. The second is the rise of global rules established by treaties or international organizations, but addressed to States and private actors. These international norms penetrate domestic legal systems, thus affecting national administrative laws.

These two developments are distinct, but related. The first, which will not be analyzed here, are the global rules that govern international bodies. Of particular interest here, however, is the second development, which represents an intrusion of global rules into national administrations. It is important to understand how the interference of the global with the national occurs, whether it corresponds to the practices of other international legal systems, and whether international regulatory forms resemble national ones.

---

[162] This formulation comes from D. Donati, and is cited and discussed in S. Battini, *Amministrazioni senza Stato: profili di diritto amministrativo internazionale*, Milan, Giuffrè, 2003, p. 31.

[163] O. Mayer, *Le droit administratif allemand*, Paris, Giard-Brière Editeurs, 1906, p. 354.

3. INTERNATIONAL REGULATION

There are many different kinds of international administrative norms. These norms can have either an ad hoc character or a permanent one. Examples of ad hoc norms are the World Bank Operational Policies, which require public consultation on the environmental assessment of projects proposed for Bank financing.[164] Under these policies, national law is obliged to respect the principle of private participation in administrative proceedings. A national administration that disregards this norm cannot obtain financing.

Even more interesting are the permanent norms. Four of these, examined here, all follow the same model. They are set forth in the following legal instruments: the Agreement on the Application of Sanitary and Phytosanitary Measures (SPS Agreement),[165] the Agreement on Technical Barriers to Trade (TBT Agreement),[166] the General Agreement on Trade in Services (GATS),[167] and the Principles for Food Import and Export Inspection and Certification (FIEIC).[168] The first three instruments belong to the legal system of the WTO,[169] while the fourth was

---

[164] See S. Battini, *Amministrazioni senza Stato*, cit., p. 262.

[165] Agreement on the Application of Sanitary and Phytosanitary Measures, Apr. 15, 1994, WTO Agreement, Annex 1A, The Legal Texts: The Results of the Uruguay Round of Multilateral Trade Negotiations 59 (1999), 1867 U.N.T.S. 493, *available at* http://www. wto.org./english/tratop_e/sps_e/ spsagr_e.htm (last visited Feb. 20, 2005) [hereinafter SPS Agreement].

[166] Agreement on Technical Barriers to Trade, Apr. 15, 1994, WTO Agreement, Annex 1A, The Legal Texts: The Results of the Uruguay Round of Multilateral Trade Negotiations 121 (1999), 1868 U.N.T.S. 120, *available at* http://www.wto.org/english/docs_e/legal_e/17-tbt.pdf (last visited Feb. 20, 2005) [hereinafter TBT Agreement].

[167] General Agreement on Trade in Services, Apr. 15, 1994, WTO Agreement, Annex 1B, The Legal Texts: The Results of the Uruguay Round of Multilateral Trade Negotiations 284 (1999), 1869 U.N.T.S. 183, *available at* http://www.wto.org/english/docs_e/legal_e/26-gats.pdf (last visited Feb. 20, 2005) [hereinafter GATS].

[168] Principles for Food Import and Export Inspection and Certification System, Doc. No. CAC/GL 20-1995, *in* Codex Alimentarius Comm'n, Food Import and Export Inspection and Certification System – Combined Texts 1 (2000), *available at* http://www.fao.org/documents/show_cdr.asp?url_file=/DOCREP/005/X4489E/x4489e02.htm.

[169] On the WTO, see J. H. Jackson, *The World Trading System: Law and Policy of International Economic Relations*, Cambridge and London, The MIT Press, 1997, 2d ed.; A. F. Lowenfeld, *International Economic Law*, Oxford, Oxford University Press, 2002; P. Picone and A. Ligustro, *Diritto dell'Organizzazione Mondiale del Commercio*, Padova, Cedam, 2002; G.

adopted by the Joint FAO/WHO Food Standards Program *Codex Alimentarius* Commission.[170]

Although varying in their details, these four instruments present common characteristics. First, the norms in these instruments are aimed at ensuring the balancing of conflicting interests. They seek to guarantee free trade, but also to protect health and consumer interests. The SPS Agreement seeks to reconcile free trade with the sanitary and phytosanitary measures necessary to protect human, animal, and plant health. The TBT Agreement seeks to balance the needs of international commerce with the safety of products and processes, because excessively and unjustifiably complex national rules governing products, processes, and methods of production might discriminate against foreign products.[171] The GATS seeks to limit the professional requirements one must meet and procedures one must follow to practice a profession, in order to prevent such rules from operating as barriers to the free circulation of services. The FIEIC seeks to facilitate international trade in foodstuffs while ensuring adequate protection of consumer health. All these instruments aim at preventing restrictions on trade in goods and services through disguised barriers, like health or technical requirements, which would favor national products and impede the importation of foreign ones.

Second, these instruments establish a link – and require a balance – among collective public interests, one of which is international trade.

Venturini, *L'Organizzazione Mondiale del Commercio*, Milano, Giuffrè, 2000; J.H.H. Weiler (ed.), *The EU, the WTO and the NAFTA: Towards a Common Law of International Trade?*, Oxford, Oxford University Press, 2000 [hereinafter *The EU, the WTO and the NAFTA*]. On the WTO's dispute settlement systems, see E.-U. Petersmann, *The GATT/WTO Dispute Settlement System: International Law, International Organizations and Dispute Settlement*, London, Kluwer Law International, 1997; E.-U. Petersmann (ed.), *Studies in Transnational Economic Law: International Trade Law and the GATT/WTO Dispute Settlement System*, London, The Hague, Boston, Kluwer Law International, 1997.

[170] The Food and Agriculture Organization of the United Nations (FAO) and the World Health Organization (WHO) created the *Codex Alimentarius* Commission in 1963 to develop food standards, guidelines, and related texts such as codes of practice under the Joint FAO/WHO Food Standards Program. FAO/WHO Food Standards, *Codex Alimentarius*, at http://www.codexalimentarius.net/web/index_en.jsp.

[171] On the balancing relative to the TBT agreement, see WTO Appellate Body, *European Communities – Measures Affecting Asbestos and Asbestos-Containing Products*, WT/DS135/AB/R, Doc. No. 01-1157 (March 12, 2001).

The four instruments considered here are only some of the many existing "linkages," or "trade ands," because the pervasiveness of trade connects it with a host of other concerns, such as the environment, employment, competition, corporate law, foreign investments, development, immigration policy, and poverty.[172]

Third, these instruments contain five types of common provisions, relating to transparency, harmonization, equivalence, consultation, and control procedures. To ensure transparency, these instruments require national administrations to publish their requirements promptly so that they can be made known to other national administrations and interested parties. A reasonable period should be allowed before a new requirement takes effect in order to allow producers in exporting countries to adapt their products or methods of production. To the same end, Members must establish enquiry points to provide information to other States or to private actors. However, there are some variations in how the agreements discussed here implement this norm. For example, some instruments require Members to supply requested documents to nationals of other Members at the same price, while others require Members to provide information and assistance.[173]

Fourth, to ensure harmonization, these instruments encourage national administrations to base their measures on international standards, guidelines, or recommendations.[174] These norms are formally non-binding, but measures based on them are presumed to be consistent with the relevant international provisions of the treaties. Standards, guidelines, and recommendations are not set forth by the agreements themselves. Instead, they are issued by other international organizations in which the Member States are required to participate. Examples of

---

[172] See generally S. Battini, *Amministrazioni senza Stato*, cit., pp. 236–237; J. H. Jackson, "Afterword: The Linkage Problem – Comments on Five Texts", in *American Journal of International Law*, 2002, vol. 96, p. 118 (commenting on how the five articles in the issue addressed "the problem of linkage between 'nontrade' subjects and the World Trade Organization" and making some general observations on the subject); M. Nettesheim, "Legitimizing the WTO: The Dispute Settlement Process as Formalized Arbitration", in *Rivista trimestrale di diritto pubblico*, 2003, p. 711, 716, 719, 722-724.

[173] GATS pt. II, art. III; SPS Agreement annex B, ¶¶ 1-3; TBT Agreement art. 2, ¶ 11 and arts. 10, 12; FIEIC, cit., p. 3-4, ¶¶ 14 – 17.

[174] GATS pt. II, art. VI, ¶ 5(b); SPS Agreement art. 4; TBT Agreement art. 2, ¶ 4 and art. 5; FIEIC, cit., p. 3, ¶ 12.

such international organizations include the *Codex Alimentarius* Commission, the International Office of Epizootics, the International Plant Protection Convention, the International Organization for Standardization (ISO), and the International Electrotechnical Commission (IEC).

Fifth, to ensure equivalence, all four agreements provide that Members should accept the measures of other States as equivalent if the exporting State objectively demonstrates that its measures achieve the importing State's level of protection. The obligation to demonstrate equivalence rests with the exporting country. The Member States may also sign bilateral and multilateral agreements on the recognition of the equivalence of specified measures.[175]

If no international standards, guidelines, or recommendations exist, or if a national measure does not respect the international standard, guideline, or recommendation, the Member shall follow a procedure of notification and consultation that involves publishing a notice of the measure to enable interested Members to become acquainted with it, notifying other Members of the products to be covered by the regulation, providing other Members with copies of the proposed regulation, and allowing other Members reasonable time to make comments, discuss them upon request, and take the comments and the results of the discussion into account.[176] In the case of sanitary and phytosanitary measures, for example, a State may choose a higher level of protection, but it must demonstrate that this is justified and does not result in arbitrary discrimination.

Finally, these four international agreements set forth restrictions on national procedures of certification and control. National procedures must respect the following principles: equivalence of assessment and control procedures for imported and domestic products, expedient execution of the procedures (without undue delays) and the avoidance of undue delay in considering an application, no overly burdensome requirements,

---

[175] GATS pt. II, art. VII; SPS Agreement art. 4, ¶ 2; TBT Agreement art. 2, § 7; FIEIC, cit., p. 3, ¶ 13.

[176] SPS Agreement annex B, ¶ 5; TBT Agreement art. 2, ¶ 9; FIEIC, cit., p. 3-4, ¶ 15; WTO Council for Trade in Services, *Disciplines on Domestic Regulation in the Accountancy Sector*, S/L/64, Doc. No. 98-5140 (Dec. 17, 1998) (see the section on "Transparency").

confidentiality, reasonableness and proportionality, and a procedure for reviewing decisions.[177]

4. THE REGULATORS

The body of legal rules summarized here derives both from international agreements and from decisions of the collegial bodies established by the agreements themselves.[178] The distinction between the agreements and the collegial bodies they create is important because standards derived from interstate agreements—that is, agreements between States—disciplining State administration are acts of self-restraint undertaken by the States themselves. By contrast, standards established by the collegial bodies of international organizations represent an external limitation, even if State representatives belong to these bodies. This distinction is not only formal, but also substantive. Interstate agreements are the work of national governments and the legislative bodies that ratify them. The collegial organs of international organizations, by contrast, are made up of national civil servants.

The Committee on Sanitary and Phytosanitary Measures is one such collegial body. Adopting guidelines in June 2000 envisaged by Article 5, Paragraph 5 of the SPS Agreement for applying the concept of the appro-

---

[177] GATS pt. II, art. VI; SPS Agreement annex C; TBT Agreement art. 5, ¶¶ 1–3; FIEIC, cit., p. 4, ¶ 19. There is abundant literature on the SPS, TBT, and GATS cited in P. Picone and A. Ligustro, cit. See also C. Arup, *The New World Trade Organization Agreements—Globalizing Law Through Services and Intellectual Property*, Cambridge, Cambridge University Press, 2000; A.O. Sykes, *Product Standards for Internationally Integrated Goods Markets*, Washington, D.C., The Brookings Institution Press, 1995; J.P. Trachtman, "Lessons for the GATS from Existing WTO Rules on Domestic Regulation", in A. Mattoo and P. Sauvé (eds), *Domestic Regulation and Service Trade Liberalization*, Oxford, Oxford University Press, 2003, p. 57; M. Djordjevic, "Domestic Regulation and Free Trade in Services—A Balancing Act", in *Legal Issues Economic Integration*, 2002, vol. 29, p. 305; T. P. Stewart and D. S. Johanson, "The SPS Agreement of the World Trade Organization and International Organizations: the Roles of the Codex Alimentarius Commission, the International Plant Protection Convention, and the International Office of Epizootics", in *Syracuse Journal of International Law and Commerce*, 1998, vol. 26, p. 27.

[178] These bodies include the Committee on Sanitary and Phytosanitary Measures, regulated by SPS art. 12 and art. 5, ¶ 5; the Committee on Technical Barriers to Trade, regulated by TBT art. 13; the Council for Trade in Services, regulated by GATS arts. XXIV and VI, ¶ 4; the *Codex Alimentarius* Commission; and the Committee on Import/Export Inspection and Certification Systems.

priate level of protection, it declared that new measures must be based on a comparison with the previous ones, with national measures addressing analogous risks, with measures adopted by international bodies, and with measures adopted in other countries and based on technical opinions.[179] The Committee on Technical Barriers to Trade, another example of these collegial bodies, has established norms for the implementation of Articles[180] concerning transparency and notification obligations, recommending that Members designate the government authority or agency that will examine comments, acknowledge receipt of the comments, specify the ways in which the comments will be taken into account, and provide further information when necessary.[181] A third example, the Council for Trade in Services, adopted disciplines[182] intended to facilitate the liberalization of trade in accounting services by ensuring that domestic laws do not constitute unnecessary barriers to such trade. Under these disciplines, Members are required to designate a national administrative authority, notify other Members of new measures, and establish professional licensing criteria and predetermined qualification requirements that are publicly available, objective, proportional, and reasonable.[183] In international law, as is common in European law, these committees are made up of national bureaucrats rather than government representatives. They function as clearinghouses for national interests, as connecting bodies, and as centers of secondary rulemaking.

International agreements do not themselves fix the standards, guidelines, and recommendations to which the Members are invited to conform, nor do they entrust this job to the bodies constituted by the agreements themselves; instead, they route this job to other international bodies, using a connection technique known as "borrowing regimes." There is, therefore, a schism between the regulators on the one hand,

---

[179] WTO Committee on Sanitary and Phytosanitary Measures, *Guidelines to further the practical implementation of Article 5.5*, G/SPS/15, Doc. No. 00-2955 (July 18, 2000).

[180] TBT Agreement art. 2, ¶ 9–10; art. 3, ¶ 2; art. 5, ¶¶ 6–7; and art. 7, ¶ 2.

[181] WTO Secretariat, Transparency Provisions of the TBT Agreement (2002), *available at* http://www.wto.org/english/tratop_e/tbt_e/booklet_transparency_e.doc.

[182] Disciplines on Domestic Regulation in the Accountancy Sector [hereinafter Disciplines] in GATS art. VI, ¶ 4.

[183] WTO Council for Trade in Services, cit.

and the authors of the regulation on the other. In the context of the WTO, it has been observed that,

> on the one hand, the WTO avails itself of the Codex Commission's work for the harmonization of national regulations likely to prejudice free international trade; that is the interest protected by that organization. On the other hand, the Codex Commission, in order to guarantee the safety of foodstuffs, borrows from the greater institutional effectiveness of the WTO system: its standards are not in themselves binding upon States, but the degree of their observance has markedly increased owing to the application of these standards by the dispute resolution bodies of the WTO.[184]

The WTO stands at the heart of the system. Through the medium of trade, the WTO ultimately regulates—or, better yet, lends its regulatory force to—different authorities to implement rules regarding very diverse sectors, such as the environment, agriculture, plants, health, and food safety. There is, in this sense, a certain resemblance between the WTO and the European Union (EU): both revolve around the circulation of goods and services (though the EU also protects the free circulation of persons and businesses). Both ultimately penetrate other sectors in order to balance competing and conflicting interests. The process of EU transformation from a sectoral authority into a general public authority is, however, substantially more advanced.[185]

The agreements require that the Members designate a government authority responsible for performing the activity subject to international

---

[184] S. Battini, "Il sistema istituzionale internazionale. Dalla frammentazione alla connessione", in *Rivista Italiana di Diritto Pubblico Comunitario*, p. 969-986 (quotation translated for use in this section); see also A. von Bogdandy, "Legitimacy of International Economic Governance: Interpretative Approaches to WTO Law and the Prospects of Its Proceduralization", in S. Griller (ed.) *International Economic Governance and Non-Economic Concerns: New Challenges for the International Legal Order*, Wien-New York, Springer, 2003, p. 103, 109; S. Charnovitz, "Triangulating the World Trade Organization", in *American Journal of International Law*, 2002, vol. 96, p. 50-55. Borrowing regimes is a widespread phenomenon: for example, the International Monetary Fund and the World Bank lend their own power to the rules and criteria established by the Basel Committee, asking that national administrations apply them and verify their observance.

[185] On the difference between the WTO and the EU, see A. von Bogdandy, *Legitimacy of International Economic Governance*, cit., pp. 122-126.

obligations[186] or designate an enquiry point.[187] In this way, the State is substantially disaggregated: the designated national office becomes the body of reference for the international organization. The paradigm of the State as a unit is thus cast aside and the internal administrative organization of the State takes on greater international importance.[188]

5. THE REGULATED

The second noteworthy aspect of this international regulation lies in how it operates. It has a vertical effect, in the sense that it penetrates within the State, circumventing national legislation in order to address national public administrations directly. This is the product of harmonization. International regulation is not directed solely at States, however. It is also addressed to sub-State entities and even to private ones. The TBT Agreement, for example, concerns not only central governments but also the local governments and non-governmental bodies that establish technical rules. The Agreement regulates the preparation, adoption, and application of technical regulations and procedures for the assessment of conformity by central government bodies[189] and local government and non-governmental bodies.[190] The member States must ensure that local governments and non-governmental bodies comply with requirements established by the TBT, but addressed directly to the sub-State bodies.

International regulation also produces a horizontal effect, in the sense that it requires a kind of dialogue between States. This dialogue unfolds in two different ways. First, national public administrations are

[186] See, e.g., SPS Agreement, Annex B, ¶ 10.

[187] See, e.g., SPS Agreement, Annex B, ¶ 3 and TBT Agreement, art. 10, ¶ 1. The latter states, "Each Member shall ensure that an enquiry point exists which is able to answer all reasonable enquiries from other Members and interested parties in other Members."

[188] On this, see S. Battini, *Amministrazioni senza Stato*, cit., p. 211. See generally S. Cassese, *Relations Between International Organizations and National Administrations*, in XIX International Congress of Administrative Sciences, Berlin (West), proceedings, 1983, p. 159, pp. 177-180 (examining the international role of domestic bureaucracies).

[189] TBT Agreement arts. 2, 5.

[190] TBT Agreement arts. 3, 7-8.

required to compare continuously their own and other countries' measures. Second, national public administrations are encouraged to enter into equivalence or mutual recognition agreements. Global regulation thus not only imposes itself vertically on States, but also requires States to open themselves up reciprocally—laterally, as it were—respecting procedural rules in their relations.

This twofold effect, vertical and horizontal, and the relationship between international organizations and States, also can be seen in the EU. Here, too, harmonization is required from on high and is accompanied by mutual recognition.

Differences between international and European administrative law nevertheless abound. Whether in the vertical or the horizontal sense, global regulation is addressed to national public administrations. But private parties, active within States, also are increasingly interested in it. They participate in the processes of legislation, administration, and adjudication. One example of private participation in the legislative process is the Disciplines. The International Federation of Accountants (IFAC) and national organizations like the National Council of Accountants and Business Consultants in Italy have played an important role in promoting, preparing, and developing global standards, first in the Working Party on Domestic Regulation, then in the Council for Trade in Services.[191] National organizations (be they public or private, as dictated by the national law governing professional organizations) and (private) international organizations have thus taken part in the formation of substantive global law. One example of the administrative process allowing and accepting private participation is the TBT, according to which, "[e]ach Member shall ensure that an enquiry point exists which is able to answer all reasonable enquiries from other Members and interested parties in other Members."[192] Another example of private participation is in adjudication—American companies working

---

[191] On the role of the IFAC, see C. Trolliet and J. Hegarty, "Regulatory Reform and Trade Liberalization in Accountancy Services", in A. Mattoo and P. Sauvé (eds), *Domestic Regulation and Service Trade Liberalization*, cit., p. 147. Information on the role of the Italian National Council of Accountants and Business Consultants was obtained by direct research in the Council's archives.

[192] TBT Agreement art. 10, ¶ 1.

with U.S. public authorities "to challenge foreign trade barriers before the WTO legal system."[193]

Despite such examples, one view of the global legal system is that it leaves no place for private actors. According to that view, private actors stand in a legal relationship to the States alone, and the States must mediate their relationship to the global legal system. That view considers the global and domestic legal orders to be two separate systems, existing upon different levels, in which there would be no unmediated relations between private actors and global organizations.

However, legal relationships do exist between the infra-State and the global levels, however difficult and incomplete they might still be. Thus, it is foreseeable that when, for example, the Disciplines are complete and have been incorporated into the GATS, accountants from one country, acting through their own national authorities, will be able to contest the legitimacy of the behavior of public authorities in another country (for example, charging that they violated the duty of transparency) before the judicial bodies of the WTO. This will create a triangle consisting of an accountant in one country (acting through his own national authority), the global judicial authority, and the public authority of the other country.

6. THE REGULATORY PROCESS

The third noteworthy aspect of international regulation has to do with the regulatory process. State obligations deriving from international regulation are related to procedures—obligations such as consultation and discussion, respect for the principles of reasonableness and proportionality, and the duty to give a response within a fixed period. By requiring national legal systems to respect the procedural obligations of consultation, transparency, reasonableness, and proportionality, the global system thus imports legal principles into national systems, and thereby "denationalizes" the relevant areas or sectors.[194]

---

[193] G. C. Shaffer, *Defending Interests: Public-Private Partnership in WTO Litigation*, Washington D.C., The Brookings Institution Press, 2003, p. 5.

[194] Because "the Appellate Body proceduralizes the substantive WTO obligations" it has extended "basic elements of the democratic principle and the rule of law to aliens." See A.

The regulatory process at the international level also incorporates the practice of mutual recognition. This is a widespread practice that overcomes the dualism between international and domestic law by enabling a national authority to make decisions that have direct effects in other national legal systems. In the EU, where the principle of mutual recognition originated before spreading to international law,[195] it was developed by the European Court of Justice (ECJ), while at the global level, it is the outcome of interstate agreements and is thus a matter of voluntary consent.

The notice and comment procedure also has been borrowed from other legal systems, this time from national ones. Still, this too is very different from the analogous procedures practiced in domestic legal systems. In fact, at the national level, the actor that notifies, receives comments, and decides is a State authority and is superior to the commenting party. Transposed into international law, the procedure is structurally similar, but functionally different. At the international level, it is a State that listens to another State,[196] and there is no higher authority that decides. International law is inspired by domestic administrative law, but the function of the institution, transplanted into a different context, changes. The notice and comment procedure becomes an instrument of consultation and debate among equals subject to no higher authority.

Finally, the public arena phenomenon manifests itself in the global legal space as well as in the national one. There are multiple levels of

---

von Bogdandy, *Legitimacy of International Economic Governance*, cit., p. 128, 132. The phenomenon of proceduralizing substantive obligations is also evident in other cases, like in the Poverty Reduction Strategies of the World Bank and International Monetary Fund. These two organizations grant loans to low-income countries on the condition that national programs are prepared with the participation of government and administrative bodies, as well as interested parties such as civil society organizations, minorities, unions, and research institutes, and that the results of such participation be taken into account in preparation of the programs. See The World Bank Group, Topics in Development, Poverty, Poverty Reduction Strategies, *at* http://web.worldbank.org/WBSITE/external/topics/extpoverty/extprs/0,menuPK:384207~pagePK:149018~piPK:149093~theSitePK:384201,00.html.

[195] A. Alemanno, "Gli accordi di reciproco riconoscimento di conformità dei prodotti tra regole OMC ed esperienza europea", in *Diritto del commercio internazionale*, 2003, p. 379.

[196] But note the arguments of the previous paragraph on the growing participation of private actors.

government (that is, international organizations and national administrations) in potential conflict with each other, as well as interested parties that can exploit the differences between the regulators by playing off one against the other.[197]

7. THE LEGAL STATUS OF THE RULES

The rules created by international organs in furtherance of the treaties are defined in different ways through disciplines, guidelines, and standards.[198] These rules do not create direct, legally binding obligations on the States.[199] For some of these rules, the relevant international organization debated the question of their legal status and decided not to make them binding. For example, the international rules governing accountants, set forth on the basis of "Additional Commitments" in Article XVIII of the GATS, are binding only when they are voluntarily inscribed in a Member's schedule. Currently, the Working Party on Domestic Regulation is trying to extend this regime to other professions. At the end of this process, the "disciplines on domestic regula-

---

[197] S. Cassese, *L'arena pubblica. Nuovi paradigmi per lo Stato*, in S. Cassese (ed.), *La crisi dello Stato*, Laterza, Rome-Bari, 2002, p. 74.

[198] See, e.g., GATS pt. II, art. VI, ¶ 4 (disciplines); SPS Agreement art. 5, ¶ 5 (guidelines); TBT Agreement art. 2 (standards).

[199] The question of the direct application of norms and of their higher status has been discussed with respect to the norms contained in the WTO Agreement, not with reference to secondary norms. See, e.g., A. von Bogdandy, "Legal Equality, Legal Certainty, and Subsidiarity in Transnational Economic Law—Decentralized Application of Art. 81.3 EC and WTO Law: Why and Why Not", in A. von Bogdandy et al. (eds), *European Integration and International Co-ordination, Studies in Transnational Economic Law in Honour of Claus-Dieter Ehlermann*, The Hague, Kluwer Law International, 2002, p. 13 [hereinafter *European Integration*] (concluding that the direct applicability of WTO law is undesirable "because of the total lack of mechanisms which provide for legal equality between competitors from different jurisdictions and which guarantee legal security"); J. H.J. Bourgeois, "The European Court of Justice and the WTO: Problems and Challenges", in *The EU, the WTO and the NAFTA*, cit., p. 71-123 (exploring the question why WTO law raises specific problems and challenges for the European Court of Justice); J. H. Jackson, *The Jurisprudence of GATT and the WTO: Insights on Treaty Law and Economic Relations*, Cambridge, Cambridge University Press, 2000, p. 297-366 (examining the effect of treaties in domestic law in the United States and setting forth a policy analysis of the status of treaties in domestic legal systems).

tions" should become an annex to the GATS and thus assume a binding character.[200]

Still, it cannot be said that global standards will have no effect until they are incorporated into an international treaty. The example of the Disciplines for services, adopted in the context of the GATS, is illuminating. First, the standstill provision found in GATS Article VI, Paragraph 5, in fact applies to them. Even before the Disciplines are enforced, Member States that have assumed "specific commitments"[201] may not apply

---

[200] See GATS pt. IV, art. XX, ¶ 3 (providing that "[s]chedules of specific commitments shall be annexed to this Agreement and shall form an integral part thereof"). There has been far-reaching discussion of developing GATS Disciplines on the domestic regulation of services. For an understanding of the issues involved, see the Papers Presented at the "*Workshop on Domestic Regulation*" organized by the WTO Working Party on Domestic Regulation (Mar. 29–30, 2004), *at* http://www.wto.org/english/tratop_e/serv_e/workshop_march04_e/workshop_programme_march04_e.htm; WTO Working Party on Domestic Regulation, *Report on the Meeting held on 30 September 2003: Note by the Secretariat*, S/WPDR/M/23, Doc. No. 03-6313 (Nov. 27, 2003); WTO Working Party on Domestic Regulation, *Communication from the European Community and Its Member States: Proposal for Disciplines on Licensing Procedures*, S/WPDR/W/25, Doc. No. 03-3734 (July 10, 2003); WTO Working Party on Domestic Regulation, *Communication from Singapore: GATS Article VI:5 and its relation to the future Article VI:4 Disciplines*, JOB(03)/113 (June 11, 2003); WTO Working Party on Domestic Regulation, *Communication from the European Communities and Their Member States: Applicability of the Disciplines on Domestic Regulation in the Accountancy Sector to Other Professional Services*, S/WPDR/W/5, Doc. No. 00-2053 (May 19, 2000); WTO Council for Trade in Services, *Article VI:4 of the GATS: Disciplines on Domestic Regulation Applicable to All Services: Note by the Secretariat*, S/C/W/96, Doc. No. 99-0769 (Mar. 1, 1999); WTO Council for Trade in Services, Decision on Disciplines Relating to the Accountancy Sector: Adopted by the Council for Trade in Services on 14 December 1998, S/L/63, Doc. No. 98-5102 (Dec. 15, 1998); WTO Working Party on Professional Services, *Report to the Council for Trade in Services on the Development of Disciplines on Domestic Regulation in the Accountancy Sector*, S/WPPS/4, Doc. No. 98-4965 (Dec. 10, 1998); European Commission, Directorate General I, *Note to the Member States: GATS Working Party on Professional Services Draft Disciplines on Domestic Regulation in the Accountancy Sector*, DGI/M/1/FLM D(98) (Jan. 22, 1998).

[201] M. Krajewski, *National Regulation and Trade Liberalization in Services: The Legal Impact of the General Agreement on Trade in Services (GATS) on National Regulatory Autonomy*, The Hague, Kluwer Law International, 2003, p. 45 (explaining that WTO members have market access commitments that prohibit them from "maintain[ing] certain specified restrictions of market access" and national treatment commitments that require them to "treat foreign services and service suppliers no less favourable than their own like services and suppliers" in "those service sectors which a WTO member specifically committed to these disciplines in its Schedule of Specific Commitments").

domestic standards that "nullify or impair [the Disciplines]."[202] Second, there is no need to incorporate the Disciplines into the treaty. Mutual recognition agreements have been created between developed countries for already internationalized professionals like architects, accountants, and engineers. These agreements are based on "common international standards" as set forth by Article VI, Paragraph 5, of the GATS.[203] Third, the doctrine of consistent interpretation must be applied: when domestic law lends itself to multiple interpretations, it ought to be interpreted so as to conform to international law.[204]

The decisions of international bodies have direct legal consequences, even before they are incorporated into international treaties.[205] Thus, global standards produce their effects in different and more complicated ways than national standards do. For example, international law techniques for enforcing decisions differ from domestic ones in providing for a retaliation mechanism that functions as an ultimate rule of the global legal system.[206] Although the WTO system borrows rules from other international systems (such as the Food and Agriculture Organization of the United Nations (FAO), World Health Organization (WHO), *Codex*

---

[202] See *id.* p. 117-119 (discussing non-violation and impairment of specific commitments, and explaining that a Member that brings a non-violation nullification and impairment complaint must "establish that a benefit it could have reasonably expected to accrue to it under a specific commitment of another member was nullified and impaired through the application of a measure"); see also *id.* p. 151-153 (discussing the impact of the disciplines on domestic regulations found in GATS Article VI, Paragraph 5).

[203] But only for a limited set of countries.

[204] See generally T. Cottier, "A Theory of Direct Effect in Global Law", in *European Integration*, cit., p. 99, p. 109-110 (discussing the doctrine of consistent interpretation). The doctrine of consistent interpretation is a principle that is applied by judges to treaties and common law. It is not clear why the domestic legal order, in the face of many possible interpretations, should not also conform to non-binding international rules, especially when one considers that "WTO law is influenced by Anglo-American legislation which ... has a tradition of explicit and detailed regulation. As a practical matter, these texts thus can often assist in interpreting broad and open textured language in domestic law." *Id.*

[205] As noted, non-binding standards often gain binding force through borrowing and enforcement by way of the WTO.

[206] In the WTO, the offended State may, following the dispute resolution procedure set forth in Articles 21–23 of the DSU, take countermeasures in the form of tariffs so as to penalize the exports of the condemned country and obtain compensation for the losses incurred by the violation.

Alimentarius, etc.), it also lends those rules muscle, so that they are effectively respected.

8. CONCLUSION

The parts of the global legal system examined here appear as a network of sectoral regulators. These regulators, however, are not separate, but rather reinforce each other mutually. They do not make up a structural unit, but they do become a functional one, thanks to mutual ties and the division of labor between standardization bodies and bodies charged with imposing standards.

In the global legal system, one can see the use of many forms otherwise specific to States and supranational bodies like the EU: regulators, committees, harmonization, and consultation procedures. These forms rarely appear in the global legal order in the same way as in national or mature supranational systems. Here, the regulator is not unitary, as in the States, but split in two: one body sets the rule and another imposes it. Harmonization is encouraged, but not imposed from on high, as in the EU. The consultation procedures are carried out by actors in a position of equality, while in domestic law, the State authority that hears the views of the "administered" before making its decision is superior to them.

Why do these different institutions not correspond to their national or European models? Perhaps because they are transformed by the different context.

> [W]e will have occasion to stress the importance, when transposing concepts of administrative law to the international sphere, of evaluating with prudence and circumspection the extent to which they are fully applicable at a particular stage of development, with due regard to the contrast between the infancy of international organization and the maturity of the modern State.[207]

---

[207] C. Wilfred Jenks, *The Proper Law of International Organisations*, London, Stevens and Sons Ltd.,1962, p. XL.

It is not just that national and global administrative law are developed to a greater or lesser degree. There are also some important qualitative differences between the two.[208] First, national administrative laws rotate around a single axis—the State, or the national government—even if in federal or regional States many authorities may establish primary rules. Global administrative law, by contrast, is multi-polar. It lacks a hierarchically superior power similar to the power of the central State, which prevails over the other powers in the domestic legal system. The global administrative law system is characterized by sectoral authorities, and sometimes just sectoral networks of national authorities. It is also for this reason that here it is better to speak of "governance" than "government" or "regimes."

Second, the various authorities of the global legal system have developed differently than States have. A strong lawmaking power exists in both systems, and there are many legal prescriptions in the global legal system. But the executive power is weak at the global level, because (for various reasons) sectoral enforcement is carried out by, or delegated to, State executive powers or their offices. There are judicial authorities at the global (for example, the WTO) and the supranational (for example, the EU) levels, and their development is directly related to the influence of the global system over national legal systems.[209]

That executive powers in the global system are underdeveloped creates a third kind of difference between global and State administrative law: the former is characterized by an "indirect rule" that consists of national authorities carrying out the functions belonging, in fact, to the global system. This enables the global system—in a way similar to the EU—to be effective using just a modestly sized administration of its own. But it also creates—as in the EU—serious enforcement problems. A modest administration means having limited tools to guarantee enforcement.

Finally, the global legal system is of a mixed or composite character, as it is made of both a State and an "ultra-State" dimension. The latter,

---

[208] On global administrative law, see generally E. D. Kinney, "The Emerging Field of International Administrative Law: Its Content and Potential", in *Administrative Law Review*, 2002, vol. 54, p. 415.

[209] This can be seen by comparing the EU with Mercosur, for example.

functioning as a kind of common law, not only requires national laws to conform to it, but also enables them to communicate with each other. This communication takes place in two ways: (1) through the circulation of capital, goods, and services (and, to a lesser degree, businesses and persons); and (2) by the State legal system's opening up to recognize other legal orders. Both of these ways enable a choice of the most favorable law and may lead to regulatory competition. The communication between different legal systems, made possible by the consolidation of higher and common rules, does not, however, unfold in a regular, symmetrical way. Rather, there are important differences between sectors, goods, and objectives.

The above analysis leads to two final points. The first has to do with the distinction between domestic and international law. The second concerns the functions of these two kinds of law in relation to private parties.

International law has long been dominated by a dualistic conception of its separation from domestic law. The States, the only subjects of international law, functioned as a screen dividing the one kind of law from the other.[210] The examples considered in this section belie this conception. The power of State intermediation is in fact attenuated. The State itself, in acting, must respect the standards established at the international level.

The authority of domestic administrative law is imperative. It imposes itself on the public, issues orders, grants permission, and establishes obligations. From this comes the characterization of substantive administrative law as the point of equilibrium between State authority and individual liberty. The authority of international administrative law functions differently. It does not set limits upon individuals, but rather upon States. It is a higher law that imposes procedural obligations upon national authorities. Its function is the inverse of domestic administration. International administrative law serves to widen, rather than to narrow, the sphere of private liberty by limiting the action of the State.[211]

---

[210] On this distinction, see S. Battini, *Amministrazioni senza Stato*, cit., p. 4–5, p. 10.

[211] J. H. Jackson has noted that "[t]he basic purpose of the General Agreement [on Tariffs and Trade] is to constrain governments from imposing or continuing a variety of measures which restrain or distort international trade." J. H. Jackson et al., *Legal problems of International Economic Relations: Cases, Materials and Text on the National and International Regulation of*

This reversal in the function of international administrative law, compared to its domestic counterpart, requires a reconsideration of the principles that ground the two systems, taking care not to apply them mechanically in extraneous contexts. Values and rules that have one meaning domestically assume another one internationally. It is enough to give two examples, concerning accountability and participation.

Accountability serves to protect individual liberties. The national administration is asked to respect the law (the principle of legality) because the law comes from the legislature. Citizens elect the legislature, and in so doing, consent to the limits imposed upon them by the public administration. The legislature and its laws thus protect citizens against the executive power, which limits their sphere of activity. At the international level, this conceptual order does not hold. Here, in fact, there is no executive power; the public authority functions to enrich the sphere of private liberty, and the procedural standards of international bodies are enforced against States in order to limit their power.

An analogous observation can be made for participation. This assumes a different significance in the international arena. In domestic law, it is private actors who participate, and this participation has two connected purposes: to ensure the cooperation of citizens in the decision-making process and to give them voice, in order to protect them in their relations with the public power. In international administrative law, the situation is different. Here, it is the State that is generally called on to participate,[212] and it participates not as a defendant but as a vindicator of rights. Therefore, the international community must listen to the point of view of each State if it wishes to maintain general collective control over States' actions. Finally, in international administrative law there is no higher authority that decides after the consultation, because the decision is remanded to bilateral or multilateral collective decision-making.[213].

Transnational Economic Relations, St. Paul, West Group, 1995, 3d ed., p. 290. National administrative law also imposes limits on the public administration (for example, the duty to provide a hearing and judicial review). But these limits serve to constrain the executive power of the administration, which is its primary function.

[212] But, as noted above, private actors are playing a greater role.

[213] This is part of the larger issue of democracy and law in global governance. See generally A. C. Aman, Jr., "Globalization, Democracy and the Need for a New Administrative Law", in

IV. RULING INDIRECTLY: JUDICIAL SUBSIDIARITY IN THE ECHR*

1. DEFERENTIAL STANDARDS OF REVIEW: FROM THE MARGIN OF APPRECIATION TO SUBSIDIARITY

The European Convention on Human Rights provides protection exceeding that ensured by national law, a protection that is based on certain common, shared, and therefore uniform principles (as is the case with European Union law[214]). This uniformity is balanced with a respect for national identities, through the requirement of the prior exhaustion of national remedies (according to Article 35(1) of the Convention, "[t]he Court can only deal with the matter after all domestic remedies have been exhausted...")[215] and the doctrine of the margin of appreciation (that leaves a certain degree of discretion to national governments, "a mild form of immunity"[216]).

Indiana Journal of Global Legal Studies, 2003, vol. 10, p. 125; A. von Bogdandy, *Demokratie, Globalisierung, Zukunft des Völkerrechts – eine Bestandsaufnahme*, in *Zeitschrift für ausländisches öffentliches Recht und Völkerrecht*, 2002, vol. 63, p. 853; J.H.H. Weiler, "The Rule of Lawyers and the Ethos of Diplomats Reflections on the Internal and External Legitimacy of WTO Dispute Settlement", in *Journal of World Trade*, 2001, vol. 35, n. 2, p. 191 ff.

* I want to express my gratitude to Giuliano Amato, Barbara Randazzo, Marta Cartabia and Marco Pacini for their comments on previous versions of this section.

[214] In the context of which this development was noticed by Judge Alberto Trabucchi ("*un droit ...à une protection juridique qui dépasse les limites traditionnelles de leur système nationale*") in a famous note on the *Van Gend en Loos* case (now in *La formazione del diritto europeo*, Quaderni della Rivista di diritto civile, n. 14, Padua, Cedam, 2008, pp. 171-177). See also M. Cartabia, "Fundamental Rights and the Relationship among the Court of Justice, the National Supreme Courts and the Strasbourg Court", in CJEU, *50ème Anniversaire de l'arrêt Van Gend en Loos*, Actes du colloque 13 mai 2013, Luxembourg, Office des publications de l'UE, 2013, p. 156.

[215] The related principle of due consideration by a domestic tribunal, introduced by Protocol No. 14 into Article 35 of the Convention (now Article 35(3)(b)) for the purpose of "ensur[ing] that every case receives a judicial examination whether at the national level or at the European level, in other words, to avoid a denial of justice. The clause is also consistent with the principle of subsidiarity, as reflected notably in Article 13 of the Convention, which requires that an effective remedy against violations be available at the national level" (ECtHR, First Section Decision as to the Admissibility of Application no. 25551/05 by V. P. Korolev against Russia).

[216] D. Spielmann, *Allowing the Right Margin. The European Court of Human Rights and the National Margin of Appreciation Doctrine: Waiver or Subsidiarity of European Review?*, Centre

Both the prior exhaustion requirement and the margin of appreciation doctrine regulate the interplay between legal orders and ensure judicial dialectics. However, while the first is legal in character, because it is established in the Convention, the second has a judicial nature, because it is the product of the Court's case-law.

While the first has been accepted as a common principle in international law, the second, introduced in 1958 and established with the *Handyside* case of 1976, has been criticized for its vagueness and incoherence, for being "a quirk of language", "an unfortunate Gallicism", "the most controversial 'product' of the ECtHR"[217].

Deferential principles originating in law and in case law are common to many composite legal orders, such as the World Trade Organization (WTO) and the European Union[218].

As regards the WTO, deferential standards of review are provided by Article 176 of the Anti-Dumping Agreement, which rules out *de novo* reviews and evaluations of facts, while the Dispute Settlement Body allows for a "margin of appreciation", for example in light of the gravity of the breach[219], and uses the "necessity test" and the "least restrictive test" as margin-of-appreciation techniques[220].

As for the European Union, the Treaty on the European Union (Article 5(3)) provides that "[u]nder the principle of subsidiarity... the Union shall not act only if and in so far as the objectives or the proposed action cannot be sufficiently achieved by the Member States, either at

---

for European Legal Studies, University of Cambridge, Faculty of Law, Working Paper Series, February 2012, p. 2.

[217] D. Spielmann, *Allowing the Right Margin, cit.*, p. 28. A detailed account of the margin of appreciation as subsidiarity is available in J. Christoffersen, *Fair Balance: Proportionality, Subsidiarity and Primarity in the European Convention on Human Rights*, Leiden-Boston, Martinus Nijhoff, 2009, pp. 236 ff.

The margin of appreciation doctrine is subject to multiple interpretations by the Strasbourg Court, such as in the recent case of *S.A.S. v. France*, App. no. 43835/11 (wide margin of appreciation to leave room to the democratic process, in matters of general policy on which opinions may differ widely).

[218] Y. Shany, "Toward a General Margin of Appreciation Doctrine in International Law?", in *European Journal of International Law*, 2005, vol. 16, n. 5, pp. 907 ff.

[219] WTO/DS 222/ARB Canada – Export Credits and Loan Guarantees for Regional Aircraft (15 February 2003), para. 3.44.

[220] F. Fontanelli, *Whose Margin is it? State discretion and judges' appreciation in the necessity quicksand*, available at http://ssrn.com/abstract=1687216, DS 363 (2009).

central level or at the regional and local level, but can rather, by reason of the scale or effects of the proposed action, be better achieved at Union level".

The European Court of Justice has recognized a margin of discretion to national governments, on the assumption that "specific circumstances which may justify recourse to the concept of public policy may vary from one country to another"[221], or when community rights must be balanced with national rights[222], such as in the context of freedom of expression, or simply because diversities exist between the nations[223].

2. PROTOCOL NO. 15

Returning to Strasbourg, Protocol No. 15 has embedded the principle of subsidiarity into the legal system of the European Convention on Human Rights. The most important question is: is this a new principle, or is it simply the codification of a principle derived from the system[224] or established by the Court?

---

[221] CJEU, C-36/02, *Omega v. Oberbürgermeisterin* (14 October 2004), para. 31.

[222] CJEU, C-421/70, *Frede Darmgard* (2 april 2009), para; C-112/00 *Eugen Schmidberger v. Austria* (12 June 2003), para. 81-82; C-71/02, *Herbert Karner v. Troostwijk* (25 March 2004), para.s 50 – 53.

[223] CJEU, C-41/74, *Yvonne van Duyn v. Home Office*, (4 December 1974), para. 18; C-244/06, *Dynamic Medien v. Avides Media* (14 February 2008), para. 44. See, in general, J. Schwarze, "Balancing EU Integration and National Interests in the Case-Law of the Court of Justice", in *The Court of Justice and the Construction of Europe: Analyses and Perspectives on Sixty Years of Case-law*, The Hague, Asser, 2013, pp. 257 ff. and M. Cartabia, *Fundamental Rights*, cit. E. Benvenisti, *Margin of appreciation, consensus and universal standards*, in *International Law and Politics*, 1999, vol. 31, pp. 843 ff., writes that "where national procedures are notoriously prone to failure, most evident when minority rights and interests are involved, no margin and no consensus should be tolerated".

[224] As noticed by Judge Villiger in his partly dissenting opinion in *Vinter and Others v. UK*, App.s no. 66069, 130/10 and 3896/10 (2013): "the principle of subsidiarity underlying the Convention". As a matter of fact, the principle of subsidiarity may be derived from Articles 1, 13 and 35 of the Convention.
According to F. Fabbrini, *The Margin of Appreciation and the Principle of Subsidiarity. A Comparison*, University of Copenhagen Faculty of Law, iCourts Working Paper Series, no. 15, 2015, p. 9, "whereas the Eu principle of subsidiarity and the ECHR doctrine of the margin of appreciation share a similar constitutional function, their legal nature and institutional focus is different"; "the principle of subsidiarity is to be interpreted as a neutral concept, which includes both a

To answer this question, it is necessary to consider the genesis of Article 1 of this Protocol. The subsidiarity principle was first mentioned, in passing, in the "declaration" of the High-Level Conference held in Izmir on 26-27 April 2011 (para. A.3).

The declaration adopted at the following Conference, held in Brighton on 19-20 April 2012, contains a paragraph on the "interaction between the Court and national authorities" (see para. 10-12). The reasoning set out therein is rather tortuous. It commences by mentioning the Court's case law on the margin of appreciation. Then, it states that this "reflects [the fact] that the Convention system is subsidiary" to the national level and national authorities, and that the margin of appreciation goes hand in hand with supervision under the Convention system. Third, the Court is encouraged to give great prominence to, and to apply consistently, the principles of subsidiarity and the margin of appreciation doctrine. Finally, the declaration jumps to a proposal to include, in the Preamble to the Convention, "a reference to the principle of subsidiarity and the doctrine of the margin of appreciation as developed in the Court's case law". In this respect, two points are unclear: was the margin of appreciation doctrine considered to be part of the principle of subsidiarity, or was it rather deemed to be a separate and different principle? Where were the grounds for the subsidiarity principle to be found: in the Court's case law, or in the Convention system?

As a result of the Brighton Conference, Article 1 of Protocol 15, not yet in force, added a new recital to the Preamble of the Convention: "the High Contracting Parties, in accordance with the principle of subsidiarity, have the primary responsibility to secure the rights and freedoms defined in the Convention and the protocols thereto, and in doing so they enjoy a margin of appreciation, subject to the supervisory jurisdiction of the European Court of Human Rights...".

The Explanatory Report to the Protocol states that the reference to the principle and the doctrine is "intended...to be consistent with the doctrine of the margin of appreciation as developed by the Court in its case law". The Opinion of the Court on the Draft Protocol expressed

---

negative and a positive dimension, whereas the margin of appreciation must be seen as limited to the negative dimension only"; "the principle of subsidiarity is mainly addressed to the legislature [...] the margin of appreciation, instead, is mainly concerned with the exercise of jurisdiction by the ECHR [...]".

reservations on the text, but emphasized the drafters' intentions to not "alter either the substance of the Convention or its system of international, collective enforcement". It is well known that the new recital of the Preamble to the Convention was a compromise, which sought to take into account the British reaction to the ECtHR's judgment in the *Hirst* case, which concerned the voting rights of British prisoners[225].

Reading the text, it is difficult to establish why deferential standards of review were introduced by the new Protocol. The reason may have been, simply, functionality (for example to address case overload, or a lack of resources and expertise to conduct investigations or reviews of fact by the Strasbourg Court[226]). Alternatively, to recognize the diversity of national identities. Or deference to sovereignty, to minimize restrictions[227]. Or deference to democracy, along the lines of those who believe that judicial review can be guided by subsidiarity "to enhance their specifically democratic legitimacy" and that "the margin of appreciation … is a main example of… a democratically informed standard of review"[228].

Let us consider whether the new recital is a sign of continuity or, on the contrary, traces a dividing line with the past.

First, subsidiarity and the margin of appreciation are addressed in the new recital as two different principles, as if they had different contents. This will pose, to the Court, the difficult task of establishing the peculiarities of the first *vis-à-vis* the second.

Secondly, the fact that the Convention system relies on national systems, and that the latter must provide effective remedies to the parties whose rights are infringed, is part of the Convention. But the Convention – as interpreted by the Court – may, in several cases, provide protection that is additional to that ensured at the national level. For these cases, the Court had developed, as judge-made law, the margin of appreciation doctrine. This is a self-imposed restraint. However, from

---

[225] E. Benvenisti, *The Law of Global Governance*, The Hague, Academy of International Law, 2014, p. 238.

[226] A. von Staden, *Democratic Legitimacy of Judicial Review beyond the State: Normative Subsidiarity and Judicial Standards of Review*, available at http://ssrn.com/abstract=1969442, p. 24–25.

[227] A. Follesdal, *The Principle of Subsidiarity as a Constitutional Principle in International Law*, New York University, Jean Monnet Working Paper 12/11, 2011, p. 26.

[228] A. von Staden, *Democratic Legitimacy, cit.*, p. 1, p. 5 and p. 12.

now on, both the subsidiarity principle and the margin of appreciation doctrine are imposed on the Court by the Convention. Both are now grounded on another source of law, that is not judge-made law, but Convention law. Until Protocol No. 15 was drafted, the margin of appreciation was granted or recognized to member States by the Court. From Protocol No. 15 onwards, member States are *entitled* to resort to the principle of subsidiarity and to the margin of appreciation doctrine.

This change entails a significant number of consequences. The margin of appreciation doctrine – as a judge-made doctrine – was liable to be overruled. Now, this is no longer possible, as the judge-made doctrine is enshrined in the Convention.

The new legal statement features a second peculiarity. Subsidiarity and the margin of appreciation can be "activated" by third parties (member States) "against" the Court: they can argue, before the Court, to have the primary responsibility in securing the rights and freedoms defined in the Convention and Protocols.

A third peculiarity is that, while the content of the margin of appreciation doctrine has been, and will continue to be, carved out by the Court, the content of the subsidiarity principle reaches the Court loaded with its entire history and all of its ambiguities.

Finally, with the margin of appreciation becoming a legislative doctrine, doubt may be cast on the fact that a double interpretation can still be envisaged by the Court, for countries that provide less protection at the national level and for countries that provide more[229].

I will make one last point in relation to subsidiarity. This principle displays a long-standing and rather unsuccessful[230] tradition in rulemaking and in adjudication. In the context of the Convention system, it was introduced to regulate neither the first nor the latter of these, but rather to regulate judicial review. It is addressed to the Court, as the Conven-

---

[229] On the double standard, J.-L. Flauss, "Faut-il transformer la Cour européenne des droits de l'homme en juridiction constitutionnelle?", in *Dalloz*, 2003, p. 1639, ft. 2 and L. Favoreu, "Corti costituzionali nazionali e Corte europea dei diritti dell'uomo", in *Rivista di diritto costituzionale*, 2004, n. 1, pp. 8-9.

[230] P. Craig, *Subsidiarity, a Political and Legal Analysis*, University of Oxford, Legal Research Paper Series, no. 15, April 2012.

tion's main actor; and judicial subsidiarity is different from legislative or administrative subsidiarity.

Subsidiarity has been used to distribute functions along a vertical line, between the centre and the periphery. In this context, the main purpose of subsidiarity is to allocate functions so that centralization can be avoided, and to ensure an efficient allocation of power. An example is Article 118 of the Italian Constitution: this article provides that administrative tasks are to be allocated among municipalities, provinces, regions and the central government in accordance with the principle of subsidiarity. The same is true for the principle of subsidiarity in the context of the European Union, in which it regulates the distribution of functions between European and national authorities.

Subsidiarity, as an instrument for avoiding centralization, has not been effective. Some attempts have been made to make it work by "proceduralizing" it (e.g. by requiring the advice of lower levels of government before rules can be issued by the higher levels[231]).

The use of subsidiarity in Protocol No. 15 is new, because the context is new. It does not apply to rulemaking or adjudication, but to judicial review. The purpose is not to allocate functions, but to check the uniformity of the application of supranational principles and rules in national contexts. The only precedent of which I am aware, of this type of application of the principle of subsidiarity, is that enshrined in Article 51 and in the Preamble to the Charter of Fundamental Rights of the EU (2010/C 83/02).

3. "COMPETING ASPIRATIONS TOWARDS UNITY AND DIVERSITY"[232]: SUBSIDIARITY AS INDIRECT RULE

We must now turn to the principle of subsidiarity as such. Subsidiarity "has a long and colorful history"[233] and possesses at least thirty different meanings. For this reason, it has been referred to as a program,

---

[231] M. Cartabia, "Unione europea, sussidiarietà e diritti fondamentali", in P. Donati (ed.), *Verso una società sussidiaria*, Bologna, Bononia University Press, 2011, pp. 121-141.

[232] J. H. Elliott, *A Europe of Composite Monarchies*, in *Past and Present*, 1992, p. 71.

[233] T. Horsley, "Subsidiarity and the European Court of Justice: Missing Pieces in the Subsidiarity Jigsaw?", in *Journal of Common Market Studies*, 2012, vol. 50, n. 2, p. 268.

a magic formula, an alibi, a myth, a fig leaf, an aspiration[234]. Subsidiarity was "the word that saved the Maastricht Treaty"[235]. It has been written that subsidiarity "cannot on its own provide legitimacy or contribute to a defensible allocation of authority between national and international institutions e.g. regarding human rights law"[236].

The function of subsidiarity is less unclear, as this principle is caught in a tension with the principle of universality[237], to "affirm internationalism...without the temptation for a super-State or other centralized global authority"[238]. Subsidiarity has many faces: it acts as a devolving mechanism in favour of lower authorities, it is the ground for substituting the lower level with the higher level, and it is the basis for the support provided by the higher level to the weaknesses of the lower level.

Subsidiarity is one of the many applications of a fundamental organizational principle: indirect rule. This principle is as important as the separation of powers. While the latter operates horizontally, the former operates vertically.

Whenever different legal systems integrate and lose their exclusivity[239] – no matter what kind of integration occurs – they assume a set of common general principles and are endowed with a reviewing court,

---

[234] S. Cassese, "L'aquila e le mosche. Principio di sussidiarietà e diritti amministrativi nell'area europea", in *Foro italiano*, 1995, V, pp. 373 ff.

[235] D. Z. Cass, "The Word that Saves Maastricht? The Principle of Subsidiarity and the Division of Powers Within the European Community", in *Common Market Law Review*, 1992, vol. 29, n. 1, pp. 1107 ff.

[236] A. Follesdal, *The Principle, cit.*, p. 31.

[237] E. Benvenisti, *The Law*, cit., pp. 207, 233 ff. and 238.

[238] P.G. Carozza, "Subsidiarity as a Structural Principle of International Human Rights Law", Notre Dame Law School Scholarly Works, 2003, no. 564, p. 78 (also in *American Journal of International Law*, 2003 and, in Italian, in P. G. Grasso (ed.), *Europa e Costituzione*, Napoli, ESI, 2005, pp. 129 ff).

[239] On legal orders losing their character of legal monads and their exclusivity, E. Cannizzaro and B. I. Bonafè, "Beyond the Archetypes of Modern Legal Thought. Appraising Old and New Forms of Interaction Between Legal Orders", in M. Maduro, K. Tuori and S. Sankari (eds.), *Transnational Law. Rethinking European Law and Legal Thinking*, Cambridge, Cambridge University Press, 2014, pp. 78 ff., especially pp. 95-96.

indirect rule is instrumental to avoid collisions, by "ordering pluralism"[240] and by putting together "planets and the universe"[241].

Indirect rule was instrumental first to the establishment of the Roman Empire and then to the expansion of the British Empire. The British could have ruled their empire as the French did theirs, by replacing local institutions with their own metropolitan institutions. Instead, they chose to govern by indirect rule, by super-imposing some of their own general rules, institutions, procedures, and personnel to local institutions and letting them operate as usual. This kind of adaptive, evolutionary process ensures compatibility and tolerance between different values and rules.

Governing by indirect rule in contemporary times is more difficult, as supranational legal systems superimpose only rules, institutions and procedures; they do not send persons to command national legal systems.

Legal orders lose their exclusivity, overlap, and must strike a balance between two sets of competing values: on the one hand, respect of local rules and diversity, and on the other, compliance with the common principles incorporating, in the decision-making process, those interests that are formally excluded and constrain national sovereignty[242].

Indirect rule and its applications must act as shock absorbers, to avoid collisions between converging legal orders. Therefore, they must remain open enough to be worked out over time, and to be adjustable to different conditions. Attempts to establish a precise catalogue and taxonomy of the applications of indirect rule are destined to fail. Fluidity and flexibility[243] are the rule.

4. DEFINING AND CONSTRAINING SUBSIDIARITY

Where does the higher law end, and where does national law begin? It is important to respond to this question by defining and constrain-

---

[240] M. Delmas-Marty, *Ordering Pluralism. A Conceptual Framework for Understanding the Transnational Legal World*, Oxford, Hart, 2009.

[241] B. Simma and D. Pulkowski, "Of Planets and the Universe: Self-Contained Regimes in International Law", in *European Journal of International Law*, 2006, vol. 17, n. 3, pp. 483 ff.

[242] F. de Witte, "Sex, Drugs & EU Law: The Recognition of Moral and Ethical Diversity in EU Law", in *Common Market Law Review*, 2013, vol. 50, pp. 1552 ff.

[243] P. G. Carozza, *Subsidiarity*, cit., p. 79.

ing subsidiarity, to ensure achievement of the Convention's objectives, to reduce the risk of domination by the Court and Convention bodies – which can abuse their flexibility – and to protect both the Court and Convention bodies with respect to more powerful States[244]. Neither the Court nor the contracting Parties (and their respective domestic courts) should be left "wandering in deserts of uncharted discretion"[245].

First, in which areas does the subsidiarity principle apply? The answer is clear: only where there are shared, concurring competences, and therefore where both levels, the national and the supranational, have equal possibilities of action; it does not apply, instead "in areas which do not fall within [the Union's] exclusive competence", as established by Article 5(3) of the Treaty for European Union. This dividing line is blurred for a purely internal reason: it is difficult, for unitary legal orders, as are national ones, to recognize certain rights only in certain circumstances, and not in others. For example, how could a national government and its citizens tolerate that the right to a hearing be protected in certain areas, and not in others, simply because the second falls within the exclusive competence of national authorities? In other words, different sectors and areas within any single national legal order are interconnected and communicate with one another; and citizens are in search of the best protection possible. This is the reason why the impact of the European Union law extends to areas and matters other than those upon which the Union has a direct bearing[246].

Second, when can the subsidiarity principle be invoked? Again, the answer should be clear: only "in connection with those articles of the Convention that have 'limitation clauses'"[247], and not, instead, where "absolute rights" (e.g. the right to life: Article 2; or prohibition of torture: Article 3) are guaranteed[248].

---

[244] A. Follesdal, *The Principle*, cit., p. 29.

[245] US Supreme Court, *Exxon Shipping Co. v. Baker*, 2008, 128 S. Ct. 2605, n. 7 – 219, citing M. Frankel, *Criminal Sentences: Law Without Order* (1973).

[246] A. von Bogdandy et al., "Solange ribaltata. Proteggere l'essenza dei diritti fondamentali nei confronti degli Stati membri dell'UE", in *Rivista trimestrale di diritto pubblico*, 2012, n. 4, pp. 4-5.

[247] I. Rasilla del Moral, "The Increasingly Marginal Appreciation of the Margin-of-Appreciation Doctrine", in *German Law Journal*, 2006, June, no. 6, p. 613.

[248] G. Raimondi, "Corte di Strasburgo e Stati: dialoghi non sempre facili", interview by Diletta Tega, in *Quaderni costituzionali*, 2014, n. 2, p. 463; see also G. Raimondi, "La dichiarazione

Third, can subsidiarity be subject to different interpretations, giving way to narrow/wide and double applications, as is the case with the margin of appreciation doctrine? If – as we concluded in the previous pages – subsidiarity is part of a larger *genus* of institutional arrangements called indirect rule, and if indirect rule is a flexible device *par excellence*, the answer to this question is necessarily in the affirmative.

Fourth, how can the principle of subsidiarity be translated into practice[249], and how can "brakes" be introduced, to make the subsidiarity principle effective? The European Union provides a good example with Protocols 1 and 2 to the Lisbon Treaty (respectively, political controls and judicial controls). These brakes, however, are not entirely effective[250].

As a flexible tool, subsidiarity can have varying impact, depending upon the distinctive features of each national legal order. For example, those that do not have a written constitution are more exposed to the percolation of supranational law. The United Kingdom has been obliged to adapt with the Human Rights Act 1998.

One final point on defining and restraining subsidiarity is a *caveat*. It should not be believed that, where supranational authorities have a subsidiary role, sovereign States have a free hand. Sovereignty is illusory for four reasons. Being subsidiary means that national authorities (mainly courts, in our case) must comply with some common, shared principles, as are those listed in the Convention and its Protocols. Being subsidiary also means to be subject to a supervising jurisdiction and court. Subsidiarity makes State action discretionary *vis-à-vis* the higher law, as is the case for national administrative authorities and judicial review. Finally, being part of a collective agreement, national authorities are not only accountable to the higher bodies (in our case, the ECtHR), but also to the other parties to the Convention (horizontal accountability).

---

di Brighton sul futuro della Corte europea dei diritti dell'uomo", in *Associazione italiana dei costituzionalisti, Rivista telematica giuridica*, 2012, n. 3.

[249] P.G. Carozza, *Subsidiarity*, cit., p. 79.

[250] P. Craig, *Subsidiarity*, cit.

5. CONCLUSION: TO WHAT CAN SUBSIDIARITY LEAD?

To what can subsidiarity lead the European Convention on Human Rights? Which developments can be foreseen?

One possible development is a potential restraint on the ECtHR[251], by limiting its jurisdiction, for example by endowing it with a power of review that is limited only to patent violations of the Convention, e.g. that occurring in the *Bosphorus* case ("if the protection of Convention rights is manifestly deficient": para. 156).

A second development that can be envisaged is national political bodies or national courts introducing external controls on the implementation of the subsidiarity principle, in defense of their "territories", as defined by the subsidiarity principle.

A third development is that the role of national courts as judges of the Convention will be enhanced, on the example of the European Union judicial system. Along those lines, national courts could become, at least functionally, part of the judicial branch of the Council of Europe's legal system, acting upon delegation with the task of reviewing the conventionality of national decisions, with the Strasbourg Court entitled to act as a guiding body through a system of preliminary reference[252].

While all three developments could lower the number of cases brought before the Strasbourg Court, none should be accepted as a means to revive national interests against the obligations accepted with the signature of the Convention. The process of globalization of human rights has witnessed, and will continue to witness, tensions between national governments and supranational bodies.

However, it cannot reduce its efforts to set global brakes to, and controls over, national legal orders. Over time, these display ever more faults and "lacunae", as they are instruments that are far from perfect. "Human rights, democracy and the rule of law now face a crisis unprecedented since the end of the Cold War", wrote the Secretary General of

---

[251] T. Horsley, *Subsidiarity*, cit., pp. 267 and 281.

[252] One must also consider the consequences of the Union's participation in the Convention and the impact of Protocol no. 16, that provides for the issuance of "advisory opinion[s] on questions of principle relating to the interpretation or application of the rights and freedoms defined in the Convention or the Protocols thereto".

the Council of Europe in his May 2014 Report[253]. Therefore, it becomes necessary to complement the controls from below (popular elections) with checks from above.

A second reason for not allowing the revival of the protection of pure national rights in Europe is that human rights are not guaranteed only in this area of the world, but are rather part of a general set of global rules, under the aegis of the United Nations Organization. Then, how could Europeans escape control by Strasbourg-based supranational institutions, while being submitted to other international treaties such as the Universal Declaration of Human Rights, the International Covenant on Civil and Political Rights, the International Covenant on Economic, Social and Cultural Rights, and the UN Convention against Torture, and to such global institutions in charge of confining and promoting democracy, the rule of law and human rights, as are the United Nations, the United Nations Democracy Fund, and many more ancillary institutions? How could Europe remain behind the Organization of American States (and the American Convention on Human Rights, with the Inter-American Court of Human Rights), and the Economic Community of West African States (with the African Court on Human and Peoples' Rights), whose protection of human rights has, in many countries, been incorporated in national law, that also ensures judicial remedies for private parties?

V. THE DEVELOPMENT OF GLOBAL ADMINISTRATIVE LAW

1. THE DIMENSIONS OF GLOBAL ADMINISTRATIVE LAW

In administrative law's two hundred years of history, the most important change has been the development of global administrative law (through the inception of two thousand global regulatory regimes, sixty thousand international non-governmental organizations, over a hundred

---

[253] *State of Democracy, Human Rights and the Rule of Law in Europe*, 14th Session of the Committee of Ministers, Vienna, 5-6 May 2014, p. 5.

international courts, and a similar number of quasi-judicial bodies – against "only" a hundred and ninety-three States). Global administrative law (GAL) is partly linked to the State, and partly connected with global institutions[254].

Until a few decades ago, both administrative systems and administrative law developed in the specific context of the nation-State. The legal environment that favoured the development of administrative systems and administrative law was a national government, which was run by a political body called the "State". Public administrations were conceived of as belonging to national communities, and as being structurally dependent upon national governments. Administrative law was thus fundamentally *State* law.

As a consequence, an exclusive link was established between the State and administration, the best expression of which is the famous formula "the administrative State", coined in 1948 by the American political scientist Dwight Waldo[255]. Where there is a State, there is an administrative system – and vice-versa. Administrative systems and administrative law were shaped according to the needs of the different State models; as each national State developed along divergent lines, administrative systems diverged too. Therefore, public administrations and their respective systems of administrative law became the ultimate enclaves of nationalism.

The development of global regulators and of global rules altered this traditional picture: State administrative law was monistic, while GAL has a dualistic dimension. State administrative systems diverge, while GAL has some unitary features and drives national administrative systems toward convergence.

As noted above, GAL has a double relationship – one with national governments, and one with global regulatory regimes. However, contrary to a commonly held opinion, GAL is not a layer of regulation that

---

[254] S. Cassese, "Il diritto amministrativo europeo presenta caratteri originali?" (2003), in S. Cassese, *Il diritto amministrativo: storia e prospettive*, Milan, Giuffrè, 2010, p. 388-389. With regard to the number of international judicial bodies, see *The Project on International Courts and Tribunals. The International Judiciary in Context*, directed by Cesare P.R. Romano (November 2004), which distinguishes existing, extinct, aborted, dormant, nascent, proposed international judicial bodies, including quasi-judicial, implementation control and other dispute settlement bodies.

[255] D. Waldo, *The Administrative State: A Study of the Political Theory of American Public Administration*, New York, Ronald Press Co., 1948, rev. ed. New York, Holmes & Meier, 1984.

is superimposed upon State regulation, and administrative law is not a multi-level system, because global regulation percolates into national legal orders and the result is a mixture of national and global measures.

Consequently, in the global perspective, the concept of publicness is also subject to change, because it is influenced by the State in connection with global regulators. The State remains the protagonist, but new actors play the part of deuteragonist (or vice-versa).

As a result of this overlap between the State and supranational rulers and rules, the divergence of administrative systems and of national administrative legal systems is limited by a body of basic common rules – shared among the various global regulatory regimes – with which all members of the international community are expected to comply.

A second problem for the field's identity is the use of the adjective "global" rather than "international". Historically, the latter term was used with reference to inter-State relations, assuming the paradigm of the State as a unit, while "global" also refers to civil societies and to the fragmented State[256]. GAL captures three dimensions: civil societies (and not only national rulers and ruling bodies); national institutions (but not as part of a unitary legal person); and supranational, international and transnational institutions. From this perspective, GAL is characterized not only by a "trilateral" relationship (between civil societies, national institutions and institutions beyond the State), but also by the emergence of "new alliances": as local and global interest converge, global institutions establish alliances with individuals or national civil societies against States[257]. For example, the regimes for protection of the global environment or cultural heritage use civil society members as "fire alarms" against the action of national governments. Choosing the term "global" instead of "international", is not, therefore, a matter of mere

---

[256] According to M. Mazower, Jeremy Bentham, who coined the word international, wanted to stress two points: the need for a sharp distinction between law within a State and law between States, and the distinction between legal disputes affecting individuals and those affecting the sovereign States (see M. Mazower, *Governing the World. The History of an Idea, 1815 to the Present*, New York, Penguin, 2012, p. 20).

[257] The development of global regimes is strictly linked with the aim to verify the compliance of national systems with relevant guarantees provided in favour of individuals (as underlined by S. Battini, "L'impatto della globalizzazione sulla pubblica amministrazione e sul diritto amministrativo: quattro percorsi", in *Giornale di diritto amministrativo*, 2006, p. 341).

terminology, because the former refers to the world as an interconnected whole[258].

2. ADMINISTRATION WITHOUT A CONSTITUTION?

One of GAL's peculiarities is the fact that it is much more developed than its constitutional foundations. The latter are limited to a body of basic human rights, and there is no global government. Conversely, GAL comprises a large number of global rules and regulators which basically reproduce the organizational styles and procedural paradigms that are well known within States, such as the right to a hearing, the duty to provide reasons, judicial review, and the due process of law generally. Therefore, the world is more united by the global administrative standards established, rather than constitutional principles; by the regulation of trade and the environment, more than by law and order or defence; and by the global definition of matters of low politics, rather than of high politics. This peculiarity differentiates GAL from national administra-

---

[258] On GAL in general, B. Kingsbury, N. Krisch and R. Stewart, "The Emergence of Global Administrative Law", in *Law and Contemporary Problems*, 2005, vol. 68, Summer-Autumn, n. 3-4, p. 20; E.D. Kinney, "The Emerging Field of International Administrative Law: Its Content and Potential", in *Administrative Law Review*, 2002, vol. 54, Winter, n. 1, p. 415; B.S. Chimni, "Co-Option and Resistance: Two Faces of Global Administrative Law", in *Journal of International Law and Politics*, 2005, vol. 37, Summer, n. 4, p. 799; C. Harlow, "Global Administrative Law: The Quest for Principles and Values", in *European Journal of International Law*, 2006, vol. 17, n. 1, p. 187; A. von Bogdandy, R. Wolfrun, J. von Bernstorff, P. Dann, M. Goldmann (eds.), *The Exercise of Public Authority by International Institutions: Advancing International Institutional Law*, Heidelberg, Springer, 2009; B. Kingsbury, "The Concept of "Law" in Global Administrative Law", in *European Journal of International Law*, 2009, vol. 20, n. 1, pp. 23-57; B. Kingsbury and L. Casini, "Global Administrative Law Dimension of International Organizations Law", in symposium on "Global Administrative Law in the Operations of International Organizations" (eds. L. Boisson de Chazournes, L. Casini, and B. Kingsbury), *International Organizations Law Review*, 2009, vol. 6, n. 2, p. 326, nt. 23 *Global Administrative Law Dimensions of International Organizations Law*, cit., p. 319. See also, in the French literature, J.-L. Halperin, *Profils des mondialisations du droit*, Paris, Dalloz, 2009 (tracing the history of legal globalization, from Roman law to constitutionalism and codification), but mainly J.-B. Auby, *La globalisation, le droit et l'Etat*, Paris, L.G.D.J., II edition, 2010. In the Italian literature, M. R. Ferrarese, *Diritto sconfinato. Inventiva giuridica e spazi nel mondo globale*, Roma – Bari, Laterza, 2006 and S. Cassese, *Il diritto globale*, Torino, Einaudi, 2009.

tive law, which is instead subject to a process of constitutionalization and is fundamentally ruled by constitutional principles.

Another peculiarity derives from the absence of a single government and of a single comprehensive legal order at the global level. In the global space, several global regulatory regimes act without subjection to one hierarchically superior regulatory system. This is the empire of the "ad-hoc-cracy", because there is no uniformity and no common pattern. This fragmentation is balanced in various ways: links between otherwise self-contained regimes, cross-references between area regulations, the use of "precedents" taken from different regulatory regimes diffuses, and so on[259].

However, a process of convergence of the different regulatory regimes is under way, as "norms, standards and expectations that have crystalized in most domestic legal systems have migrated to global governance bodies and now frame perceptions about the legitimacy of their decision-making processes and decisions. At the same time, this process of migration creates pressure for convergence, in what sociologists would call a process of isomorphism"[260]. Also "[...] the substantive norms of administrative law [...] are generally similar in most domestic and global systems, and are certainly undergoing a process of assimilation [...]".[261]

In conclusion, while GAL largely includes national administrative legal orders, it remains significantly different from the administrative laws developed within national governments.

3. THE "MARBLED" STRUCTURE OF GLOBAL ADMINISTRATION: THE ROLE OF GLOBAL REGULATORY REGIMES

The American political scientist and diplomat Henry Kissinger has written that "The contemporary, now global Westphalian system – what colloquially is called the world community – has striven to curtail the anarchical nature of the world with an extensive network of international

[259] S. Cassese, *The Global Polity. Global Dimensions of Democracy and the Rule of Law*, Sevilla, Global Law Press, 2014, p. 22 ff.

[260] E. Benvenisti, *The Law of Global Governance*, Hague Academy of International Law, 2014, p. 195 and 196.

[261] Ibid 196.

legal and organizational structures designed to foster open trade and a stable international financial system, establish accepted principles of resolving international disputes, and set limits on the conduct of wars when they do occur. This system of States now encompasses every culture and region. Its institutions have provided the neutral framework for the interactions of diverse societies – to a large extent independent of their respective values"[262].

The American historian Mark Mazower has observed that "[t]oday there is more global policymaking, in more varied form, than ever before [...]. There are military alliances, such as NATO and WEU; intergovernmental organizations in the classic mold, from the UN to specialist agencies such as the ILO, ICAO, ICC, WHO, and GATT; regional bodies, like the Council of Europe, the European Commission, and the Organizations of American and African States; post-imperial clubs, like the Commonwealth and the *Organisation international de la Francophonie*; quasi-polities like the European Union; and regular summit conferences like the G-20. Nor should one ignore the vast number of NGOs of all kinds, many of which now play a more or less formalized role in shaping global politics". [263] He has also written that "ninety per cent of international NGOs have been formed since 1970, and there has been a quickening of associational life on a scale not seen since before the First World War: a 1994 *Foreign Affairs* article referred to a "Global Associational Revolution".[264]

The American political scientist Anne-Marie Slaughter has written that "[t]here is an entire infrastructure of global governance that is not at the UN, or at the World Bank, or at the International Monetary Fund or at the World Trade Organization. It is the networks of antitrust officials, of police officials, prosecutors, financial regulators, intelligence operatives, militaries, judges and even, although lagging behind, legislators"[265].

Global regulatory regimes cover many fields: "forest preservation, the control of fishing, water regulation, environmental protection, stand-

[262] H. Kissinger, *World Order. Reflections on the Character of Nations and the Course of History*, Allen Lane, The Penguin Press, 2014, p. 6.

[263] M. Mazower, *Governing the World* cit., p. XVII and 417.

[264] Ibid 417.

[265] A.-M. Slaughter, "A New UN for the New Century", in *Fordham Law Review*, 2006, vol. 74, n. 6, p. 2961 – 2970.

ardization and food safety, financial and accounting standards, internet governance, pharmaceutical regulation, intellectual property protection, refugee protection, coffee and cocoa standards, labor standards, antitrust regulation, regulation and finance of public works, trade standards, regulation of insurance, foreign investments, international terrorism, war and arms control, air and maritime navigation, postal services, telecommunications, nuclear energy and nuclear waste, money laundering, education, migration, law enforcement, sport, and health"[266].

Richard B. Stewart has classified global regulators into four basic types: "(1) formal treaty-based international or intergovernmental organizations (such as the WTO, the Security Council, the World Bank, and the United Nations Framework Convention on Climate Change regime); (2) transnational networks of domestic regulatory officials (such as the Basel Committee on Banking Supervision); (3) private regulatory bodies (such as international sports federations, the Society for Worldwide Interbank Financial Telecommunication, and the Forest Stewardship Council, constituted by non-State actors, including business firms, trade and professional associations, and NGOs); and (4) hybrid public-private regulatory bodies (such as the International Conference on Harmonisation of technical requirements for registration of Pharmaceuticals for Human Use, the World Anti-doping Agency, ICANN, and the Global Fund to Fight AIDS, Tuberculosis and Malaria (Global Fund) – composed of non-State actors and international organizations and/or governments"[267].

The growth of global regulatory regimes is explained in different ways. Statisticians, geographers, engineers, physicians believe that the "fundamental unity of the world [is] a scientific fact"[268]; politicians think that "internationalism [is] preeminently a movement to restore sovereign power to the peoples of the world and those who governed in their

[266] S. Cassese, *The Global Polity*, cit., p. 20.

[267] R.B. Stewart, "Remedying Disregard in Global Regulatory Governance: Accountability, Participation, and Responsiveness", in *American Journal of International Law*, 2014, vol. 108, p. 216 – 217.

[268] M. Mazower, *Governing the World*, cit., p. 95. See also J. Renn (ed.), *The Globalization of Knowledge in History*, Max Planck Research Library for the History and Development of Knowledge. Studies 1, 2012, Berlin. epubli (Edition Open Access).

name"[269]; public administrators have been themselves the architects of modern international organizations[270].

Global regulatory regimes present many peculiar features. First, despite the rapid expansion of their material scope and the proliferation of regulators, they are still at an early stage of development and have not yet reached maturity. Legal scholars are therefore obliged to take into account the fact that the subject they are studying is, as yet, *in itinere*.

Second, they are composite organizations, as they include global bodies, national authorities and personnel, representatives of civil society, transnational networks, members of epistemic communities, and various types of stakeholders, with no clear dividing line or hierarchy between the local and the global; in many ways, they can be compared to the European empires of the seventeenth to nineteenth centuries[271].

Third, there is no unitary government and rule, but rather a multiplicity of diverse elements, which are fragmented and often not interconnected because there is no superior unifying authority (and no national legal system is currently willing to recognize a superior authority having general competences). This allows for a certain degree of flexibility and ability to adjust to different situations, but also leads to a lack of uniformity, coordination and planning; these drawbacks are compensated by the establishment of links between global regulatory bodies and procedures[272].

---

[269] M. Mazower, *Governing the World*, cit., p. 421 – 422; see also p. 152 - 153. From a similar perspective, see A.L. Paulus, "Law and Politics in the Age of Globalisation", in *European Journal of International Law*, 2000, vol. 11, n. 2, p. 465–472.

[270] M. Mazower, *Governing the World*, cit., p. 155 ff.; see also p. 281 ff., 299 ff., 317 ff, 359 ff. Also in the European context, public administrators acted as architects of a ultra-State model of public administration, "whose area overlaps with the space of European Union, incorporating the effects of globalization": A. Matei and L. Matei, *Globalization and Europeanization. A Projection on a European Model of Public Administration*. Paper presented at the 27th International Congress of Administrative Sciences, organised by the International Institute of Administrative Sciences in Abu Dhabi, United Arab Emirates, on 9-14 July 2007 (available at http://ssrn.com/abstract=1310129).

[271] See J. Leonhard – U. von Hirschhauser, *Imperi e stati nazionali nell'Ottocento*, Italian translation, Bologna, Il Mulino, 2014, p. 7 – 8.

[272] Elsewhere, I have written: "National governments are unitary and have an executive body at their centre. In the global space there are several different regulatory regimes and there is no single executive. In national legal orders, a central executive is accompanied by a body of general rules, which is then divided into sector-specific norms. The former confer coherence

Fourth, there are no strong executives; global institutions lack enforcement powers, and in the great majority of cases rely upon nation-States as enforcers[273]. The absence of a centre is balanced by the presence of a great array of collegial bodies, in which administrators meet to discuss, convince, and reach compromises, similarly to the Spanish Empire's "polisinodality".

Fifth, since GAL features a double link – one with the State and one with global institutions – and the State's influence is weakened, the public-private divide is blurred, and hybridism prevails (for example, in procedural matters, the WTO places national governments and private producers, exporters, importers, and interested parties all on an equal footing).

---

and uniformity to the latter. At the global level, the situation is different. Almost all human activities are regulated by global norms. The latter are highly diverse. Some establish only framework legislation, for States to flesh out through regulatory activity; some provide guidelines for national authorities; others directly impose certain obligations upon private parties; other norms can rely on global authorities for implementation or to control implementation; some rely on national authorities for these activities; some provide instruments of judicial conflict resolution, while others yet are devoid of such mechanisms and resort only to negotiation or national judges. However, they do present a common trait, outlined above: these normative entities are all sector-based; there is no general set of rules (or meta-rules) to operate as a unifying element. The global legal space compensates for the disadvantages of this sectoralism in several ways. The first and most common course is a process of accretion and accumulation of legal principles, as highlighted by the first decision issued by the Arbitral Tribunal established by the Convention on the Law of the Sea. The second is the establishment of horizontal connections between different normative bodies. For example, the standards established by the *Codex Alimentarius Commission* were voluntary prior to 1995, but have since acquired legal force because the WTO required parties not wishing to observe them to prove their capacity to guarantee an adequate level of protection. These connections are usually established starting from, and surrounding, the most important global normative bodies, such as that on trade, which, due to their scope, exert gravitational pull on other sector-based regulations. Thus, the various regulatory bodies are distinct but not separate. As established by the first decision issued by the Appellate Body of the WTO, the global laws on trade are not to be interpreted in isolation, separate from general international law. This gave rise to the ever-closer connections between rules on trade, on one hand, and those on environmental protection, worker protection standards etc. on the other" (S. Cassese, *The Administrative State in Europe*, in A. von Bogdandy, P. M. Huber, S. Cassese (eds), *The Max Planck Handbooks in European Public Law. The Administrative State*, Oxford, Oxford University Press, 2017, vol. I, p. 91).

[273] For more details on enforcement mechanisms in the global administrative space, see S. Cassese, E. D'Alterio and M. De Bellis, "The Enforcement of Transnational Private Regulation: A Fictitious Oxymoron", in F. Cafaggi (ed.), *Enforcement of Transnational Regulation. Ensuring Compliance in a Global World*, Cheltenham, Edward Elgar Publishing Ltd., 2012, p. 331 ff.

Sixth, due to the fact that global regulators are fragmented, and there is no single global hegemonic government, it is necessary to rule indirectly. Global regulators thus act as standard-setters and gatekeepers, and rely upon national authorities as implementers. In doing so, global regulators break away from the paradigm of the "State as a unit", and establish direct links with the national bodies empowered to act in the relevant fields, often bypassing national executives and Parliaments.

Finally, in the relations between global and national bodies, the crucial point is that of enforcement. The former have experimented with several ways to enforce their decisions: by gaining support from below, i.e. civil society, which sounds a "fire alarm" and pressures national authorities to enforce; by making it expedient to comply with decisions taken at the global level, through incentives and rewards; by sanctioning non-compliance with expulsion measures; by exploiting conflicting interests and introducing retaliatory measures under judicial control. However, despite all these indirect measures, the final word for enforcement still falls to national governments. This is advantageous in that it is reassuring for States, which can delegate powers to global bodies more easily; but it also has a cost, as enforcement is irregular and ultimately relies upon voluntary compliance.

4. DIFFERENT TYPES OF RULE OF LAW

As noted above, the global space is replete with rules that impose transparency, as well as affirmations of the right of stakeholders to a hearing, the right to be informed and consulted, the duty to provide reasons, and the right to a judge and to the judicial review of decisions. Procedural rights are more broadly present in some contexts, and more limitedly in others.

One of the most striking features of the global legal space is the speed at which principles of the rule of law have developed within the different legal orders[274]. Institutions that took decades or even centuries to develop within States quickly expanded beyond the State, sometimes

---

[274] J. Agudo Gonzalez, "The Evolution of Administrative Procedure Theory in 'New Governance' Key Point", in *Review of European Administrative Law*, vol. 6, n. 1, p. 73-109.

even more proficiently than in the State context. It is likely that the reason for this rapidity lies in the fact that all States have experienced a historical phase of absolutism, during which the principle of authority prevailed and no administrative rights were granted to citizens. It took centuries for certain basic rights to be recognized against the executive agencies of national governments.

The global context exemplifies the influence of American institutions and culture, as most of its rules follow the model of the 1946 US Administrative Procedure Act. However, the due process clauses of the global space do not have the same structure and function as those of their national counterparts.

First, these clauses are provided by global rules, but are imposed upon national authorities, not upon global regulators. They endow nationals with additional rights *vis-à-vis* national governments, rights that are not provided by national law. Paradoxically, global rules are less generous in providing people with access to and voice against global institutions; hence the observation made by certain scholars that global regimes "operate in an essentially closed and opaque manner"[275].

Second, these procedural requirements play a different role also from a functional point of view. They act as fire alarms: global bodies cannot patrol the whole world to ensure compliance on part of national governments, and must therefore rely upon information from nationals, individuals or associations. Thus, they also act as an instrument for mobilization and integration. Global bodies grant access to citizens, whose participation is not allowed by national law, and foster strategic alliances between global institutions and civil societies against national governments. In the meantime, they level the playing field, diffusing certain basic administrative rights throughout the world or within supranational regions, and opening the path to dialogue.

In giving citizens a voice and imposing upon national authorities an obligation to openness and to give reasons, due process clauses also perform a legitimating role for the global bodies that act as guarantors of civic rights. The expanding role of global rules and bodies as guarantors may, one day, become a weak surrogate for global democracy.

---

[275] With regard to the WTO, see R.B. Stewart and M. Ratton Sanchez Badin, "The World Trade Organization: Multiple Dimensions of Global Administrative Law", in *International Journal of Constitutional Law*, 2011, vol. 9, n. 3-4. p. 556-586.

One may conclude that due process principles, when transplanted into the global space, become different from the analogous procedural rights established by national rules against national authorities – that they are not new, but rather become different in a new context.

Similar conclusions can be traced for reviewing mechanisms. Not all two thousand global regulatory regimes provide such mechanisms; however, some ten or fifteen percent do have either courts, tribunals, panels, compliance committees, inspections panels, or assessment panels[276].

The reviewing bodies established at the global level are affected by four problems. First, they are called upon mainly to review decisions taken by national authorities, and not decisions taken by global institutions. They are therefore instrumental to global regulators' control of national bodies' compliance with global standards. They trigger a fire alarm system through popular participation (complaints), legitimate global rules and maximize the power of global regulators. They also raise a question that is much debated in the United States: since national governments agree to become parties to treaties establishing global regulatory regimes, and thus acquire an obligation to comply with global standards, could not national courts be in a better position to provide such review?

Second, the review bodies act in a space that is not entirely developed as a unitary entity which adopts the parameter of legal reasonableness, appearing to prefer more flexible standards such as suitability, appropriateness, or expediency, or even simply technical standards (e.g. the International Civil Aviation Organization's Universal Security Audit Program Continuous Monitoring Approach). This integration of review standards raises many questions. Are the members of the reviewing bodies the most suitable parties to evaluate such a broad scope of standards? Are adversarial procedures appropriate to these evaluations? Could it be more appropriate to delegate these evaluations (which examine the merits of decisions subject to review) to independent and non-accountable bodies?

---

[276] M. Mazower, cit., p. 397 ff. and 402 ff. and S. Cassese, *When Legal Orders Collide: The Role of Courts*, Sevilla, Global Law Press, 2010. See also C.P.R. Romano, "A Taxonomy of International Rule of Law Institutions", in *Journal of International Dispute Settlement*, 2011, vol. 2, n. 1, p. 252.

Third, this type of review is not only reactive, but is often proactive. Reviewing bodies are also required to make proposals, to direct training to ensure compliance in the future, and to make suggestions.

Fourth, while reviewing bodies must adjudicate, they either do not have or have primitive rules of procedure. Certain bodies adopt reviewing procedures on a case-by-case basis. Many reviewing bodies require national authorities to ensure transparency, openness, participation, but are themselves neither transparent nor open, and do not provide full hearings.

Finally, the decisions taken by reviewing bodies are necessarily limited to the specific field concerning which the rules are enacted. However, many of these tribunals and quasi-judicial bodies make reference to decisions taken by reviewing bodies acting in other regulatory regimes; they therefore establish bridges to one another, and contribute to the de-fragmentation of the global space and the development of certain common jurisprudential principles. In so doing, they act as promoters, developers, accelerators, and system builders of a global legal order.

5. DEVELOPMENT MECHANISM

GAL has developed rapidly, but in an incremental and even accidental fashion. Its development has been rapid, taking place in the space of only twenty or thirty years; incremental and accidental, because it has grown without a prior plan or a design, prompted by two types of pressures. First, governments are challenged by new problems that are of a global scale and thus require global solutions: global warming, global terrorism, the organization of Olympic games, the disposal of nuclear waste, the financial crisis. Second, local problems now become global: local environmental associations require UNESCO's assistance to protect sites that are registered as world heritage (e.g. the Yellowstone National Park in the United States); and national governments ask the UN for advice and support in prosecuting crimes (e.g. the case of Guatemala).

Under these pressures, global rules, institutions and procedures have developed under the strong influence of American examples – not necessarily as part of a process of "colonization", but mainly as a process of contamination and intellectual influence.

This process of development is necessarily incomplete and therefore presents several black and grey holes. It has begun at the edges, and is slowly moving towards the centre. However, it is not ephemeral, nor will it disappear. A new constitution will eventually emerge from this fabric of administrative law, reversing the succession known within national governments in which administrative law has usually developed on the basis of a stable constitution, growing out of constitutional law.

6. THE STUDY OF GLOBAL ADMINISTRATIVE LAW

The study of GAL must overcome two important difficulties. One relates to ideological prejudices, approaches and biases. The second concerns traditional legal scholarship.

The first danger is that of becoming imprisoned in one of two opposing points of view, one optimistic and one pessimistic. The optimist finds, in globalization, the solution to all of the world's social and economic problems. The pessimist finds that globalization is either not relevant or even dangerous.

The second danger, instead, is of remaining enslaved to the nationalistic approach developed by legal positivism: States are monopolistic law-makers, the subject of legal scholarship is the law, and therefore lawyers are always bound to study State law. This approach – defined by Raymond Saleilles as one of "*nationalisme étroit*" – has suffocated the research of more general laws that transcend the State. On this view, openings to other legal systems have been accepted only in terms of legal comparison, and not as the study of transplants, circulation, dialogue, hybridism, convergence, or common core principles.

All these developments are not entirely new: Jeremy Bentham (1748 – 1832) already distinguished local and universal forms of jurisprudence; Giandomenico Romagnosi wrote a book on the "*Diritto pubblico universale*" ("Universal public law", 1833) and Raymond Saleilles wrote that "*toute science juridique est forcément internationale et universelle*" ("all juridical science is necessarily international and universal", 1904)[277].

---

[277] R. Saleilles, "Le Code civil et la Méthode historique", in *Le Code Civil 1804-1904* Livre du Centenaire publié par la Société d'Etudes Législatives, tome premier, Paris, Librairie Edouard Duchemin, 1904, reprinted 1969, p. 127. Author's translation.

VI. GLOBAL ADMINISTRATIVE LAW: THE STATE OF THE ART

Global institutions are about twenty years old, but they have developed rapidly. Indeed, globalization enhances the role of law and of legal systems, because globalization is achieved mainly through legalization. These institutions have attracted a great deal of intellectual interest, since scholarship has reacted quickly to global administrative law. Indeed, there exists today a very rich literature on the subject, and some general accounts or overviews of the field[278].

And yet, the definition of global administrative law is still very much contested; its relations with international law and constitutional law are not yet settled; and no single account of the field has attained the status of orthodoxy.

The definition of global administrative law is contested by the German school of Heidelberg, whose scholars, such as Armin von Bogdandy, believe that it is more appropriate to speak of an "exercise of international public authority"[279]. Eyal Benvenisti, on the other hand, finds it more appropriate to speak of the "law of global governance"[280].

The dividing line between administrative and constitutional law is blurred: Gunther Teubner, in his work entitled *Constitutional Fragments. Societal Constitutionalism and Globalization*[281], observed that global administrative law "is the latest candidate for the constitutionalization of world society" and that "most of the authors avoid the language of constitutionalism and content themselves with general principles of administrative law, without adequately addressing the basis of their validity in the transnational sphere".

---

[278] B. Kingsbury, N. Krisch and R. B. Stewart, "The Emergence of Global Administrative Law", in *Law and Contemporary Problems*, 2005, vol. 68, n. 3-4, pp. 15 ff.; S. Cassese, *The Global Polity. Global Dimensions of Democracy and the Rule of Law*, Seville, Global Law Press, 2012; and E. Benvenisti, *The Law of Global Governance*, The Hague, AIL – Pocket, 2014.

[279] A. von Bogdandy et al. (eds), *The Exercise of Public Authority by International Institutions. Advancing International Institutional Law*, Heidelberg, Springer, 2009.

[280] E. Benvenisti, *The Law of Global Governance*, cit.

[281] G. Teubner, *Constitutional Fragments. Societal Constitutionalism and Globalization*, Oxford, Oxford University Press, 2012, p. 50 and footnote n. 31.

The relations with international law are not yet settled. Scholars of the growing field of global administrative law (GAL) share the idea that it transcends international law, because it also includes national civil societies among its actors. However, international law experts tend to consider global administrative law as a part of their discipline.

No single account of the field has reached the status of orthodoxy, because there are globalists and skeptics. Richard Stewart and Benedict Kingsbury may be considered to fall within the former category[282]; and Eric Posner in the latter[283].

It is now clear that global administrative law is not only global, not only administrative, and not only law. It is not only global, because it includes many supranational regional or local agreements and authorities. It is not only administrative, because it includes many private and constitutional law elements (although the administrative component prevails, because constitutions and private regulation, involving "high politics" matters or societal interests, resist globalization). Global administrative law is not only law, because it also includes many types of "soft law" and standards.

The rich literature on global administrative law has focused on especially two problems: the reasons for global administrative law, and its peculiarities – the "why" and the "how". However, in both respects, many questions remain unanswered.

As for the reasons, one set of explanations is clear: global problems require global institutions. To organize Olympic Games and control doping; to fight global terrorism; to control epidemics, world trade, international finance, the Internet; to protect highly migratory species; or to reduce global warming, one cannot proceed at the national level – one must go global.

Less research has been done on why global administrative law develops to address national problems – for example, on the global institutions established to enhance national democracy or the rule of law, to increase mutual accountability between nations, or to reduce the asymmetries between nations.

---

[282] B. Kingsbury, N. Krisch and R. B. Stewart, "The Emergence of Global Administrative Law", in *Law and Contemporary Problems*, cit.

[283] E. Posner, *The Perils of Global Legalism*, Chicago, University of Chicago Press, 2009.

As for global administrative law's peculiarities, three in particular have been studied. Global administrative law is de-territorialized. Global regulatory regimes feature legislation (treaties, rules, policies, standards, soft law) without legislatures, dispute settlement functions with only a limited number of courts (but a great number of quasi-judicial reviewing bodies), implementation without an executive branch (through indirect rule, and by monitoring and controlling implementation and enforcement through national bodies). Global administrative institutions lack the usual legitimacy and accountability mechanisms, but possess capacity-based authority[284] and are kept under control through surrogates.

However, the literature on global administrative law has yet to capture all the peculiarities of the field. I wish to focus on four features of GAL.

First, global administrative law is undergoing constant development, change, and improvement; and this is not a unidirectional or linear process. In reaction to healthcare tourism, national actors travel abroad to find patients. Through its *maquiladoras*, the United States exports jobs but also pollution, thus provoking strong reactions from Mexico. A large part of the imports from Mexico to the United States originated in the United States itself. To avoid importing the economic crisis, governments react to globalization by establishing new gates[285].

Second, the literature on global administrative law underestimates the role played by States in the global space: States are managers of non-State authority, establish networks with international governmental and non-governmental organizations, and are indispensable instruments of global institutions ("more non-State rule requires more State authority, not less"[286]). Global administrative scholars tend to consider global actors as the protagonists, while there is also a deuteragonist: the State. Suffice it to note that the Italian State participates in more than twenty international military (peace-keeping and stabilization) missions around

---

[284] In this connection, see T. Büthe, in D. D. Avant, M. Finnemore, and S. K. Sell (eds.), *Who Governs the Globe?*, New York, Cambridge University Press, 2010.

[285] See "*The Gated Globe*", a special report from *The Economist*, 12 October 2013.

[286] P. Genschel and B. Zangl, *The Rise of Nonstate Authority and the Transformation of the State*, Paper presented at the Seminar on the State, Oxford, Nuffield College, December 2013.

the world[287]. The State and its interaction with global regulatory regimes should be reintroduced into the context of global administrative law.

Third, in the global space, legitimacy and accountability mechanisms and processes are horizontal, not vertical. It is therefore a mistake to search for a *demos* and to bring the same paradigms of the State into global administrative law – a mistake no less dangerous that committed by Theodor Mommsen (1817-1903), who brought the German "*Staatsrecht*" approach into the study of Roman law[288]. Another mistake is to continue using the concept of State sovereignty, challenged by the submission of States to the rules and implementation mechanisms of global law. In Europe, monetary currencies, a symbol of sovereignty, were once thirty-seven, while they are now twenty. Because global administrative law is an entirely new legal entity, it is not possible to rely on methodological nationalism[289]. New paradigms must be developed.

Fourth, because global administrative law is a complex network of cooperative measures after all, it can be expected that new forms of cooperation will develop, called "creative coalitions"[290]. These will include governments, multilateral organizations, business, charities, and nongovernmental organizations. It can also be expected that these cooperative measures will be different depending upon the area or field involved, and that they will develop practices and traditions worthy of study, just like judge-made law.

Despite these shortcomings, the literature on global administrative law is making a unique contribution to the progress of administrative law scholarship around the world. During its two centuries of life, administrative law has been largely parochial, because it was studied as a purely national intellectual effort, based solely on national rules. The scholarship on global administrative law adds a new layer and a common language, contributes to the emphasis of similarities against differences, and establishes some unitary features in a field that, since the decline of the natural law doctrine, has been conceived as only national.

---

[287] See Law N. 28 of 2014.

[288] L. Capogrossi Colognesi, *Storia di Roma tra diritto e potere*, Bologna, Il Mulino, 2012.

[289] A point advanced by Benoît Frydman in J.-Y. Chérot and B. Frydman (eds.), *La science du droit dans la globalisation*, Brussels, Bruylant, 2012.

[290] Oxford Martin School, *Now for the Long Term, The Report of the Oxford Martin Commission for Future Generations*, October 2013.

It is often lamented that global administrative law is mere technocratic governance and does not involve civil societies. According to Europol, out of three thousand and six hundred organized crime groups, only one-quarter can be said to possess a "main nationality", and some may even operate in a dozen countries. Is not this, too, an important indicator of civil societies' involvement in globalization?

CHAPTER IV

JUDGING AND GLOBALIZATION

I. LEGAL COMPARISON BY THE COURTS

1. JUDICIAL COMPARISON

O N July 2, 2009[1], the Delhi High Court ruled that consensual sexual acts between adults in private are not criminal, and therefore declared that Section 377 of the Indian Criminal Code violates Articles 21, 14 and 15 of the Constitution.

In decriminalizing homosexuality, the Delhi Court had considerable recourse to foreign law. It established that Article 21 of the Constitution of India includes the recognition of human dignity, by making reference to Canadian Supreme Court judgements. It concluded that the freedom of speech and expression protected by Article 19 of the Constitution extends to the "right to be let alone", making extensive reference to the US Supreme Court cases on privacy. It established that targeting homosexuals as a class is contrary to the principle of equality under Article 14 of the Constitution, reasoning on the basis of Supreme Courts decisions and dissenting opinions from the US, Canada and South Africa.

It argued that there is a global trend towards the protection of the privacy and dignity of homosexuals by referring to the European Court of Human Rights and the Supreme Courts of South Africa, the US, New Zealand, Hong Kong, and Australia. It held that public morality is not a valid basis for restricting the fundamental rights of homosexuals, quoting decisions of US, UK and South African courts.

Lastly, it described the role of the judiciary as one of protecting the counter-majoritarian safeguards set out in the Constitution, citing the

---

[1] Judgement WP (C), No. 7455/2001.

arguments of US Supreme Court Justice Robert Jackson in *West Virginia State Boards of Education v. Barnette* (1943).

On 21 April 2010[2], the United Kingdom Supreme Court ruled that certain notification requirements for sexual offenders constituted a disproportionate interference with their right to privacy (Article 8 of the European Convention on Human Rights), because they made no provision for review of individual cases.

The Supreme Court relied on a number of reasons in reaching this conclusion. These included the fact that registration requirements for sexual offenders exist in France, Ireland, the seven Australian States, Canada, South Africa and the United States, and almost all of these contain provisions for individual review.

Not every court decision that makes use of comparison with foreign law does so to such an extent as the Indian court in developing constitutional standards. Not every court asked to review national law in the light of the European Convention on Human Rights makes reference, as did the British court, to European and non-European legal systems. But recourse to comparison is widespread, in spite of recurring arguments against the application of foreign law. A recent bibliography on the use of foreign precedents by constitutional courts lists more than five hundred examples. Assuming that such an extensive group of scholars did not decide to write about a figment of the imagination, it can be concluded that recourse to comparison by constitutional judges is far from limited.

It must be added that constitutional courts often prepare their decisions taking foreign law into account, but subsequently give minor importance to the comparative argument in their reasoning. For example, the Italian Constitutional Court was recently invited to verify the constitutionality of a statute that made illegal immigration a criminal offense, sanctioned with a fine and with expulsion from the State. The documents prepared prior to making this decision included a thorough examination of foreign law: German, British, French, Spanish, Austrian, Dutch, Greek, Danish, Finnish, Portuguese, and American. The judge-

[2] *R (on application of F (by his litigation friend F)) and Thompson (FC) (Respondents) v Secretary of State for the Home Department (Appellant)* 2010 UKSC17.

ment, however, made only a cursory mention of this thorough investigation, in spite of the influence that it had on the decision[3]

2. WHY IS JUDICIAL COMPARISON SPREADING?

Judicial comparison is becoming more widespread for many reasons:

a. Recourse to foreign law is increasingly provided for in national law. This is the case of Section 39 of the South African Constitution: "when interpreting the Bill of Rights, a court, tribunal or forum (....) may consider foreign law"; or the case in which national regulation of conflicts of law provide for the application of the most favorable rule (this requires an examination of foreign law, a comparison between that and local law, and an evaluation of which is more favorable).

b. National legal orders, face similar problems and it is, therefore, expedient to consider foreign law, to seek advice from others who have confronted the same problems, in order to find better solutions (e.g. by evaluating the advantages/disadvantages of different solutions to a common legal problem): for instance, courts everywhere are engaged in the review of statutes enacted to fight international terrorism, and it is useful for them to make reference to foreign judicial decisions.

c. National legal orders are increasingly bound together in supranational and global regulatory regimes, which facilitate the opening up of national legal systems towards each other. The rise of world constitutionalism renders constitutional borders permeable and acts as a bridge, encouraging local courts to look beyond national borders. For example, if a national court is called upon to define the notion of "refugee", and if that court belongs to a country that has ratified the UN Convention relating to the Status of Refugees (July 28, 1951), it may be expedient for that court to consider the inter-

---

[3] Judgment n. 250/2010.

pretation given to that instrument, and to that term, by other courts of UN Member States.

d. Some principles are universal (for example, human rights) and command respect in every domestic legal order.

e. Comparison can assist constitutional courts in identifying changes in national standards, traditions and values (using foreign constitutional practices as a form of "rear-view mirror"). For example, Canada, Australia, and New Zealand have, since the 1970s, faced similar problems with their indigenous communities and have had to change their approach to the rights of these groups. In doing so, their supreme courts referred to each other's decisions (and to those of the US Supreme Court) when adjudicating these rights[4].

3. WHAT WEIGHT TO ATTACH TO FOREIGN LAW?

How much weight should be attached to foreign law? There are two answers to this question:

a. Foreign law is binding as national law: an example is provided by the "*lex alius loci*" a principle followed by national courts in Europe throughout the seventeenth and eighteenth centuries: this area was ruled by a "*ius commune*" (a common law) and, when a provision in a domestic legal order was missing, courts were entitled to use foreign law to fill the "lacuna". This practice came to an end with the codifications of the nineteenth century. In this case, foreign law becomes a rule or norm in the "borrowing" legal order, just as it is in the "lending" legal order.

A similar case is that of the "common constitutional traditions" of European countries. The European Court of Justice has frequently referred to these traditions in order to establish some basic common principles (such as the right to a hearing or access to justice), thus

---

[4] See, for example, *Supreme Court of New Zealand, Wi Parata v. Bishop of Wellington* (1878) 3 NZ Jur (NS) SC 72, and *Supreme Court of Canada, R. v. Van der Peet* (1996) 2 S. C. R. 507.

helping to make the national legal systems in the European legal space more porous.

    b. Foreign law is merely a means of interpretation: given that comparison is a universal method of interpretation, and judges are interpreters of law, judges are of necessity comparatists. Comparison for courts is not, therefore, simply erudition or "soft law"; nor does it furnish mere influential or persuasive guidelines that require respectful consideration. Rather, it plays the same role as other methods of interpretation.

4. ARE THERE RULES OF INTERPRETATION BY COMPARISON?

Having ascertained that comparison is a method of judicial interpretation, I want now to turn to the following questions: What makes one court more likely to use this method than another? And should there be at least some basic rules of interpretation by comparison? At the outset, let me make one basic distinction:

    a. interpretation may be regulated by the legislator, as in the South African case;

    b. or, as in the majority of countries, interpretation can be left free to the authorized interpreter. In this case, the interpreter is not obliged to have recourse to foreign law or to compare it with national law. It is important here to ascertain which variables are most important in influencing the recourse to foreign law by national courts.

    The use of a language that is common to many countries (English, Spanish) may facilitate comparison (and the widespread use of translating judgements of constitutional courts into English may enhance such comparison);

    – Given that interpretation is based on legal culture, the greater the legal culture in question is open to comparison, the more willing the courts are to perform this function;

    – Some countries are by tradition exporters of legal models and cultures (think, for example, of the United Kingdom, and the United

States), whereas some are by tradition importers of models and cultures: in general, courts in the latter will be more open to comparison;

– The common law pays more attention to practices: as a consequence, common law has more frequent recourse to judgements;

– Common legal traditions (e.g. in the Commonwealth, or in the European legal space) establish basic conditions for dialogue and comparison;

– Judicial networks are growing, and constructing step-by-step an epistemic community: most constitutional courts translate their judgments into English; many courts have regular, periodic exchanges with their foreign equivalents (for example, members, of the Italian Constitutional Courts attend some fifteen meetings per year with their colleagues from foreign countries); and many courts employ staff regularly charged with reading and summarizing foreign decisions.

– Some countries belong to a region where trans-judicial communication is easier: for example, North America, in which US and Canadian law communicate frequently.

5. TOWARDS BETTER JUDICIAL COMPARISON

If the court as interpreter is free to choose foreign law, is it possible to formalize the basis upon which this is done, or this is a field in which cherry-picking must be the rule? To which limits should judicial discretion conform in choosing which foreign law to consider? From this point of view, a few issues are crucial:

   a. Which country to choose for comparison? Should a court choose only foreign law of countries which share the same constitutional commitments? Or should comparison also take into account the foreign law of countries that take different approaches, and balance the various solutions?

    The answer to this question is simple. A good comparison must not take into account only one or two foreign legal systems, chosen because they belong to the same area or region, or because they share the same values, or simply because they have a common language. A court - like any good comparatist - should consider the various legal "families" and weigh the differing solutions on offer, before arguing that one or more foreign legal systems provides a good example because it is more effective, or because it ensures more benefits, or because it is more congenial to the borrower's legal order.

b. What forms of foreign law should be involved: legislation, judgments, scholarship? As comparison is, at least for our purposes here, the task of courts, should they pay attention only to foreign judge made law?

Again, the answer is simple. Given that the law generated by legislatures, judges and, indeed, by scholars do not represent self-contained worlds, courts should have recourse to all: to foreign legislation, and to interpretations provided by both judges and law professors. One famous example of this approach is the Supreme Court of Canada's decision on the Quebec secession[5], in which a variety of statutes, regulations and international treaties, beginning with the Magna Carta were considered.

c. Should judicial comparison also take into account the different contexts in which laws apply?

Contrary to the prevailing opinion, national legal systems make use of a growing number of similar legal instruments (think of the "Ombudsman", the notice and comment procedure, the proportionality principle). These legal instruments are, however, applied in different contexts, as history, social values, and national constitutions differ from one country to another. These contexts render the legal institutions different: although structurally similar, they are functionally diverse. It is, therefore, crucial to take into account not only the legal institution to be compared, but also the legal environment in which it is applied.

d. How should foreign law be used? It can be used as a source of solutions to common problems, or to strengthen or support a decision, or as a benchmark to evaluate national law.

---

[5] *Supreme Court of Canada*, [1998] 2 S.C.R. 217.

6. THE SO-CALLED "LEGITIMACY PROBLEM" OF JUDICIAL COMPARISON

Finally, there is the problem of legitimacy. As democracy tends to "nationalize" the law, borrowing foreign law may appear as a non-democratic move to those who support "legal particularism" and resist the use of foreign ideas. This question has generated much discussion in the US, where, in any event, many courts (including the Supreme Court) make reference to foreign law; and where those who oppose the use of foreign law by American courts do not, to my knowledge, also oppose the use of US law by foreign courts.

This problem of legitimacy is wrong. Making reference to foreign law does not mean that national courts surrender State sovereignty. A court acting as comparatist does not renounce its decision-making responsibility. It simply enlarges the "discussion" that precedes and informs the decision, by admitting to that "conversation" also actors that are foreign to the legal order in question.

This conclusion has been supported quite recently by the US Supreme Court in *Graham v. Florida*[6], on the question of imposing sentences of life without parole on juveniles who committed homicide: "The Court has looked beyond our Nation's borders for support for its conclusions that a particular punishment is cruel and unusual", and "the Court has treated the law and practices of other nations and international agreements as relevant to the Eighth Amendment not because those norms are binding or controlling but because the judgement of the world's nations that a particular sentencing practice is inconsistent with basic principles of decency demonstrates that the Court's rationale has respected reasoning to support it".

7. CONCLUSIONS

Much of the literature on judicial comparison examines both the use of supranational (and global) law and of foreign law, and focuses on the "to do or not to do" question.

---

[6] *United States Supreme Court*, No. 08-7412, May 17, 2010.

This section has approached the question from a different point of view. It has established a clear dividing line between supranational and global law on one hand, and foreign domestic law on the other. The first cannot be considered as foreign, as it stems from obligations undertaken by national governments. Supranational and global law can, however, facilitate the use of foreign domestic law.

Secondly, if judges interpret the (local) law, and if comparison is one of the methods of interpretation, then the right question to ask is not *whether* judges are entitled to make such comparisons, but rather *how* they should do so.

II. THE CONSTITUTIONAL FUNCTION OF SUPRANATIONAL COURTS: FROM GLOBAL LEGAL *SPACE* TO GLOBAL *LEGAL* ORDER

> "*Philosopher.* What hope then is there of a constant Peace in any Nation, or between one Nation, and another?
> *Lawyer.* You are not to expect such a Peace between two Nations, because there is no Common Power in this World to punish their Injustice [....] Peace at home may [....] be expected durable, when the common people shall be made to see the benefit they shall receive by their Obedience and Adhesion to their Sovereign".
>
> T. Hobbes, *A Dialogue between a Philosopher and a Student of the Common Laws of England* (1681), Oxford, Clarendon Press, 2005, p. 12.

1. *RAISON D'ÉTAT* IN THE EUROPEAN COMMUNITY COURTS

Van Parys NV, a Belgian firm, had imported bananas from Ecuador into the European Community for more than twenty years. In 1998-9, it asked the Belgisch Interventieen Restitutiebureau (BIRB) for the authorization to import a certain quantity of bananas. The BIRB authorized the importation, but only of a lesser amount.

Van Parys subsequently brought two actions before the Belgian Council of State, contesting the BIRB's decisions denying it import licenses for the full amounts requested. The firm argued that the Community regulations governing such authorizations violated the rules of the World Trade Organization (WTO). The judicial organ of the World Trade Organization, the Dispute Settlement Body (DSB), had in fact ruled that the Community regulations in question were inconsistent with the rules of the Organization. The Belgian Council of State stayed the proceedings and referred the prejudicial question (review of the validity of the regulations with respect to the GATT agreements) to the European Court of Justice for a preliminary ruling.

The Court of Justice held that, before assessing the validity of the Belgian regulations, it had to address the question "whether the WTO agreements give Community nationals a right to rely on those agreements in legal proceedings challenging the validity of Community legislation where the DSB has held that both that legislation and subsequent legislation adopted by the Community in order, *inter alia*, to comply with the relevant WTO rules are incompatible with those rules" (Par. 38). The Court said no: "an operator, in circumstances such as those in the main proceedings, cannot plead before a court of a Member State that Community legislation is incompatible with certain WTO rules, even if the DSB has stated that that legislation is incompatible with those rules" (Par. 54)[7].

The Court's reasoning was as follows: the WTO dispute resolution system accords an important role to inter-state negotiation. "In those circumstances, to require courts to refrain from applying rules of domestic law which are inconsistent with the WTO agreements would have the consequence of depriving the legislative or executive organs of the contracting parties of the possibility afforded by Article 22 of that memorandum of reaching a negotiated settlement, even on a temporary basis" (Par. 48); moreover, "to accept that the Community Courts have the direct responsibility for ensuring that Community law complies with the WTO rules would deprive the Community's legislative or executive bodies of the discretion which the equivalent bodies of the Community's

---

[7] C-377/02 of 1 March 2005 *Van Parys NV v. Belgish Interventie-en Restitutiebureau (BIRB)* (2005). See also the relevant precedents: C-149/96 *Portugal v. Council* (1999); C-377/98 *Netherlands v. Parliament and Council* (2001); C-93/02P *Biret International v. Council* (2003).

commercial partners enjoy. It is not in dispute that some of the contracting parties, which are amongst the most important commercial partners of the Community, have concluded from the subject-matter and purpose of the WTO agreements that they are not among the rules applicable by their courts when reviewing the legality of their rules of domestic law. Such lack of reciprocity, if admitted, would risk introducing an anomaly in the application of the WTO rules" (Par. 53).

This case is instructive for a number of reasons. In the first place, the European Court affirmed the superiority of the global law (of international trade) over the supranational (Community) law, but only on condition of reciprocity between the different national legal orders. Thus, it linked the vertical relationships between the WTO and European Union with the horizontal relationships between the States. Only if all States were to allow their courts to review the legitimacy of their domestic law in light of the global law, could the Court of Justice review the conformity of Community regulation (already held by the DSB to be illegitimate) with WTO rules. In other words, the horizontal dimension, which is characterized by equivalence or reciprocity, was held to be just as important as the vertical, hierarchical one.

Furthermore, considering that negotiation is recognized in the global law, it is given priority; there is a place for judicial review, but only on condition of reciprocity, when it is permitted in all of the States. As a result, the European Union (notwithstanding the fact that it is a community of law, according to the Court of Justice) did not consent to the judicial review of the consistency of its norms with the admittedly superior global ones.

This decision raised a problem. The Court of Justice asked to examine the conformity of the "inferior" Community law with the "superior" global law, ought to have played a mediating role between the two legal systems. But it decided not to, in defense of a Community *raison d'État*, in order not to weaken the bargaining power of the Union with respect to other States.

This case illustrates the constitutional role of courts in the global arena. They are charged with a twofold task: to determine the *vertical* relationships between the different legal orders and to *horizontally* integrate different self-contained regulatory systems.

This section examines the problem raised by the *Van Parys* decision. The analysis is divided into three sections. In the first section, I shall examine the question in its general terms, comparing the situation as it arises within States and beyond them. In the second part, I will analyze the contributions of courts, in the European and global dimensions. Part 3 traces the implications emerging from the analysis for the role that courts have in transforming the global legal *space* into a global legal *order*.

2. NATIONAL LEGAL SYSTEMS AND THE GLOBAL LEGAL SPACE

National legal systems have two special tools - which are lacking in the global legal space - for regulating both their domestic laws and their relationships with other legal systems.

First of all, national legal systems are grounded in constitutions. These constitutions are vested with a sovereign function, in so far as they serve as an interface between national and international legal systems[8]. For example, Article 10 of the Italian Constitution provides that "Italian law shall conform to the generally accepted norms of international law" and Article 11 provides that "Italy [...] agrees, on condition of equality with other states, to the limitations of sovereignty necessary for an order that ensures international peace and justice [...]". These constitutional norms hinge the Italian legal system to international law, and filter its relations to it.

Secondly, national legal systems are organized according to principles of unity, hierarchy and competence; these principles do not admit of lacunae and thus have special rules for overcoming them (for example, according to the Italian Civil Code, "if a controversy cannot be resolved according to a specific provision, regard shall be made to the provisions regulating similar cases or analogous areas. In case of further doubt, the controversy shall be decided according to the general principles of the legal system of the State").

Each institution or body in the national legal system has a specific legal position and a recognized area of substantive activity, for which there is a division of tasks and a differentiated relationship to State power.

---

[8] T. Ginsburg, "Locking in Democracy: Constitutions, Commitment and International Law", University of Illinois College of Law, *Law and Economics Working Papers*, 2006, n. 55.

National legal systems also have specific paths for the migration of principles from one sector to another, so that concrete cases can be resolved, even in the absence of express rules regulating them.

In the legal space beyond the State, global bodies cannot make use of solemn acts (constitutions), aimed at regulating their relations with other legal systems. The global legal space lacks a connective tissue establishing the jurisdiction of each entity or body. There is no hierarchy nor mutual ties between them, and there are no systematic rules for overcoming lacunae.

A constitution (in the formal sense) is the act of sovereignty *par excellence*. Only States have constitutions, not the global legal system.

The global legal space is loaded with self-contained regulatory regimes, but there is no clear separation of competences nor a hierarchical relationship between them[9]. For example, human rights protection is the work of both specialized, sectoral bodies (like the International Labour Organization and the United Nations Educational, Scientific and Cultural Organization – UNESCO), *ad hoc* bodies (like the High Commissioner for Human Rights, an organ of the UN, or the European Court of Human Rights, an organ of the Council of Europe), and other bodies as well, due to linkages between trade and human rights, for example. Criteria for the prevalence of one regime over another in the global legal space have to be defined in an *ad hoc*, cooperative way, through negotiated agreements. These agreements regulate a specific case, but have no further value. There are no general rules establishing the hierarchical relationship between interests or between the bodies that look after them, and thus apply to all cases.

The global legal space is *cloisonné*, in the sense that it is made up of relatively impermeable systems, between which there is no communication or migration of rules or principles, nor is there a method for filling normative gaps, because there are no common platforms which could enable the recourse to analogies and the formation of common principles. For example, if the right to defense or participation in administrative proceedings is guaranteed in one system, this principle does not immediately apply in other systems as well, because they are not a part of

---

[9] There is a simple explanation for this: it is easier to overcome States' resistance when the transnational coordination has a sectoral basis.

a single legal order governed by common general principles, nor part of a system in which principles rooted in one sector may migrate to other sectors by means of analogical analysis.

Finally, there is no higher "regulator" in the global legal space; here, even the attribution of a controversy to one regulatory regime rather than another is uncertain. For example, a case regarding the maritime carriage of hazardous substances could be classified as a question regarding trade, or maritime transport or environmental protection or the law of the sea, and thus be subjected to different regulatory regimes accordingly[10].

The global legal space is not an "anarchical society" (in the expression of Hedley Bull)[11], nor is it a "free floating mélange of legal organizations,"[12] because it is not comprised of fragmented and separate[13] "self-contained regimes."[14] But neither can it be regarded as a "global legal regime,"[15] insofar as it is comprised of an aggregate of special regulatory systems; there is not exactly a void in the space between these systems, but the prerequisites of unity are lacking. There is contiguity, but not continuity. The general and unifying law has a low density.

---

[10] This example is given by M. Koskenniemi, "The Fate of Public International Law: Between Technique and Politics", in *The Modern Law Review*, 2007, vol. 70, n. 1, p. 8.

[11] H. Bull, *The Anarchical Society - A Study of Order in World Politics*, Oxford, 1977 (second edition, New York, Columbia University Press, 1999). See also M. Koskenniemi, *Global Legal Pluralism: Multiple Regimes and Multiple Modes of Thought*, paper presented at Harvard University, 5 March 2005, p. 4.

[12] R. Post, "The Challenge of Globalization to American Public Law Scholarship", in *Theoretical Inquiries in Law*, 2001, vol. 2, n. 1, p. 8.

[13] International Law Commission, Fragmentation of International Law: Difficulties Arising from the Diversification and Expansion of International Law, UN General Assembly, A/CN.4/L.682 13 April 2006. On this report, see P.-M. Dupuy, "A Doctrinal Debate in the Globalisation Era: On the 'Fragmentation' of International Law", in *European Journal of Legal Studies*, 2007, vol. 1. An entirely different point of view is expressed by E. Benvenisti and G. W. Downs, "The Empire's New Clothes: Political Economy and the Fragmentation of International Law", in *Stanford Law Review*, 2007, vol. 60, p. 595 ff., which argues that fragmentation is the product of a strategy created by the most powerful States to preserve their supremacy in the world.

[14] A. Lindroos and M. Mehling, "Dispelling the Chimera of 'Self-Contained Regimes'. International Law and the WTO", in *European Journal of International Law*, 2005, vol. 16, n. 5, p. 857 ff.

[15] C. H. Koch, "Judicial Review and Global Federalism", in *Administrative Law Review*, 2002, vol. 54, 2002, pp. 491 and 494.

It is not coordinated from on high, but is rather established by the very bodies which it seeks to regulate. Precisely because it is "without any author,"[16] global law forms an extreme example of "legal pluralism."[17]

3. THE ROLE OF COURTS IN THE GLOBAL LEGAL SPACE

To remedy the absence of such national tools, global legal actors - whether they be international organizations, supranational bodies or even States - must use the classical tool of international law, negotiated agreements, in order to connect the global legal space with other legal orders or to determine the internal order of global norms.

Still, with the recent increase in the number of supranational courts (there are now more than one hundred), we see a new phenomenon: courts are starting to regulate the relations between different levels of government (in the vertical sense) and to create norms for filling in the voids between different supranational regulatory regimes (in the horizontal sense). This leads to the question that I hope to answer in this section: do these courts contribute to the creation of a common legal fabric, which is able to cover the lack of a general global law, and thus become main actors in the development of global law[18]?

My purpose is thus to examine supranational (regional and global) legal systems as separate legal orders, which regulate themselves through these courts. The main questions that I would like to address are:

a. how do the courts perform this function?

b. what are the consequences of the performance of this function by courts?

---

[16] R. Post, *The Challenge of Globalization to American Public Law Scholarship*, cit., p. 7. The unity of a legal system presupposes a single coherent or consistent sovereign will: C. W. Hermann, *Much Ado about Pluto? The 'Unity of the Legal Order of the European Union' revisited*, EUI Working Papers, RSCAS 2007/05, p. 20.

[17] M. Koskenniemi, *The Fate of Public International Law*, cit., p. 14 ff.

[18] A different but related issue is examined by A.-M. Slaughter, "A Global Community of Courts", in *Harvard International Law Journal*, 2003, vol. 44, p. 191, analyzing the ties between different national high courts.

I am specifically concerned with whether supranational courts, in performing their particular functions, contribute to the transformation of the global legal *space* into a global legal *order*.

4. THE IMPORTANCE OF THE JUDICIAL CONSTRUCTION OF A GLOBAL LEGAL ORDER

The importance of the above questions calls for an explanation. As already mentioned, in the global arena there are only laws for specific regulatory regimes. The construction of a *general* law requires the recognition of a system of principles, values, rules, and a systematic way to think about their ramifications and interconnections; finally, it requires the promotion of forms of cooperation based on legal proceedings rather than agreements. All of this is implied by the idea of legal system.

Now, this construction of a legal system can be carried out through legislative will - or more generally, through politics - or by the judiciary. In national legal systems, legislators and judges usually converge in this work.

These two different paths for constructing a legal system do lead to different outcomes. If the judiciary contributes to the formation of a general system of principles, the system thus develops on the basis of legal criteria, independently of political evaluations and accords a secondary role to the States. If, by contrast, political and administrative bodies are driving the integration, the political and governmental components will weigh more heavily upon the system, and the system itself will be less oriented to rules than to negotiations (the typical approach of international relations).

Very instructive in this sense is the development of the European Union. Though created as an economic union on the basis of treaties, it has become a community of law through the work of the Court of Justice. International agreements produced economic integration, while judicial activity has created a legal system. The global legal space is, however, different from the European one. The principle of European unity was contained, *in nuce*, in the treaties. These treaties established a single body, the Community (though one with two executives, the Council and the Commission).

The judicial creation of a legal system in the global space has a second important consequence. The bodies operating in this space have only an indirect legitimation, through the States. This leads to complaints about a "democratic deficit." However, judicial respect for the *règle de droit* confers a legitimation upon global bodies that makes up for their democratic insufficiency.

Thirdly, the judicial evolution of the global legal order has important consequences for its hold upon the States, because it is only through law, and certainly neither through force nor popular investiture, that supranational powers may impose themselves upon national legal systems.

5. A HIERARCHY OF LEGAL SYSTEMS?

Supranational courts recognize that the regulatory systems operating in the global legal space cannot all be located at the same level, but are ordered in a graduated or even hierarchical formation. Global standards prevail over Community norms (though in different ways from how Community norms prevail over national ones). The clearest assertion of this prevalence was made by the Appellate Body of the World Trade Organization (WTO) in the *Sardines* case[19], affirming that Community activity ought to be performed on the basis of the standards established by the international *Codex Alimentarius* Commission and the World Health Organization.

The European Community Court of First Instance held in the *Kadi* case that "[....] the obligations of the Member States of the United Nations under the Charter of the United Nations clearly prevail over every other obligation of domestic law or of international treaty law including, for those of them that are members of the Council of Europe, their obligations under the ECHR and, for those that are also members of the Community, their obligations under the EC Treaty."[20]

The European Court of Justice held in the *Demirel* case that "a provision in an agreement concluded by the Community with non-member

---

[19] WTO AB *European Communities - Trade Description of Sardines*, WT/DS 231/AB/R 26 September 2002. See also the *Hormones* case, AB *EC Measures Concerning Meat and Meat Products (Hormones)*, WT/DS26/AB/R - WTDS48/AB/R 18 January 1998.

[20] CFI, 21 September 2005, Case T- 315/01, *Yassin Abdullah Kadi*, par. 181.

countries must be regarded as being directly applicable when, regard being had to its wording and the purpose and nature of the agreement itself, the provision contains a clear and precise obligation which is not subject, in its implementation or effects, to the adoption of any subsequent measure."[21]

Such prevalence, however, is not absolute. The Community courts have distinguished agreements with third countries "which introduce a certain asymmetry of obligations, or create special relations of integration" from "reciprocal and mutually advantageous arrangements,"[22] and ruled that the WTO agreements could not serve as a yardstick for reviewing the legality of Community measures, except when the Community intended to implement a specific obligation[23].

There is thus a graduated order rather than a clear hierarchy. Such a hierarchy would have to be based on uniform, rigid criteria defining the different levels and the different legal force of the norms.

Some might object that the obligations mentioned above are no different than the contractual obligations characteristic of international law. Consider, however, the following three features.

First of all, we are not dealing here with obligations derived from international agreements (except for those assumed by the European Union Member States and transmitted by them to the Union), but rather obligations deriving from supranational agreements between international organizations.

Second, treaty-derived rights and obligations are only the starting point for the development of other rights and obligations, which regard the implementation phase, and come from the legislative or administrative measures of a recognized, "higher-order" organization. This issue is very well illustrated by the measures adopted for addressing international terrorism in the global and European contexts. Here, the Community has powers previously exercised by the States, in an area governed by the United Nations Charter, and in exercising these powers is

---

[21] C-12/86, 30 September 1987, par. 14.

[22] Court of Justice, *Portugal v. Council*, Case C-149/96 of 23 November 1999, par. 42-46 and Case C-377/98 of 9 October 2001, par. 50-55.

[23] See the *Biret* case, *supra* n. 1. *Portugal v. Council*, *id.*, par. 49.

obliged to adopt all measures necessary to carry out the Security Council's decisions[24].

Third, the obligations assumed through agreements, and their derivatives, do not only bind the parties to the agreement, but also penetrate into their national legal systems[25].

6. A UNITARY ORDER?

Supranational courts develop general principles common to different specialized regulatory systems, as well as linkages between one regulatory regime and another.

In the *Gasoline* case[26], for example, the WTO Appellate Body held that "trade agreements are not to be read in clinical isolation from public international law." In the *Korea* case[27] the WTO Panel affirmed that "customary international law applies generally to the economic relations between the WTO Members. Such international law applies to the extent that the WTO Treaty agreements do not 'contract out' from it." In its judgment in *Fogarty v. the United Kingdom*[28], the European Court of Human Rights held that "[t]he Convention [....] cannot be interpreted

---

[24] This situation is discussed by the CFI in the *Minin* judgment, T-362/04 *Minin v. Commission*, 31 January 2007, especially paragraphs 67-69.

[25] Thus creating effects similar to obligations *erga omnes* which hover over States (P. Picone, *Comunità internazionale e obblighi "erga omnes". Studi critici di diritto internazionale*, Naples, Jovene, 2006, p. XI-XII). See J.-P. Jacqué, *Droit constitutionnel national, droit communautaire, CEDH, Charte des Nations Unies. L'instabilité des rapports de système entre ordres juridiques*, in *Revue française de Droit constitutionnel*, 2007, n. 69, p. 3 ff., which observes, relative to the relations between Community law and UN measures, that "*la primauté est admise tant qu'elle n'implique pas de déroger à quelques principes fondamentaux*" (p. 34) and observes that "*l'expérience montre qu'heureusement la sagesse a prévalu jusqu'à présent grâce à l'attitude coopérative des juridictions suprêmes. La solution est toujours la même et semble universellement pratiquée. Elle consiste en une acceptation des autres systèmes assortie des réserves en ce qui concerne quelques principes fondateurs dans l'ordre juridique concerné. La coexistence est acceptée, mais elle s'accompagne du refus d'une subordination totale qui ferait disparaître l'identité du système*" (p. 36).

[26] *United States - Standards for Reformulated and Conventional Gasoline*, WT/DS2/AB/R.

[27] *Korea - Measures Affecting Government Procurement*, WT/DS163/R. See also International Law Commission, *op. cit.*, p. 87. See, finally, M. Koskenniemi, *The Fate of Public International Law*, cit., p. 9.

[28] *Fogarty v. United Kingdom*, Judgment of 21 November 2001, ECHR 2001-XI, par. 36.

in a vacuum. The Court must be mindful of the Convention's special character as a human rights treaty, and it must take the relevant rules of international law into account. The Convention should as far as possible be interpreted in harmony with other rules of international law of which it forms a part [....]." In the *Feldman* case[29], the NAFTA Arbitration Tribunal directly invoked general principles for the interpretation of an article of the NAFTA relating to the regulation of cigarette exports. In other cases, the courts have referred only to the principles of international law, without expressly defining (the scope of) their application[30].

In the above cases, the courts exploited the difference between jurisdiction, on the one hand, and applicable law, on the other. The jurisdiction of these courts is limited by the treaties instituting them. But the treaties do not limit the scope of the applicable law (and might be actually extended by them, when they provide that other, compatible norms of international law may be applied)[31]. As a result, courts can appeal to principles drawn from general international law, or other international conventions, or even from State constitutional or legislative traditions[32].

In this way, such common principles as the respect for certain fundamental rights (human rights), rule of law, due process, the duty to State reasons for administrative decisions, transparency, justiciability (right to judicial protection) have penetrated into the different global regulatory regimes.

Let us examine three specific cases. First is the *Shrimp-Turtles* case, decided by the WTO Appellate Body[33]. Article X:3 of the 1994 GATT provides only that "[e]ach Member shall administer in a uniform, impar-

---

[29] *Feldman v. United Mexican States*, Award of 16 December 2002, ICSID, Case no. ARB(AF)/99/1, ILR, vol. 126, (2003), pp. 58-65, par. 98.

[30] *Brazil - Measures Affecting Desiccated Coconut*, WT/DS22/AB/R; *European Communities - Regime for the Importation, Sale and Distribution of Bananas*, WT/DS27/R; *India - Patent Protection for Pharmaceutical and Agricultural Chemical Products*, WT/DS50/AB/R; Shrimp, WT/DS58/AB/R; *United States - Measures Affecting Imports of Woven Wool Shirt and Blouses*, WT/DS33/AB/R.

[31] International Law Commission, *op. cit.*, p. 29.

[32] This last case raises the further possibility of the transplant of principles or rules from the national legal space to the global one, thus establishing a direct communication between the two spheres.

[33] WTO AB *United States - Import Prohibition of Certain Shrimps and Shrimp Products*, AB-1998-4, especially paragraphs 180-183.

tial and reasonable manner all its laws, regulations and rulings [....]."
From this provision, the judicial body has derived the principle that the
States ought to follow "a transparent, predictable certification process,"
thus respecting "certain minimum standards for transparency and procedural fairness in the administration of trade regulations [....]."

Next, take the *Steel* case, also decided by the WTO Appellate
Body[34]. Here, Article 3.1 of the Agreement on Safeguards envisages
"reasoned conclusions." The court requested "an explanation supporting its conclusions." The reason for this was that in order "to enable a
panel to determine whether there was compliance with the prerequisites that must be demonstrated before the application of a safeguard
measure, the competent authority must provide a 'reasoned and adequate
explanation.'"

Finally, let us look at the *Nold* judgment of the European Court of
Justice[35]. The Court declared that: "as this court has already stated, fundamental rights form an integral part of the general principles of law, the
observance of which it ensures. In safeguarding these rights, the court
is bound to draw inspiration from constitutional traditions common to
the Member States, and it cannot therefore uphold measures which are
incompatible with fundamental rights recognized and protected by the
constitutions of those States. Similarly, international treaties for the protection of human rights on which the Member States have collaborated
or of which they are signatories, can supply guidelines which should be
followed within the framework of Community law."

But this "corpus" of common legal principles is drawn from different
sources; it is applied by judges to different contexts; it does not lend itself
to easy generalizations. Such principles might be developed by courts proceeding from the specific treaty norms that they are seeking to enforce;
or they might be drawn from other international norms; they might also
be inspired by national constitutional traditions. Supranational courts,
moreover, apply these principles to both the national legal orders as well
as to the supranational global orders. But this application cannot be truly
regarded as general, except in terms of its potential, because so far only a

---

[34] WTO AB *United States - Definitive Safeguard Measures on Imports of Certain Steel
Products*, WT/DS 248-259/AB/R, 10 November 2003, especially paragraphs 278-286.

[35] Court of Justice, Case C-4/73 of 14 May 1974, par. 13.

few regulatory regimes even have courts, and those global courts that do function (as already mentioned, just a little over one hundred) are almost all of recent establishment (on average, less than ten years).

Notwithstanding these uncertainties, a general global law is emerging within the specialized regimes and the rules of individual regulatory systems[36]. And this law is affirmed by courts, thus counterbalancing the principle of speciality, the basis of self-contained global regulatory regimes, structured as "closed legal systems."[37]

7. A COURT-ORDERED WORLD?

The above analysis suggests that though global regulatory regimes are "self-contained," they do not however float in an empty legal space, but rather are subject to general principles and communicate between each other. But all of this is due to the work of the courts. Global courts perform this constitutional function, weaving a connective tissue between specialized regimes, and thus slowly producing the missing unity. But courts' work is ephemeral in a sense, especially if we compare the (judicial) decision in each concrete case with the stability of the laws (dictated by legislators). Thus, though global legal systems are not separate, it is still hard to explain how the work of supranational courts contributes to their unity.

The International Law Commission of the United Nations recently confronted this paradox when it had to face the problem of the fragmentation of global regulatory systems; examining the jurisprudence of supranational courts, it concluded that fragmentation did not exist. But the connective tissue of principles, rights and linkages exists because of the work of the courts, not by the will of the global "legislators," whose jurisdiction is, in any case, always limited by the principle of speciality.

The world order, once dictated by sovereigns, is now established by judges. And judicial world government presents both advantages and disadvantages.

---

[36] International Law Commission, cit., pp. 287, 288.

[37] A. Lindroos and M. Mehling, *Dispelling the Chimera of "Self-Contained Regimes" International Law and the WTO*, cit., p. 862.

One source of weakness in a judicially-constructed order comes from the formal position of supranational courts. They are located in individual regulatory systems (regulating trade, the law of the sea, the regional European system, etc.), not in a hierarchical system of courts, as are the European judges with respect to national ones. It follows that each court, no matter how open and ready to establish connections with other legal systems, takes its own regulatory system as the unit of measure[38]. Here the inherent danger of conflicts produces interpretative differences[39] that no higher court can reconcile.

Another disadvantage of a judicially-constructed global legal order lies in the danger that supranational courts may overreach, due to the lack of a political community equipped with representative bodies[40]. National systems have experienced functioning judicial systems, which serve as a counterweight to the powers of popularly-elected bodies and vigorous executives. In the global legal space, by contrast, there are no directly representative bodies, and the secretariats of international organizations are weakened by the presence of both a transnational and a multinational component[41].

---

[38] M. Kumm, *Constitutional Democracy Encounters International Law: Terms of Engagement*, New York University Public Law and Legal Theory Working Papers, 2006, n. 47, p. 2.

[39] This danger has been signaled for the European Community by G. F. Mancini, *Le sfide costituzionali alla Corte di giustizia europea*, in G. F. Mancini, *Democrazia e costituzionalismo nell'Unione europea*, Bologna, Il Mulino, 2004, p. 71. On conflicts between supranational jurisdictions, T. Treves, "Conflicts Between the International Tribunal for the Law of the Sea and the International Court of Justice", in *International Law and Politics*, 1999, vol. 31, p. 809-821 and E. Cannizzaro, "Metodi di soluzione di conflitti fra giurisdizioni internazionali: il contributo della sentenza della CIG sul caso del genocidio (Bosnia Erzegovina c. Serbia e Montenegro)", in *European Journal of Legal Studies*, I, April 2007. There is also an additional danger specific to national judges: "*Il est véritablement dur pour des magistrats qui, en conscience, ont toujours estimé qu'ils n'étaient pas qualifiés pour instaurer un gouvernement des juges d'être obligés d'en instituer les principes pour le compte d'une institution extérieure à leur système national*" (P. Reuter, *L'application du droit international par le juge français*, Paris, Colin, 1972, p. 41).

[40] M. Luciani, "Costituzionalismo irenico e costituzionalismo polemico", in *Giurisprudenza costituzionale*, 2006, n. 2, p. 1663.

[41] Where this has been defined as a "cosmopolitan pluralist conception of jurisdiction": P. S. Berman, "The Globalization of Jurisdiction", in *University of Pennsylvania Law Review*, 2002, vol. 151, n. 2, pp. 311-545 and R. A. Sedler, "Law Beyond Borders: Jurisdiction in an Era of Globalization. Introduction to the Symposium", in *Wayne State Law Review*, 2005, vol. 51, pp. 1065-1103.

In this political void, supranational courts could be tempted to act as the exclusive guardians of international law[42]. This function cannot be performed by a single body, but rather depends on a wider legal system of checks and balances[43].

Finally, the judicial development of global law is destined to be incomplete: not all supranational regulatory systems make use of courts; there is no necessary symmetry between norms, on the one hand, and courts to enforce them, on the other; in the global legal space, the judicial bodies hardly make up an organic system[44]; regulation by judicial means runs into the limit of judge-made law, and is thus liable to remain the law governing the concrete case alone[45].

On the other hand, leaving the formation of a general global law up to supranational courts carries the distinct advantage implied by the incremental way in which they operate, which makes their action fluid, adaptable, and open to revision.

In substance, the global system encourages the formation of law through judicial means. It thus stimulates a "vertical" dialogue between different national, supranational and global orders. The most interesting example (though also involving the States, which stand outside the framework set forth thus far) is provided by supranational courts' appeals to common constitutional traditions and by the theory of counter-limits developed by some European constitutional courts[46].

---

[42] K. Odendahl, "Wer ist der 'Hüter des Völkerrechts'?", in *Jahrbuch des Öffentlichen Rechts*, Neue Folge, Band 55, 2006, p. 1 ff., arguing that there is currently no network of courts acting as guardians of international law.

[43] Thus national legal systems resist the development of supranational judicial review, considering it a threat to the national norms assigning functions to national courts: see H. P. Monaghan, "Article III and Supranational Judicial Review", in *Columbia Law Review*, 2007, vol. 107, n. 4, p. 833 ff.

[44] J. S. Martinez, "Towards an International Judicial System", in *Stanford Law Review*, 2003, vol. 56, p. 429 ff.; D. Sarmiento, *Poder judicial e Integración europea, la construcción de un modelo jurisdiccional para la Unión*, Thomson-Civitas, Cátedra Garrigues Universidad de Navarra, 2004.

[45] I am not concerned here with the formation of a global community of judges, but rather with the question of whether they would be able to create a community of law. But it is clear that the one community could influence the other.

[46] G. Martinico and O. Pollicino, *The European Constitution and Contemporary Constitutionalism. The Specificity of the European Judiciary Against the Background of the Judicial Glo-*

The courts' approaches represent "a shift from rules of conflict to rules of engagement. These rules of engagement characteristically take the forms of a duty to engage, the duty to take into account as a consideration of some weight, or presumptions of some sort."[47] This leads to the establishment of a "discourse between courts"[48] or a "hidden dialogue,"[49] based on law and on the duty to provide a reasoned motivation for decisions. Because of its transparency, the judicial construction of a legal order presents many advantages compared to its construction through international negotiations.

We must not underestimate the fact that the alternative to a global legal order constructed by transnational courts is the development of powerful legal orders, hierarchically organized as in an imperial system[50]. Thus, the transformation of the global legal space into a legal order presents the notable advantage of preventing the formation of aggregations of power around a regulatory regime, a geographical zone of one or more States.

8. FROM PYRAMID TO TEMPLE TO NETWORK

National legal systems have often been depicted as pyramids, a figure which clearly illustrates their unitary character and hierarchical structure.

The European legal order, by contrast, has been represented by the image of a Greek temple, supported by three pillars: the central pillar, consisting of the functions related to economic integration, and two-side pillars, one representing foreign policy and the other police and criminal law cooperation.

---

balization, paper presented at the Seventh World Congress of the International Association of Constitutional Law, Athens, 11-15 June 2007, p. 12.

[47] M. Kumm, *Constitutional Democracy Encounters International Law*, cit., p. 40.

[48] *Id.*

[49] G. Martinico and O. Pollicino, *The European Constitution and Contemporary Constitutionalism*, cit., p. 14.

[50] M. Koskenniemi, "Constitutionalism as Mindset: Reflections on Kantian Themes About International Law and Globalization", in *Theoretical Inquiries in Law*, 2007, vol. 8, n. 1, pp. 13 and 17.

It is more difficult to represent the global legal *space*, in the moment of its transformation into a global legal *order*. The regulatory systems are separate, but many have judicial bodies which recognize the existence of a common connective tissue and forge ties between different bodies. The most common representation of these multiple lines between different points resembles the metaphor of the network, as in "non-hierarchical deliberative networks."[51]

This network performs an essential function. In fact, "economic globalization has outpaced political globalization. We have a chaotic, uncoordinated system of global governance without global government, an array of institutions and agreements dealing with a series of problems, from global warming to international trade and capital flows. Finance ministers discuss global finance matters at the IMF, paying little heed to how their decisions affect the environment or global health. Environment ministers may call for something to be done about global warming, but they lack the resources to back up those calls."[52]

In this messy picture, "in less than a decade, an unprecedented concept has emerged to submit international politics to judicial procedures." This idea has led some to fear a "tyranny of judges" (because "historically, the dictatorship of the virtuous has often led to inquisitions and even witch-hunts"[53]), and others to fear the "defeat of democracy" (because a genuine *rule of law* cannot prevail in international relations until there is a common political ethics or a shared sovereignty)[54].

The fact remains that these new forms of supranational power cast doubt upon the basic assumptions underlying our notions of legal system and democracy, which we ought to re-examine before we throw up our arms in bewilderment, concern or outright fear. Let us not forget that we owe the birth of modern constitutionalism, in America, to the ingenious invention of federalism: "*[e]n qualifiant de 'constitution' un texte qui était plutôt regardé par ses auteurs comme un 'pacte' (compact) entre peuples souverains, autrement dit un traité, ils ont fait basculer une grande partie*

---

[51] M. Kumm, *Constitutional Democracy Encounters International Law*, cit., p. 4.

[52] J. E. Stiglitz, *Making Globalization Work*, London, Penguin, 2006, p. 21.

[53] H. Kissinger, *Does America Need a Foreign Policy? Toward a Diplomacy for the 21ˢᵗ Century*, New York, Simon and Schuster, 2001, cited in R. H. Bork, *Coercing Virtue: The Worldwide Rule of Judges*, Random House Canada, 2002.

[54] *Id.*, p. 205.

du droit des structures composées d'Etat qui était considéré comme du droit international vers le droit interne."[55]

III. THE CONSTELLATION OF GLOBAL AND NATIONAL COURTS: JURISDICTIONAL REDUNDANCY AND INTERCHANGE

> *"Á l'échelon de la Communauté européenne, il ne doit y avoir ni gouvernement des juges, ni guerre des juges. Il doit y avoir place pour le dialogue des juges"*
>
> Conclusion of Bruno Genevois, Conseil d'État, *Ministre de l'intérieur c/ Cohn-Bendit*, 22 December 1978

1. JUDICIAL GLOBALIZATION AND ITS DIVERSITY

According to the "Project on International Tribunals and Courts", there are one hundred and twenty-five supranational and international courts. To these, one must add an equivalent number of quasi-judicial bodies – "Compliance Committees", "Inspection Panels", "Article 1904 NAFTA Binational Panels", "Administrative Panels of the WIPO Arbitration and Mediation Centre for Uniform Domain Name Dispute Resolution", and the like. If one compares these numbers with the number of States (the Member States of the UN are currently a hundred ninety-three), it can be noticed that courts are more numerous than States.

The great majority of these courts were established in the last twenty years. Since the 1990s, the number of international courts and tribunals has grown rapidly[56]: compulsory means of quasi-judicial dispute settlement have been developed, whereby the complaining party can bring his case before an impartial body and the party against whom the complaint

---

[55] É. Zoller, *Introduction au droit public*, Paris, Dalloz, 2006, p. 129.

[56] For more details, see R. Mackenzie, C. Romano, Y. Shany, P. Sands, *The Manual on International Courts and Tribunals*, Oxford, Oxford University Press, 2010.

is brought cannot avoid a third-party decision. Not long before, there were only six operative international courts. In the last fifteen years of the twentieth century, fifteen new permanent adjudicative mechanisms and eight quasi-judicial procedures were introduced[57]. In previous times, it was generally agreed that *"law without adjudication is [...] the normal situation in international affairs"*;[58] and, according to Article 33(1) of the Charter of the United Nations, parties can choose any means they wish for the peaceful settlement of disputes.

Supranational and international courts challenge some of the most basic principles of the long-established community of Nations: the principle that disputes between States should be solved through negotiations or conflicts, and not through recourse to a third party; that States hold a monopolistic jurisdiction over disputes between their associates; and that decisions given by States' higher courts are final.

The judicialization of the global polity has attracted much criticism. It has, for example, been pointed out that there is the *"risk [of] substituting the tyranny of judges for that of governments"*[59] and that *"effective courts cannot exist without supporting government institutions, no such institutions exist at the international level"*[60]. But global courts and quasi-judicial bodies are pale imitations of national courts: therefore, one cannot simply transplant national paradigms into the global space.

The family of global courts and quasi-judicial bodies includes very diverse institutions, such as the World Trade Organization's (thereinafter: 'WTO') Dispute settlement Body, the European Union's (thereinafter: 'EU') Court of Justice (thereinafter: 'ECJ'), the Court of Arbitration for Sport, the World Bank's Inspection Panel, the Aarhus Convention Compliance Committee, the International Criminal Tribunal for the former Yugoslavia, the International Criminal Court. The latter does

---

[57] Y. Shany, *The Competing Jurisdictions of International Courts and Tribunals*, Oxford, Oxford University Press, 2003, pp. 3, 5, 7-8 and, more recently, *Regulating Jurisdictional Relations between National and International Courts*, Oxford, Oxford University Press, 2007.

[58] J. G. Merrills, *International Dispute Settlement*, Cambridge, Cambridge University Press, 2005, 4th ed., reprinted 2007, p. 237.

[59] H. Kissinger, *Does America Need a Foreign Policy?*, New York, Simon & Schuster, 2001, pp. 273 and 279.

[60] E. A. Posner, *The Perils of Global Legalism*, Chicago, The University of Chicago Press, 2009, p. 207.

not judge cases or controversies, but "situations"; the WTO Appellate Body can authorize retaliatory measures, i.e. judge-controlled infringements of the law; the Aarhus Convention Compliance Committee can impose obligations for the future, and therefore is not only a "re-active" body, but also a "pro-active" body[61].

According to Kingsbury, the global space presents an "uneven judicialisation".[62] First, there are specialized tribunals: the "[n]ew global tribunals have almost all been created as parts of specialized regimes, rather than as courts of general jurisdiction".[63] Second: there are "uneven rates of acceptance in advance of jurisdiction of international tribunals" (the most populated States tend to not accept in advance the jurisdiction of human rights courts, but accept that of economic courts; the same is true of the world's largest economies, which also tend to accept economic courts and not those of human rights).[64]

Global courts exercise public authority through judicial law-making[65], but their power can be justified neither by the traditional basis of State consent, nor by functionalist narrative. In democratic contexts, judicial law-making is embedded in a political system in which a democratic legislature holds the central role in creating norms: there is no such equivalent in the global space. Therefore, global courts are not *indirectly* legitimated in this manner. This argument, however, underestimates the existence of a large mass of global legislation (treaties, "constitutions", regulations, by-laws, "policies"). For every topic, there are rules; some "soft", others "hard"[66]. This legislation establishes the

---

[61] In other words, a quasi-judicial global body possesses a law-making function: this situation presents the benefit of an expert and impartial law-maker, but the cost of an absence of division of powers.

[62] B. Kingsbury, "International Courts: Uneven Judicialisation in Global Order", in J. Crawford and M. Koskenniemi (eds), *The Cambridge Companion to International Law*, Cambridge, Cambridge University Press, 2012, pp. 203 ff.

[63] Ibid. p. 211.

[64] Ibid. p. 212.

[65] See, e.g., A. von Bogdandy and I. Venzke, "Beyond Dispute: International Judicial Institutions as Lawmakers", in A. Bogdandy and I. Venzke (eds), *International Judicial Lawmaking*, Berlin, Springer, 2012, p. 15 ff.

[66] According to José E. Alvarez, "[t]he picture that emerges is of many International Organizations organs, not just a select few, acting as law-makers in some sense, even though few of them are given explicit authority to legislate or to recommend, and even though much of their

framework in which global courts operate. Therefore, courts do not act in a vacuum.

2. WHY IS JUDICIAL GLOBALIZATION RISING

Why have so many new bodies been created, in such a short span of time, and with such a revolutionary character?

The reasons why judicial institutions and policies have been spreading are manifold.

A first set of reasons derives from the global space: global institutions need "fire alarm" systems, and the judicial mechanism is an effective system to obtain the cooperation of the population.

For example, which system can best protect the environment? According to the Rio Declaration, it is citizens' participation.[67] The Aarhus Convention Compliance Committee rules allow a Kazakh environmental association to obtain information on the importation of nuclear waste by a Kazakh authority, Kazatomprom.[68]

A second set of reasons derive from the nation-States.

First: courts and court-like bodies can reduce tensions between national governments. The latter can find it useful to delegate power to courts, instead of negotiating with other governments. Therefore, courts can act as shock absorbers.

Second: States and institutions are utility maximizers that select their course of action on the basis of cost/benefit calculations and of the lessons learnt. Therefore, they adopt "best practices" that can attract foreign direct investments, provide competitive advantages and increase

---

work product does not fit easily into the classic sources of international obligation [....] In many, perhaps most ways, IOs do not *subdue* governments as much as *assist* them. Yet IOs are regarded, simultaneously, as the servants, agents, or instruments of governments *and* as a challenge to their authority" (*International Organizations as Law-makers*, Oxford, Oxford University Press, 2005, p. 262).

[67] Rio Declaration on Environment and Development, 14 June 1992, Principle 10, 31 ILM 874, 878.

[68] Aarhus Convention Compliance Committee, Communication by Green Salvation (Kazakhstan) regarding Compliance by Kazakhstan with the Obligations under the Aarhus Convention in the Case of Information Requested from Kazatomprom, Doc. ACCC/C/2004/01, 31 January 2005.

their legitimacy as members of the international community (think of Myanmar's participation in the ILO, in relation to the procedure to sanction forced labor in that country[69]).

Third: emulation. Currently, four international economic systems emulate the WTO dispute resolution system. Eleven regional supranational bodies have copied the European Court of Justice, introducing compulsory supranational oversight of State action which private parties, too, may access[70].

Fourth: the emergence of facilitating structural conditions, such as major international crises, the demand for institutional change and rights protection, and the need to sanction war crimes.

3. JUDICIAL INTERCHANGE

The first outcome of judicial globalization is a growing "dialogue" between national, supranational and global judges. Judges come to know each other better through the translation of the most important judgments into English, the organization of bilateral or multilateral seminars, informal consultations, and even actions such as the drafting and issuance of "joint communications", like that of 17 January 2011, by Presidents Costa and Skouris of the Strasbourg and Luxembourg Courts respectively, where a "parallel interpretation" of the Charter of Fundamental Rights of the European Union and of the European Convention

---

[69] International Labour Organization, *Report of the Commission of Inquiry* (art. 26 of the Constitution) to examine the observance by Myanmar of the Forced Labor Convention, 1930, (No. 29).

[70] K. J. Alter, "The Global spread of European style International Courts", in *West European Politics*, 2012, vol. 35, n. 1, p. 135.

The importance of the "market of institutions" has been always neglected or even overlooked. Successful national models, such as British self-government, the Scandinavian Ombudsman, British nationalized enterprises, and American federalism, have been widely adopted in other countries. The same can be said for supranational models, such as the European Court of Justice.

This "market", in which institutions are exchanged, has become even more dynamic since the use of two new instruments has proliferated in the efforts to reduce uncertainties at the global level: indicators, measuring development, integrity, democracy, rule of law, and the like; and conditionality, i.e. the creation of positive and negative incentives to spur adaptation to or adjustment of national governments or other institutions to specific models.

At the global level, this "market" ensures unilateral adjustments and produces self-harmonization.

on Human Rights by the two courts was envisaged.[71] A visible outcome of this dialogue is the growing number of citations of foreign (national, supranational and global) legislation and foreign (national, supranational and global) jurisprudence by national courts[72].

But the most important outcome of the spreading of courts beyond the State is inter-judicial interchange, at both horizontal and vertical levels.

At the *horizontal* level, each court or quasi-judicial body beyond the State belongs to a single regulatory regime: the WTO has a court, the EU has a court, the Law of the Sea system has a court, the Aarhus Convention has a Compliance Committee. Therefore, there is not only one global judicial system. But the courts, at this level, are overcoming fragmentation by developing common legal principles, by making references to the jurisprudence of other courts, by using previous judgments of other courts as precedents, or by applying general principles, as did the International Tribunal of the Law of the Sea, in the *Juno Trader* case by establishing, that "[t]*he obligation of prompt release of vessels and crews includes elementary considerations of humanity and due process of law. The requirement that the bond or other financial security must be reasonable indicates that a concern for fairness is one of the purposes of this provision*".[73]

Through horizontal judicial interchange, supranational courts, on the one hand, make interconnections between regulatory regimes possible, thus reducing the fragmentation of international law; on the other, they increase the horizontal accountability of each regime towards each other[74].

---

[71] Joint Communication from Presidents Costa (ECtHR) and Skouris (ECJ) (24 January 2011).

[72] On cross-citation, B. Kingsbury and R. Stewart, *Administrative Tribunals of International Organizations from the Perspective of the Emerging Global Administrative Law*, in O. Elias (ed.), *The Development and Effectiveness of International Administrative Law*, Leiden – Boston, Nijhoff, 2012, p. 94.

[73] *Juno Trader*, International Tribunal of the Law of the Sea, Case No. 13, Decision of 18 December 2004, para 77.

[74] This kind of accountability is quite different from vertical accountability, which does not exist for courts: we do not ask for democratic justification of courts, but want them to be accountable to the law and to other courts, not to the People. We should not therefore pose the question of how the power of international courts relates to the principle of democracy.

Horizontal judicial interchange occurs also at the national level, as a result of supranational adjudication. One development to this effect can be seen when countries that were not parties to a dispute before the European Court of Human Rights (thereinafter 'ECtHR' or 'the Strasbourg Court') apply the judgments issued by that Court, as if the Strasbourg Court were an international regulator providing solutions applicable in all the contracting States, and not a judge deciding case-by-case.

As noted above, national implementation may affect the relationship of other jurisdictions to the Strasbourg Court: "the compliance of one State with the international human rights of its citizens can affect the compliance of other States with rights of their citizens"; "[t]he opening up of national and international legal systems is a complex process, where "dialogues" may turn from ways of taking due account of Strasbourg jurisprudence to strategies of national resistance against the implementation of international human rights standards"[75].

There is a more subtle and widespread influence of Strasbourg Court's jurisprudence, that may be seen when national courts – and constitutional courts especially – before taking their own decision, must consider similar issues already decided by that Court, to avoid conflicts or clashes between legal orders. As similar questions arise in countries that are part of the European Convention, all neighboring legal systems become important for each national legal order and judge. This increases interdependence, adding a horizontal link to the vertical relations that already exist.

Judicial interchange at the vertical level is functional to the insertion of global regimes into national legal orders, and vice versa.

Contrary to a widely held point of view, globalization and global courts do not have exclusive jurisdiction. Supranational courts and national courts (mainly, constitutional courts) seek to adjust each other's competences, in the attempt to find a solution to the problem of contemporaneous allocation of authority. In this exercise of "dialogue", there are several experiences.

---

[75] M. Andenas and E. Bjorge, *The External Effects of National ECHR Judgments*, NYU Law School, Jean Monnet Working paper 07/12, p. 4 and 9.

Bottom-up, national courts accept supranational primacy, but with some exceptions, such as in the cases *Solange I*[76] and *II*[77] (the ECJ has not yet developed a measure of protection equivalent to that provided by national law), and in the *controlimiti* ("counter-limits") doctrine developed by some European national constitutional courts (i.e. granting national courts the power to review whether higher law is inconsistent with either the basic principles of the constitution or with the constitution itself)[78]. In these cases, national courts, while accepting the primacy of a supranational court, declare themselves to be courts of last resort, and establish their power to review acts of the higher legal order (two paradoxes).

A rather different reaction by a national court is that of opposition, as operated by the United States Supreme Court in the *Medellin* judgment: in that case, the national court refused to recognize the superiority of the international court *vis-à-vis* the national court.[79]

In the opposite direction, top-down, supranational courts, while assuming their superiority over national legal orders and national courts, recognize some room for maneuvering to national legal orders and courts, by resorting to doctrines of deference, subsidiarity, or to the margin of appreciation. The crucial problem is, then, how supranational courts exercise their powers of control on the use of discretion by subordinate legal orders and courts.

In this field, the richest experience is that of the ECtHR, which has developed a test of proportionality based on counting (the doctrine of consensus). This technique recalls Article 38 of the ICJ Statute, which refers to the "general principles of law recognized by the civilized nations".[80]

---

[76] *Solange I*, German Federal Constitutional Court, Case No. 2 BvL 52/71, Decision of May 1974, 37 BVerfGE 271.

[77] *Solange II*, German Federal Constitutional Court, Case No. 2 BvR 197/83, Decision of 22 October 1986, 73 BVerfGE 339.

[78] On the recent developments of the "counter-limits" doctrine, P. Mengozzi, "Corte di giustizia, giudici nazionali e tutela dei principi fondamentali degli Stati membri", in *Il diritto dell'Unione Europea*, 2012, n. 3, p. 563 ff. and G. Scaccia, *"Rottamare" la teoria dei controlimiti*, in "Quaderni costituzionali", 2013, a. XXXIII, n. 1, marzo, p. 141.

[79] *José Ernesto Medellin v. Texas*, United States Supreme Court, Case No. 06-984, Decision of 25 March 2008, 552 U.S. 491.

[80] Statute of the International Court of Justice, 26 June 1945, Art. 38 (1) (c), 1 UNTS XVI.

According to the consensus doctrine, the proportionality test is integrated with a "horizontal" test, as occurred in the case on abortion in Ireland, where the court also tested the coherence of national law to a common, recognised standard (i.e. the "consensus standard")[81]. In this case, the "higher" court must analyse and compare many different national legal orders, ascertain whether a "consensus" may be found, and balance the "superior" rule with these; therefore, the proportionality principle also acts as a facilitator in a process of reception-circulation of legal rules among parallel national legal orders; the job of courts is to evaluate the relevance of the context of each national provision[82] and establish the relevant standard (consensus inquiry) through a comparative process that leaves room for a choice among options (*"wertende Rechtsvergleichung"*)[83]. Integration of the principle of proportionality, which operates "vertically", with the "consensus" doctrine, which operates "horizontally", is extremely important. If the latter predominates, the principle of proportionality can lose its importance, as agreement among different legal orders becomes the parameter against which to evaluate State action.

But counting has also presented some problems. One is that, in counting, the ECtHR has resorted to legal solutions adopted in countries that are not among the forty-seven members of the Council of Europe, such as Canada or South Africa. Another is that the ECtHR traces a difference between relevant and non-relevant consensus.

In these cases, national and supranational courts try to balance national legal orders – that is, diversity – and supranational legal orders – that is, uniformity.

In conclusion, the creation of a constellation of global and national courts and the subsequent jurisdictional redundancy has the benefit of bringing the rule of law into the global realm[84], thus challenging the

---

[81] G. Repetto, *Argomenti comparativi e diritti fondamentali in Europa. Teorie dell'argomentazione e giurisprudenza sovranazionale*, Napoli, Jovene, 2011, pp. 129, 134, 184, 144.

[82] G. Repetto, *Argomenti comparativi e diritti fondamentali in Europa. Teorie dell'argomentazione e giurisprudenza sovranazionale*, cit., p. 127.

[83] G. Repetto, *Argomenti comparativi e diritti fondamentali in Europa. Teorie dell'argomentazione e giurisprudenza sovranazionale*, cit., p. 259 and p. 264.

[84] A. Nollkaemper, "The International Rule of Law", in *Hague Journal on the Rule of Law*, 2009, vol. 1, p. 74 – 78 and Id., *National Courts and the International Rule of Law*, Oxford,

supremacy of the political process within the global arena, but also the cost of constructing an order of which the ultimate dimension is unclear and in which uncertainty prevails, as there is no final authority or there are competing claims to final authority. This fluidity may be an important feature of judicial globalization, as a new hierarchy is difficult to establish in a short period of time and it may be better to leave the door open to experimentation.

4. COURTS AS MEDIATORS: THE CASE OF PROPORTIONALITY

I shall now return to the use of proportionality in judicial interchange, and examine two European cases. Alec Stone Sweet has written: "constitutional judges have adopted proportionality to manage intra-constitutional conflicts associated with rights"[85]. How has proportionality been used to solve inter-constitutional conflicts (i.e. conflicts between different legal orders and courts)?

The ECJ, in the *Groener* case (C-379/87), referred by the Irish High Court, established that a requirement of linguistic knowledge imposed by the Irish government is justified if it is applied in a proportionate manner: it is not disproportionate if it is applied to permanent, full-time posts of lecturer in public vocational education institutions. [86] In that case, the requirement imposed on teachers to have an adequate knowledge of a given language is not disproportionate in relation to the objective pursued. [87]

The ECtHR, in the *Handyside* case (7 December 1976, N. 5493/72), concluded that the seizure and confiscation of a book by the British government, upheld by a Magistrates' Court and, on appeal, by the Inner London Quarter Sessions, does not violate Article 10 of the

Oxford University Press, 2011, notes that the rule of law is increasingly defined by the interaction and interface between international and national law.

[85] A. Stone Sweet and J. Mathews, "Proportionality Balancing and Global Constitutionalism", in *Columbia Journal of Transnational Law*, 2008, vol. 47, n. 1, p. 72, 91.

[86] *Anita Groener v. Minister for Education and the City of Dublin Vocational and Educational Committee*, ECJ Case No. C-379/87, Decision of 28 November 1989, [1989] ECR 3967, 3994, para 24.

[87] Ibid.

European Convention on Human Rights (which guarantees freedom of expression), because it is "necessary in a democratic society" "for the protection of morals".[88] Each government – according to the Court – has a margin of appreciation in evaluating the necessity of a given measure for the protection of morals; however, such a margin is not unlimited, because the restriction must be proportionate to the legitimate aim pursued. [89]

In both cases mentioned, the principle of proportionality is judge-made (the principle of proportionality was eventually codified in European Union law, but only following the *Groener* case). [90]

The proportionality principle is used in a legal space that is not uniform and unitary, but, on the contrary, pluralist and diverse, in order to "balance" two or more opposed interests, located at different levels of government: protection or promotion of language (a national interest) and freedom of movement of workers (a European interest); protection of morals (national) and freedom of expression (European). In this context, the function of proportionality is more complex than that of merely "balancing"[91], as it must reconcile values and principles that are different and allocated to authorities at different levels of government, to give rise to a unitary framework (or identify the right measure of State limitations on certain rights). Therefore, proportionality is instrumental both to the protection of rights and to the allocation of tasks among different levels of government[92].

---

[88] *Handyside v. United Kingdom*, ECtHR Application No. 5493/72, Decision of 7 December 1976, para. 47.

[89] Ibid. para. 49.

[90] Treaty Establishing the European Community, Art. 5 (now: Treaty on European Union (TEU), Art. 5 of the Consolidated version of the TEU can be found in OJ C 83/13 (30 March 2010)). See also Charter of Fundamental Rights of European Union, Art. 49 (3). The consolidated version can be found in OJ C 326/391 (26 October 2012).

[91] On balancing by the European Court of Justice, J. Schwarze, "Balancing EU Integration and National Interests in the Case-Law of the Court of Justice", in Court of Justice of the European Union, *The Court of Justice and the Construction of Europe: Analyses and Perspectives on Sixty Years of Case Law*, The Hague, Asser Press, 2012, pp. 257 ff.

[92] E. Bjorge, "National Supreme Courts and the Development of ECHR Rights", in *I•CON*, 2001, vol. 9, n. 1, pp. 5-31 notes that "[n]ational judges in the U.K., France and Germany are fully aware that it is incumbent upon them to not only to be led, but also to give a lead to Strasbourg".

Courts resort to the proportionality test in conjunction with another doctrine, that of the margin of appreciation, or discretion. Proportionality and the "margin of appreciation" reciprocally reinforce each other: the more discretion is left to the "lower" level, the more the "higher" level has to resort to proportionality checks. Proportionality is instrumental to the purpose of adjusting two sets of legal orders, to recognise the primacy of the "superior" versus the "inferior", while leaving maneuvering room to the latter.[93] Proportionality is, in other words, a part of a more complex mechanism designed to establish indirect rule.

Proportionality requires comparison between two distinct legal orders and public interests. Comparison is an essential aspect of this use of proportionality. Proportionality is an important instrument for globalisation, as it allows global regulators to find their way in the global space, and to establish their primacy (not supremacy), while at the same time respecting pre-existing national legal orders. Compatibility and tolerance of different values and rules can be established through a mixture of "delegated" power or discretion left to the latter, while the former retain their power to measure and balance "higher"

---

[93] The term primacy, and not supremacy, is purposely used, as the relationships between supranational legal orders are not hierarchical: see Judgment N. 1/2004: "Supremacy and primacy are categories which are developed in differentiated orders. The former, in that of the application of valid regulations; the latter, in that of regulatory procedures. Supremacy is sustained in the higher hierarchical character of a regulation and, therefore, is a source of validity of the lower regulations, leading to the consequent invalidity of the latter if they contravene the provisions set forth imperatively in the former. Primacy, however, is not necessarily sustained on hierarchy, but rather on the distinction between the scopes of application of different regulations, principally valid, of which, however, one or more of them have the capacity for displacing others by virtue of their preferential or prevalent application due to various reasons. In principle, all supremacy implies primacy (which leads to its occasional equivalence, as in our DTC 1/1992, FJ 1), unless the same supreme regulation has set forth, in some scope, its own displacement or non-application. The supremacy of the Constitution is therefore compatible with application systems which award applicative preference to regulations of another legislation other than the national legislation as long as the Constitution itself has set forth said provision, which is what happens exactly with the provision set forth in Art. 93, which enables the transfer of competences resulting from the Constitution in favour of an international institution thus enabled constitutionally for the regulatory provision of matters until then reserved for constituted internal powers and the application thereto. In short, the Constitution has accepted, by virtue of Art. 93, the primacy of the Union legislation in the scope inherent to said Law, as now recognized expressly in Art. I-6 of the Treaty" (official translation).

principles with "lower" rules. Indirect rule was instrumental for the expansion of the British empire. Likewise, proportionality is instrumental to globalization. Such an arrangement has the benefit of constituting an adaptive evolutionary process, as standards can change over time.

5. *"VERALLGEMEINERUNGSFÄHIGKEIT"* AND COMPARISON

The proliferation of national, supranational and global courts obliges judges to attend their respective and reciprocal interaction. Consequently, judges take on two new tasks. They must establish an interchange with other courts. Second, they become instrumental to the "Verallgemeinerungsfähigkeit" or "universalizability"[94] of certain basic legal principles and values. As observed by Kingsbury and Stewart, "the design, work and future evolution of international administrative tribunals is both subject to and a creative influence on the development of, global administrative law".[95] International administrative courts "strike balances between demands for generality in the enunciation and application of core principles, and the need for contextualization in specific institutional and socio-cultural settings"[96].

This universalizability has a significant impact on the legal scholarship, as it adds a new quantitative and qualitative dimension to comparison. Legal scholars cannot compare one legal system to another, nor one "family" of legal systems to another; they must move towards a more complex scheme of comparison, where there are global, supranational, national, individual and set-based categories.

---

[94] A. von Bogdandy, "Prinzipien der Rechtsfortbildung im europäischen Rechtsraum: Überlegungen zum Lissabon-Urteil, des BVerfGE", in *Neue Juristische Wochenzeitung*, 2010, vol. 63, p. 1 and M. Andenas and E Bjorge, *The External Effects*, cit., p. 4 ff.

[95] B. Kingsbury and R. Stewart, *Administrative Tribunals of International Organizations from the Perspective of the Emerging Global Administrative Law*, cit., p. 103-104.

[96] Ibid., 104.

IV. INTERACTIONS BETWEEN NATIONAL AND SUPRA-NATIONAL LEVELS OF JURISDICTION*

1. SHIPS PASSING IN THE NIGHT?

Only a decade ago, the French scholar Louis Favoreu wrote that "constitutional courts are the last bulwark of State sovereignty", and that "they cannot be subject to external checks"[97].

Today, constitutional courts no longer have the final say, but dialogue with lower and superior courts. They review legislation, but are held in check by other judges. Constitutional courts are neither a bulwark nor an instrument of State sovereignty.

Ten years ago, constitutional courts could at most be defined as "ships passing in the night", to use Henry Wadsworth Longfellow's poetic metaphor; in other words, they had episodic and fleeting contacts with each other.

Today, they belong to a "choir" of courts, all committed to the same task of protecting citizens' rights.

In the last twenty years, especially since 1990s, there was a great development of the role of international courts and tribunals: independent quasi-judicial bodies have been empowered to solve disputes adopting decisions that are binding for the parties.[98].

2. THE INFALLIBILITY OF SUPREME COURTS

I will begin with a famous quote from the U.S. Justice Robert Houghwout Jackson. Appointed to the Supreme Court by Franklin

---

* Report for the IAPL Seoul Conference on "Constitution and Proceedings", 1-4 October 2014.

[97] L. Favoreu, *Corti costituzionali nazionali e Corte europea dei diritti dell'uomo*, in *Rivista di diritto costituzionale*, 2004, n. 1, p. 11. By the same author, see also "Les Cours de Strasbourg et de Luxembourg ne sont pas des cours constitutionnelles", in *Au carrefour des droits*: *Mélanges en l'honneur de Louis Dubouis*, Paris, Dalloz, 2012. Author's translations from the Italian.

[98] For further details, see R. Mackenzie, C. Romano, Y. Shany and P. Sands, *The Manual on International Courts and Tribunals*, Oxford, Oxford University Press, 2010.

Delano Roosevelt, he was later chosen by President Truman to act as Chief Prosecutor at the Nuremberg trials – the role which brought him international prominence. As a Justice of the Supreme Court, in *Brown* v. *Allen*[99] Jackson wrote the renowned phrase "we are not final because we are infallible, but we are infallible only because we are final". This statement has always been interpreted as a warning to judges, to be conscious of their own fallibility.

However, this oft-cited passage is the conclusion of a broader line of reasoning. Jackson wrote that "[c]onflict with state courts is the inevitable result of giving the convict a virtual new trial before a federal court sitting without a jury. Whenever decisions of one court are reviewed by another, a percentage of them are reversed. That reflects a difference in outlook normally found between personnel comprising different courts. However, reversal by a higher court is not proof that justice is thereby better done. There is no doubt that if there were a super-Supreme Court, a substantial proportion of our reversals of state courts would also be reversed. We are not final because we are infallible, but we are infallible only because we are final".

Thus, Jackson perceived the Supreme Court's strength to lie in its "finality", its solitary position at the apex of the legal system, pursuant to which it has the final say and *therefore becomes* infallible. If a court superior to the Supreme Court existed, he argued, many of the latter's decisions would be reversed.

Justice Jackson's theoretical hypothesis is now becoming a reality. National legal systems are opening to supranational law. The latter features courts that often decide differently from national supreme courts. These, in turn, are required to consider the decisions issued by, and dialogue with, courts beyond the State. In addition, supranational law's infiltration into national legal systems also authorizes "lower" national judges to pronounce themselves upon the constitutionality of legislation; in other words, "lower" judges can now take possession of the Constitution and evaluate the constitutionality of norms, interpreting them in a constitutionally-compatible manner, and stopping only when obliged to refer them to the constitutional court, the only body empowered to

[99] 344 U.S. 443, 1953.

strike them down[100]. Thus, reviews for constitutionality become diffuse, and at the same time, constitutional courts' once-exclusive position is eroded. This also leads to a change in the very nature of supreme courts' review for constitutionality. In other words, we have transited from a "closed" constitutional law to a "constitutional globalization".

3. THE TRANSNATIONAL LAW OF LIBERTIES

In this section, I will briefly examine the steps of this complex evolution.

The starting point is the opening of national legal systems to non-national law – the phenomenon that German jurists call *Völkerrechts-freundlichkeit*. An example is Article 25 of the German *Grundgesetz*, which states that the general rules of international law are an integral part of the federal law, that they take precedence over national law and that they directly create rights and obligations for German citizens. Also, Articles 232 and 233 of the Constitution of the Republic of South Africa state that customary international law is law in the South African legal system, unless it is inconsistent with the Constitution or with an Act of Parliament; in addition, when interpreting legislation, courts must prefer an interpretation that is consistent with international law. Further examples are Articles 10 and 11 of the Italian Constitution, according to which the Italian legal system must conform to the generally recognized norms of international law, and consents to limitations of its sovereignty. In addition, Article 5, 190 and 193 of the Federal Constitution of the Swiss Federation establish that the mandatory provisions of international law take precedence over the national constitution itself.

Therefore, national law retracts, while supranational law prevails. International treaties and agreements proliferate – this is my second point: the European Convention on Human Rights, the Charter of Fundamental Rights of the European Union, the American Convention on Human Rights, the Treaty Establishing the Economic Community of

---

[100] S. Cassese, "La giustizia costituzionale in Italia: lo stato presente", in *Rivista trimestrale di diritto pubblico*, 2012, n. 3, p. 603 ff.

West African States, the Universal Declaration of Human Rights, the International Covenant on Civil and Political Rights, the International Covenant on Economic, Social and Cultural Rights, etc.

International agreements such as these contain rules to ensure and protect citizens' rights; as if "shadow" or "surrogate" constitutions, these rules overlap (and sometimes conflict) with those enshrined in national constitutions.

Furthermore, significant problems arise with regard to the "connections" between supranational legal orders, such as that between EU law and ECHR law that the Court of Justice of the European Union is called upon to solve. The Court of Justice has stated that as long as the EU has not formally acceded to the ECHR, the latter cannot be considered a legal instrument incorporated into EU law; EU law, in turn, does not regulate relations with the ECHR nor determine the conclusions that national courts can reach if the rights protected by the Convention conflict with those enshrined in national law.

The opening up of national constitutional orders and the development of global norms give rise to a third phenomenon: "domestification"[101], the process through which international human rights become effective within national legal orders. Treaties and conventions become national law, which can be enforced in national courts.

This "incorporation" can take place in various ways. However, in all cases, international norms do not enter national systems on the basis of hierarchical or "arborescent"[102] criteria, and do not affirm themselves therein on the basis of their supremacy, but rather, by virtue of their "primacy" (a distinction first made by the Spanish *Tribunal Constitucional*), they assume a place alongside national norms, "one next to the other"[103]. The Italian Constitutional Court has noted that the different formulations of the various catalogues of rights "integrate one another,

---

[101] A. Stone Sweet, "A Cosmopolitan Legal Order: Constitutional Pluralism and Rights Adjudication in Europa", in *Global Constitutionalism*, 2012, n. 1, p. 53.

[102] M. Vogliotti, "La fine del "grande stile" e la ricerca di una nuova identità per la scienza giuridica", in V. Barsotti (ed.), *L'identità della scienza giuridica in ordinamenti multilivello*, Rimini, Maggioli, pp. 97 ff.

[103] A. Ruggeri, "Rapporti tra Corte costituzionale e Corti europee, bilanciamenti e "controlimiti" mobili, a garanzia dei diritti fondamentali", in *Associazione italiana dei costituzionalisti*, n. 1, 2001, pp. 8 and 11.

completing each other by means of interpretation"[104] (Judgment N. 388 of 1999).

However, supranational law is gradually acquiring greater strength, as recently noted also by the Swiss Supreme Court in the *Thurgovia* case (2C_828/2011, of 2012), concerning the European Convention on Human Rights.

Therefore, we are witnessing the development of what Mauro Cappelletti, twenty years ago, called the "transnational law of liberties"; a development that can be ascribed, on one hand, to the decline of the nation-State as the sole source of law and justice, and on the other, to the international opening of national legal systems[105].

4. NEW GUARDIANS OF THE LIBERTIES

My fourth point is that the plurality of national and supranational charters is accompanied by another phenomenon: a proliferation of guardians of the liberties, at both supranational/global and national levels.

In the supranational and global contexts, there are the European Court of Human Rights (ECtHR), the Court of Justice of the European Union, the Inter-American Court of Human Rights, the Court of Justice of the Economic Community of West African States, the African Court of Justice for Human and Peoples' Rights.

However, these courts are not the only guardians of the rights enshrined in the constitutional charters they apply. Indeed, due to domestification, the treaties, agreements, covenants and charters that guarantee rights and freedoms are also part of national legal systems. Therefore, national courts too are guardians of these rights and freedoms, and establish relations with supranational courts, circumventing – and therefore marginalizing – national constitutional courts.

The decisions of supranational courts on individuals' rights are binding in national legal systems, albeit in different ways, depending

---

[104] M. Vogliotti, *La fine del "grande stile" e la ricerca di una nuova identità per la scienza giuridica*, cit., p. 113.

[105] M. Cappelletti, *Giustizia*, in *Enciclopedia delle scienze sociali*, Rome, Treccani, 1994.

upon the regions and countries involved. An example is *Serap v. Republic of Nigeria*, handed down by the African Court of Justice for Human and Peoples' Rights in 2012 (ECW/CCJ/JUD 18/12). The case concerned the right to health, to adequate living standards and to protection of the environment in the Niger Delta. Another example is the decision of the Inter-American Court of Human Rights in *Padilla Pacheco* (912/2010), a case raising issues relating to the right to life, personal integrity, freedom and judicial protection.

Supranational law percolates into national legal orders in many different ways, which makes it difficult to draw a general conclusion and raises many questions. Does the European Convention of Human Rights have supra-constitutional status (as in the Netherlands), constitutional status (as in Austria) or sub-constitutional status, as in Italy[106]? Or does it rank as ordinary legislation, with the consequence that a subsequent national law can nullify rights acquired at the supranational level? How can rights granted in a broader context be coordinated with those granted at the national level?

As for judicial protection, is it better for national courts – as ordinary courts called upon to apply also supranational norms that guarantee rights – to declare the inapplicability of national law that is inconsistent with supranational law, even if the national measure was enacted subsequently? Or would it be preferable for domestic courts to refer inconsistent domestic norms to their respective constitutional courts, to be struck down?

In addition to relations between legal systems and their respective rules, there are also relations between the various courts and their respective powers. The configuration of the latter type of ties may assume several different shapes. National courts may apply supranational norms directly, or may refer decisions on domestic violations of rights to supranational courts. Domestic judges may evaluate the observance of rights enshrined in supranational norms and directly declare the inapplicability of the conflicting domestic norms (as occurs in Italy for EU law). Otherwise, once they have performed this check, national judges may also

---

[106] Most recently, see S. Bartole, "Giustizia costituzionale (sviluppi recenti)", in *Enciclopedia del diritto*, 2014, pp. 504 ff., and G. D'Amico – D. Tega, *1993 – 2013: "la Corte costituzionale tra giurisdizione e politica"*, in S. Sicardi, M. Cavino and L. Imarisio (eds), *Vent'anni di costituzione (1993-2013). Dibattiti e riforme nell'Italia tra due secoli*, Bologna, il Mulino, 2015, p. 547 ff.

defer the task of striking down the non-compatible domestic norms to other national courts (i.e. constitutional courts) as did the Italian Constitutional Court in 2007, on the European Convention of Human Rights. Domestic courts may adapt to supranational law as interpreted by supranational courts (as occurs in Italy), or may be obliged only to "consider" the interpretation of supranational law given by the relevant judges (as in Germany and the United Kingdom).

Such a complex situation requires adaptations and collaboration. The former were introduced by means of norms (e.g. the principle of the prior exhaustion of national remedies, in the case of the European Convention of Human Rights, or the principle of subsidiarity, introduced in the same context by the Protocol N. 15 recently added to the Convention), or of "judge-made law" (such as the doctrine of national margin of appreciation introduced by the Strasbourg Court in relation to the application of the European Convention of Human Rights; or the doctrines of the "supreme principles" and of "counter-limits" – *controlimiti* – formulated by the Italian Constitutional Court in relation to EU law, in Judgments N. 30 of 1971 and 183 of 1973).

Second, this complex situation requires increasingly close collaboration between judicial systems, especially between supreme or constitutional courts; this is achieved by increasing both references to each others' case law, and meetings and contacts. The influences and interconnections, the mutual legitimation, and the references to comparison as a method of interpretation that have consequently arisen, have prompted remarks as to the existence of a "*Verbund* of the constitutional courts".

However, this too is not enough, because some countries attempt to evade this system of mutual checks. An example is the United Kingdom, where it has been lamented that its free people, the historical pioneer of the path towards freedom and democracy, is forced to renounce self-government; and they wish "to make [their] Supreme Court supreme"[107]. The UK situation will not be examined in detail here; I will only recall that the reactions registered there can also be ascribed to the absence of a national written constitution, that can act as a barrier or filter to the

---

[107] D. G. Green, *The Demise of the Free State: Why British Democracy and the EU don't mix*, London, Civitas, 2014.

automatic incorporation of supranational law. Such a "gap" is not filled by the enactment of the Human Rights Act 1998.

5. CONSTITUTIONAL COURTS ARE NO LONGER ALONE

In this framework, constitutional courts' tasks are eroded from above and below, and their powers are limited by the need to take into consideration supranational courts' case law. However, while constitutional courts (partially) lose the ability to have the final say, while they must also heed the opinions of other courts, they also become less solitary bodies, as they acquire a new role: that of interlocutors with supranational legal orders, of arbiters of the opening and closing of domestic legal systems, and even of the speed at which supranational legal orders progress (consider the role of the German *Bundesverfassungsgericht* with its judgments on the Lisbon Treaty[108] and on the ECB's OMTs). The overall beneficiaries of this evolution are national civil societies, given the consequent expansion of rights and the diffusion of the checks on their observance by legislative and executive bodies.

The evolution described thus far also affects the very nature of constitutional courts' work, and the horizontal expansion of the checks on the observance of rights.

The choral nature of the checks on the compliance with national and supranational charters transforms the nature of the judgments issued by constitutional courts, enhancing a specific component thereof: the evaluation of the reasonableness and the uses of balancing techniques and control of proportionality of national measures. Constitutional courts are increasingly called upon to compare and weigh rules and their applications at both national and supranational levels: for example, courts may be asked to ascertain whether individuals deprived of their personal freedom can also be deprived of their right to vote; or whether private parties against whom judgment was delivered on the basis of irregularly-collected evidence are entitled to fresh proceedings (these cases involved the UK and Italy respectively). When dual protection is available, the

---

[108] S. Cassese, "L'Unione europea e il guinzaglio tedesco", in *Giornale di diritto amministrativo*, 2009, n. 9, pp. 1003-1007.

task of comparing, weighing, and evaluating the proportionality and reasonableness of the various feasible interpretative outcomes is enhanced. Indeed, this keeps reviewers under review, and avoids arbitrary decisions on their part.

A related aspect is the courts' task of advancing the protection of rights, a task which they pursue with highly diverse formulations, such as the "maximum expression of guarantees" asserted by the Italian Constitutional Court (Judgment N. 317 of 2009, echoing a famous phrase coined by Paolo Barile[109]); or the principle of "progressivity of protection" endorsed by the Argentinian Supreme Court, according to which "all state measures having deliberately regressive nature in terms of human rights require a more accurate consideration, and must be fully justified in terms of the entirety of rights foreseen"[110]. In these cases, courts must clearly engage in comparison and weighing.

Second, vertical openness induces horizontal openness. National courts take into consideration decisions issued by supranational courts, even though these may concern other countries and do not apply to it *stricto sensu* (e.g. the Mexican Supreme Court's report on the *Padilla Pacheco* case, mentioned above). The laws of other countries gain relevance for supranational judges who decide a case involving a different country, as occurs, for example, with the ECtHR's doctrine of consensus: according to this doctrine, when reviewing the proportionality of a country's application of its margin of appreciation, the ECtHR must consider how many ECHR Contracting States have adopted a certain measure (for example, how many have accepted abortion or divorce). Domestic courts become interested in acquainting themselves with the legal solutions adopted in other countries, due to the implications that these may have in subsequent judgments concerning the domestic system.

---

[109] P. Barile, *Diritti dell'uomo e libertà fondamentali*, Bologna, Il Mulino, 1984, p. 41.

[110] Most recently, see *Corte Suprema de Justicia de la Nación, Asociación de Trabajadores del Estado*, 18 June 2013.

6. A "GREAT DISARRAY" OR "THE GREATEST TRIUMPH OF CONSTITUTIONAL COURTS"?

Over thirty years ago, the afore-cited Louis Favoreu wondered "if, in a few years' time, we will be able to make sense of the tangle of competences on the protection of fundamental rights in Europe"[111]. Ten years ago, he returned to the subject in an even more pessimistic tone, observing that "a great disarray appears to be taking shape", a "tangle of competences", which he deemed to be "counterproductive" and "catastrophic"[112]. He described the European "jurisdictional landscape" thus: "Ordinary jurisdictions [...] apply the Constitution, the European Convention on Human Rights and general principles of European law, and soon, undoubtedly, the Nice Charter. Constitutional courts apply their own constitutions, which contain a catalogue of fundamental rights and, exceptionally, the European Convention on Human Rights; the Luxembourg Court applies the case law of the Charter of Fundamental Rights (pending the implementation of the Nice Charter) and possibly the European Convention on Human Rights; the European [Strasbourg] Court applies the European Convention on Human Rights, "imposing" its interpretations upon ordinary jurisdictions, in some cases even upon constitutional courts, but without a real "constitutional authority" to do so, since it cannot invalidate domestic acts"[113].

More recently, the Italian sociologist Maria Rosaria Ferrarese has noted that the proliferation of judicial and para-judicial bodies prompts a paradox: a "limitation of the [...] role" of constitutional courts yet, at the same time, their "triumph"[114]. The proliferation of institutions empowered to have the final say indicates that what truly matters is not who speaks last, but rather, who participates in the dialogue.

Supreme or constitutional courts are caught in a continuous conflict, or at least tension, with politics: more precisely, with legislative bodies. In addition to this tension, a new one has emerged: that between domestic

---

[111] L. Favoreu, "Avertissement – article n. 2", in *Revue internationale de droit comparé*, 1981, n. 2, vol. 33, pp. 251-253, cited in L. Favoreu, *Corti*, cit., p. 17. Author's translation from the Italian.

[112] L. Favoreu, *Corti*, cit., p. 18. Author's translation from the Italian.

[113] L. Favoreu, *Corti*, cit., p. 119. Author's translation from the Italian.

[114] M. R. Ferrarese, "Dal 'verbo' legislativo a chi dice l'"ultima parola': le Corti costituzionali e la rete giudiziaria, in *Annuario di diritto comparato e di studi legislativi*, 2011, pp. 63 ff.

legal orders on one hand, and supranational/global ones on the other. In this context, courts are often called upon to perform various functions – intermediation, limitation, prompt – and in this respect, their attitudes differ greatly. See, for example, the case of prisoners' voting rights, and the relations between the UK Supreme Court and the Council of Europe and ECtHR; the German Federal Constitutional Tribunal's decisions concerning its relations with the European Union (*Solange* and *Ja, aber* cases); the cases on relief teachers, the Italian Constitutional Court and EU law; the case of the Swiss pensions, the Council of Europe and the Strasbourg Court; and the US Supreme Court cases involving the death penalty and detention without trial.

These tensions certainly have a cost, as they introduce complexity and some confusion into legal systems. However, they also bring great benefits, both because they broaden the protection of citizens' rights, and because citizens are pushed – due to the system's provisional nature – to constantly seek new ways to obtain this protection.

In light of his dual experience as a Spanish constitutional judge and an Advocate General of the European Court of Justice, Pedro Cruz Villalón, applied the hedgehog dilemma – expounded by Arthur Schopenhauer and also by Sigmund Freud – to the "crowded house" of rights in Europe, marked by a plethora of courts, each entitled to pass judgment in the final degree. According to this dilemma, in winter, hedgehogs seek to resist the cold by becoming close to each other, however, this also places them at risk of injury from their peers' sharp quills. European courts too, like the hedgehog, must learn to strike the appropriate balance between cooperation and isolation.

SE ACABÓ DE IMPRIMIR ESTE
LIBRO EL 28 DE FEBRERO DE
2   O   I   8

www.ingramcontent.com/pod-product-compliance
Lightning Source LLC
Chambersburg PA
CBHW081807200326
41597CB00023B/4176